CHILDREN OF MARS

Ancient Warfare and Civilization

SERIES EDITORS:

RICHARD ALSTON   ROBIN WATERFIELD

In this series, leading historians offer compelling new narratives of the armed conflicts that shaped and reshaped the classical world, from the wars of Archaic Greece to the fall of the Roman Empire and the Arab conquests.

Dividing the Spoils
The War for Alexander the Great's Empire
Robin Waterfield

Taken at the Flood
The Roman Conquest of Greece
Robin Waterfield

By the Spear
Philip II, Alexander the Great, and the Rise and Fall of the
Macedonian Empire
Ian Worthington

In God's Path
The Arab Conquests and the Creation of an Islamic Empire
Robert G. Hoyland

Mastering the West
Rome and Carthage at War
Dexter Hoyos

Rome's Revolution
Death and the Republic and Birth of Empire
Richard Alston

The Plague of War
Athens, Sparts, and the Struggle for Ancient Greece
Jennifer T. Roberts

Rome Resurgent
War and Empire in the Age of Justinian
Peter Heather

Conquering the Ocean
The Roman Invasion of Britain
Richard Hingley

Children of Mars
The Origins of Rome's Empire
Jeremy Armstrong

CHILDREN OF MARS
The Origins of Rome's Empire

Jeremy Armstrong

Oxford University Press is a department of the University of Oxford.
It furthers the University's objective of excellence in research, scholarship,
and education by publishing worldwide. Oxford is a registered trade mark of
Oxford University Press in the UK and in certain other countries.

Published in the United States of America by Oxford University Press
198 Madison Avenue, New York, NY 10016, United States of America.

© Oxford University Press 2025

All rights reserved. No part of this publication may be reproduced, stored in a retrieval system, transmitted, used for text and data mining, or used for training artificial intelligence, in any form or by any means, without the prior permission in writing of Oxford University Press, or as expressly permitted by law, by license or under terms agreed with the appropriate reprographics rights organization. Inquiries concerning reproduction outside the scope of the above should be sent to the Rights Department, Oxford University Press, at the address above.

You must not circulate this work in any other form
and you must impose this same condition on any acquirer.

Library of Congress Cataloging-in-Publication Data
Names: Armstrong, Jeremy author
Title: Children of Mars : the origins of Rome's empire / by Jeremy Armstrong.
Description: [First edition]. | [New York] : [Oxford University Press], [2025] |
Series: Ancient warfare and civilization | Includes bibliographical references.
Identifiers: LCCN 2025004939 (print) | LCCN 2025004940 (ebook) |
ISBN 9780197584972 hardback | ISBN 9780197584996 epub
Subjects: LCSH: Rome—History—To 510 B.C. | Rome—History—Republic, 510–265 B.C.
Classification: LCC DG231 .A748 2025 (print) | LCC DG231 (ebook) |
DDC 937/.01—dc23/eng/20250401
LC record available at https://lccn.loc.gov/2025004939
LC ebook record available at https://lccn.loc.gov/2025004940

DOI: 10.1093/oso/9780197584972.001.0001

Printed by Sheridan Books, Inc., United States of America

The manufacturer's authorized representative in the EU for product safety is
Oxford University Press España S.A., Parque Empresarial San Fernando de Henares,
Avenida de Castilla, 2 – 28830 Madrid (www.oup.es/en).

For KJA and ARH.
I think you both would have liked this one.

CONTENTS

List of Figures	xi
Preface	xiii
1. Introduction: The Origins of Empire	1
2. Sons of Venus and Mars: Rome's Founders, from Aeneas to Camillus	13
3. Veii, the Gauls, and Rome Reborn	62
4. The Romans, the Latins, and the Samnites	102
5. Rome and the Mediterranean	145
Epilogue	187
Appendix: The Nature of the Early Roman Army	191
Timeline of Early Roman History	227
Roman Naming Conventions	229
Glossary	231
Further Reading	241
Notes	245
Index	261

LIST OF FIGURES

FIG 1	Map of central Italy. Produced by the Ancient World Mapping Center.	xvii
FIG 2	Map of Rome, the early *ager Romanus*, and the early tribes. Produced by the Ancient World Mapping Center.	xviii
FIG 3	RRC 458. Struck silver *denarius*, 47–46 BCE. Obverse: Venus, facing right. Reverse: Aeneas, carrying the palladium in his right hand and Anchises on his left shoulder. University of Auckland Collection (UOA) inv. RR74. Image: G. Morris.	21
FIG 4	*Lupa Capitolina*—The Capitoline She-Wolf. Capitoline Museum, Rome. Image: J. Armstrong.	29
FIG 5	Map of the site of archaic Rome.	35
FIG 6	*Lucretia*, 1669, Rembrandt.	50
FIG 7	A terracotta figurine of a Gallic warrior. Egypt, 220–180 BCE. British Museum, London, 1994, 1001.2.	81
FIG 8	Rome's fourth-century "Servian Walls." Semi-extant section located near the modern Termini Station in Rome. Photo: J. Armstrong.	91
FIG 9	Map of Latium and the Tyrrhenian coast. Produced by the Ancient World Mapping Center.	108
FIG 10	Map of central Italy, including Campania and northern Samnium. Produced by the Ancient World Mapping Center for *The Romans: From Village to Empire: A History of Rome from Earliest Times to the End of the Western Empire*. Used with permission.	114
FIG 11	Indicative map of Roman and allied territory by ca. 100 BCE. Map courtesy of the United States Military Academy at West Point, Department of History. Used with permission.	123
FIG 12	*Les Romains passant sous le joug* ("The Romans passing under the yoke"), 1858, Marc Charles Gabriel Gleyre.	134

List of Figures

FIG 13   Sketch by Giovanni Battista Piranesi (1756–57) of the sarcophagus of L. Cornelius Scipio Barbatus, cos. 298 BCE. Original sarcophagus is now in the Vatican Museum. The lower half bears the honorific inscription detailing his career and achievements (CONSOL · CENSOR · AIDILIS · QVEI · FVIT · APVD · VOS—TAVRASIA · CISAVNA/SAMNIO · CEPIT—SVBIGIT · OMNE · LOVCANA · OPSIDESQVE · ABDOVCIT) and is one of the earliest pieces of contemporary evidence we have for Roman magistrates and warfare. Sketch held by the University of Tokyo General Library; courtesy of the Internet Archive.   138

FIG 14   RRC 1. The first "Roman" coin. Minted in the late fourth century BCE. Struck bronze. Obverse: laureate head of Apollo, facing right. Reverse: man-headed bull walking right; PΩMAIΩN (Greek for "of the Romans") above. ACANS inv.07GS16. Image: M. Rampe.   158

FIG 15   *Regulus Condemned to the Most Horrible Torture*. Pierre Chenu after Gabriel de Saint-Aubin. Etching and engraving. Metropolitan Museum of Art. 2007.49.355.   174

FIG 16   RRC 20. "Ogulnius *didrachm*." Minted in the first half of the third century BCE. Struck silver didrachm. Obverse: head of Hercules, facing right. Reverse: she-wolf, facing right, with suckling twins. UoA inv. RR1. Image: G. Morris.   177

FIG 17   Bronze cuirass and helmet from Paestum, tomb 174, Gaudo necropolis. 390–380 BCE. Photo: J. Armstrong.   198

FIG 18   An outline of the Servian Constitution as given in Livy and Dionysius of Halicarnassus. Adapted from Armstrong (2008), 62.   200

FIG 19   Indicative model of the fourth century manipular legion, as described by Livy.   205

FIG 20   Scene from the so-called "Altar of Domitius Ahenobarbus," now in the Musée du Louvre in Paris. The frieze is dated to the late second century BCE, but the Roman soldiers it shows are broadly indicative of Livy's description. Photo: J. Serrati.   206

FIG 21   Indicative model of the second-century manipular legion, as described by Polybius.   209

PREFACE

THIS BOOK IS PART of a recent resurgence in the study of early Rome. Although Roman history has always been a popular topic, arguably since the time of the Romans themselves, not every period has enjoyed the same level of attention. The late Republic (first century BCE) of Sulla, Pompey, and Caesar, along with the early Empire (first two centuries CE), from the emperor Augustus to Marcus Aurelius and Commodus, have usually claimed pride of place in both the popular imagination and scholarly circles. With their rich, contemporary literary tradition and robust archaeological record, we have always felt relatively confident discussing these later periods. They are the settings for most Hollywood movies on Rome (e.g. *Cleopatra, Spartacus,* and *Gladiator*), and the periods that most people imagine when mentally picturing "Roman History"—with the bustling metropolis of Rome, at the head of a vast empire, full of men in togas and grand, marble buildings. While scholars have dithered over the details, the basic outline of events and the nature of society during these years are considered relatively secure. This roughly 300-year period has long represented the stable core of the modern discipline.

Early Rome (eighth through third centuries BCE), on the other hand, has often been relegated—even by scholars—to the position of a problematic, and possibly even mythic, precursor to this better-documented, later era. Although most would admit the literary narrative for early Rome is fascinating, with its colorful characters and dramatic events, we haven't always been sure what to make of it historically—in short, we can't agree on the answer to "what really happened?" Our understanding of early Roman history has traditionally been based on a collection of literary sources that were written many centuries after the fact and which are of dubious accuracy—if we are being generous. When even the authors of our ancient sources (who we know were not afraid to "tweak the facts" to make their narratives more appealing) suggest you might want to take their version of events with a rather large pinch of salt, you know you are in trouble. We have long assumed that many aspects of early Roman history were simply made up by later writers. We just haven't been able to agree on exactly which aspects. As a result, and when faced with this uncertainty, most scholars have simply either accepted the narrative offered by these literary sources at face value, or have ignored it entirely, before moving on to later periods. Knowing the answer to "what really happened?" in early Rome hasn't seemed to matter much. We were always limited by our literary evidence, which, not coincidently, also viewed early Roman history as the opening act for the "more important," later periods.

This has all changed in recent years. Armed with increasingly sophisticated approaches to the ancient literary sources, coupled with models borrowed from sociology, anthropology, and other fields, historians have started to make some sense of the problematic literary record for the early period. Although the details are still viewed with caution, some broad themes and trends are beginning to emerge. When combined with an exponentially increasing archaeological record, real advances have been possible. We are no longer confined by the limitations of the ancient literature, but can build up an equally convincing picture of early Roman and Italian society from the archaeology and material remains. While many aspects of the period are still hotly debated, there is a renewed optimism that we can finally move past the seemingly intractable issues that stymied us previously.

Early Rome has slowly emerged from the mists of history as not just the vague origin point for various later developments, but rather as a dynamic, interesting, and important period of history in its own right. We have begun to realize that knowing the answer to "what really happened?" in early Rome actually *does* matter, in part because we can't fully understand the later periods until we do. In the past several decades, a number of important books and articles have been published on the subject, with

Preface

a particular flurry in the past 10 years or so (some of which you will find listed at the end of this book). This is a field that is on the move.

This is not to say, however, that we are all moving in the same direction—at least at the moment. One of the more interesting things about this resurgence in interest is that it has been defined more by disagreement than unanimity. Rather than narrowing our view toward a single, mutually agreed position, with each new book or article the debate seems to expand a bit. Loosed from the confines of staying close to the overt narrative offered by the ancient literature, scholars have increasingly taken advantage of the freedom offered to explore new possibilities. A wide range of models for early Roman society, based on both reinterpretations of the ancient literature and analyses of new archaeological evidence, have been presented, many of which challenge our traditional assumptions about who the Romans were and what they were doing. We both know more about early Rome and have far less certainty about any aspect of it than at any time previously.

The book before you is consciously part of this more expansive and contentious conversation around early Rome, and so might feel a little different from what many readers may be used to. While some of the dates and events should be familiar to those with some background in the subject, the models and interpretations presented may come as a surprise to those used to the traditional literary narrative, which is still the basis of many of the more general histories of Rome. The wider field of ancient history, and particularly mainstream textbooks, has not yet caught up with the rapid developments occurring in the specific subfield of early Roman studies in recent years.

The arguments within this book still rely heavily on the ancient literary sources—the works of ancient writers like Livy, Dionysius of Halicarnassus, Polybius, and Plutarch—although they are not as tied to them. This book treats them critically, as products of their own times and contexts, and offers ways to account for their evident biases. The arguments in this book will also make extensive use of the models derived from the archaeological record, emphasizing actors and associations that typically fall outside of the remit of our Romano-centric literary sources. Given the confines of this book, much of this material is impossible to include

Preface

directly without lengthy digressions, so I would once again point you to the "Further Reading" and "Notes" sections at the end of book if you would like to know more about the arguments and evidence these alternative models are based on. It should also be noted that this book will not necessarily try to chart a middle path in this debate, if indeed one exists, although what it argues does fall firmly within the broad outlines of the modern debate. It presents one possible interpretation—one which I hope is at least somewhat convincing, enjoyable, and enlightening as well.

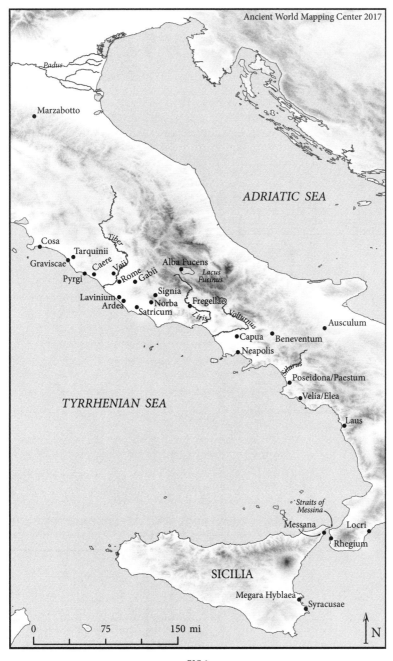

FIG 1
Map of central Italy. Produced by the Ancient World Mapping Center.

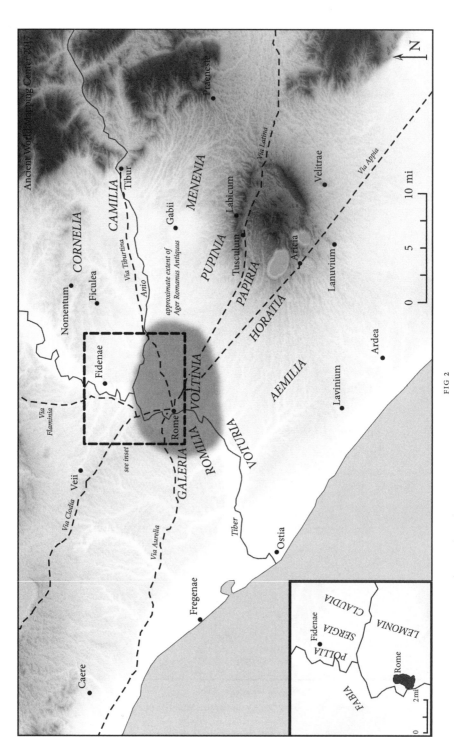

FIG 2

Map of Rome, the early *ager Romanus*, and the early tribes. Produced by the Ancient World Mapping Center.

1

INTRODUCTION

THE ORIGINS OF EMPIRE

I N 340 BCE (all dates in this book will be BCE unless otherwise noted), several thousand central Italians came together, in the shadow of Mount Vesuvius, not too far from the city of Pompeii. We do not know the exact date of this gathering, but it would have been either late spring or early summer. So it was likely a warm day, but not yet hot, and the atmosphere would have been lively. Tents of various types and colors would have been scattered across the landscape. Most were located close to the nearby Veseris River—a fancy name for what was likely little more than a small creek—and there would have been a steady stream of servants and slaves bringing water from the river back to the encampment. Cooking fires let off thin trails of smoke in the early morning air. Extended families shuffled about, meeting and mingling, catching up with friends, relatives, and acquaintances they had not seen since the previous year. Children laughed and played. Snippets of conversations in multiple languages could likely be heard—some speaking Greek, others Oscan, many conversing in Latin, and a few in Etruscan. Men emerged from tents, dressed in their finest. Animals grazed. Priests conducted sacrifices.

A casual onlooker might have easily mistaken this gathering for a festival of some sort. However, a more detailed inspection would have revealed some oddities. While many of the men seemed to wear elaborate costumes, with feathers, crests, and brightly colored cloth, they also wore pieces of bronze armor—and some were followed by boys or servants carrying shields and spears. Indeed, while women and children were almost certainly present, it would quickly become clear to our hypothetical observer that men made up the vast majority of the assembled people. Also, despite all being of similar character and composition, the collected assembly seemed to be split into two distinct groups, separated by an expanse of open terrain. While there may have been some interaction, especially between the servants and slaves down by the river, there was a clear division within the group. However, it may not have been immediately evident why.

The situation would have become clear by late morning, as the two sides came together in the open plain near the river, facing each other. The women and children would have remained with the tents, while the armored men advanced out onto the clearing—many yelling war cries, encouraging their comrades, and perhaps offering challenges to the men on the opposing side. What had been a seemingly festive context suddenly became a bit more ominous. Men slowly coalesced into small groups around standards or flags, many bearing the images of animals like wolves or boars. The clusters of men toward the front of each "army"— as it would be increasingly clear these two groups were—featured more javelins and ranged weapons, while those at the back had long thrusting spears, although it is likely all the groups or "units" would have been mixed. Equipment was highly individualized, with no two soldiers looking exactly alike. The organization of men on both sides was also loose and informal. There was no rigid rank-and-file order. Horseman slowly trotted out to the sides of the assembled armies, forming up on the wings where they could make the most of their speed and mobility. Each side watched the other cautiously, waiting for the mutually agreed sign to begin the action.

This was the lead-up to an ancient battle, and quite an important one in the history of Roman expansion and "empire": the battle of the Veseris River in the "Great Latin War" of the mid-fourth century. On the one side were the assembled forces of "the Romans," led by the consuls (Roman military commanders) Titus Manlius Imperiosus Torquatus and Publius Decius Mus. On the other side were the assembled forces of "the Latins." This battle was the culmination of tensions that stretched back over a century, with each side representing a different approach to—and vision of—power in the region.

The forces associated with Rome sought to unify the region under their leadership and consolidate power under a single banner and cause. The world around them was changing, with the rise of the ever-larger powers and kingdoms in the Mediterranean, and the men and families who had chosen to unify under the "Roman" label wanted to bring together the collected resources of their local region to compete on the same playing field as these other emerging powers. They were well aware of the rise of the kingdom of Macedon across the Adriatic. The famous battle of Chaeronea, fought between the forces of Philip II (and his son Alexander III, later known as "the Great") and the allied armies of Athens and Thebes, would occur only two years later in 338. Philip's victory would cement Macedonian dominance in Greece and allow him and his son to turn their attention east. Elsewhere, while Persia was in decline, Carthage was developing a powerful military hegemony based in North Africa, while the Greek tyrants of Syracuse in Sicily continued to fight for control of the central Mediterranean. Rome's elite families saw threats and opportunities everywhere they looked and wanted to be prepared for both.

The Latins, on the other hand, fought for their freedom. Although they were, by no means, peaceful bystanders—quite the contrary, in fact, as many of the assembled Latins were powerful, independent war leaders—they evidently did not share the same vision as their Roman counterparts. While they saw the same threats and opportunities, they did not want to join the same Roman alliance to face them. The reasons for this were varied. Some may have simply been conservative and preferred to keep things as they were—ignoring the wider Mediterranean context and continuing to focus on italian issues. Others likely also wanted to compete with other Mediterranean elites in this emerging "Age of Empires" in the fourth century but wished to do so on their own terms. They did not desire to join a more permanent Roman alliance, especially as a junior partner (the deal currently on offer). They would rather either operate independently or create their own alliance—perhaps as part of a more equal Latin federation or maybe joining with friends and allies in other parts of Italy. These men, along with their families and communities, were only unified in their resistance to the Romans and what they represented—a feature that would be increasingly common in Rome's wars over the coming centuries.

Despite this clear difference in motivations between the sides, it would have been very difficult for our hypothetical observer to differentiate the two sides on the ground. While modern film and media like to depict Roman soldiers wearing distinctive equipment and operating in a particular fashion, especially when compared with their enemies, this was certainly not the case here. The fourth-century "Romans" and the "Latins," standing on either side of the battlefield beside the Veseris River, would have been virtually indistinguishable and may not have even resembled coherent armies. Both sides would have been equipped with a wide array of equipment, would have come from a range of different communities and contexts, and would have been mobilized on the battlefield by family and tribal groups. While each side was unified, on the strategic level, by some broad goals and ambitions, on the tactical level, they would have seemed amazingly diverse and heterogeneous. The "Romans" and "Latins" were not two distinct peoples in a cultural or ethnic sense—they were all from the same region, likely spoke the same languages, worshipped the same gods, and indeed were friends and blood-relatives with those on the other side of the battlefield. Although writing centuries later, our ancient sources are probably correct in describing this as a "civil war."

The battle itself occurred over the course of the day and seems to have featured a series of distinct acts or periods—rather like a sporting event, with regular breaks, or a performance, with intermissions. Different groups charged in, engaged briefly, and then withdrew. Individuals would have called out opponents, perhaps by name, and engaged in duels. These likely attracted small audiences made up of their fellow combatants, who may have stood peacefully next to each other until the central combat concluded. Victors would have immediately stopped to gather spoils from defeated enemies and likely retreated with these to the safety of their encampment, or at least the rear of the army. It would have seemed remarkably fluid, and perhaps a bit choreographed—something not helped by the elaborate costumes and armor many wore. However, this should not downplay or diminish the violence being meted out on the field. This was a blood sport of the most brutal kind. In the end, and after a tumultuous final exchange that included the heroic death of the Roman consul Publius Decius Mus, the Roman side would emerge victorious. While the war itself would drag on for a few more years, this was the decisive moment, and in 338 the Romans would formalize their power and expansion across the region—incorporating all of the Latin clans and communities into their system, in one way or another.

This description of the battle of the Veseris River is, of course, somewhat speculative. However, we do know quite a bit about it, as it is one of the best-attested battles we have from early Roman history. The first-century Roman historian Livy spent several chapters within book 8 of his great work, the *Ab urbe condita* ("From the Founding of the City"), discussing the events in detail, which begin with the Roman commander Manlius Torquatus executing his son for indiscipline and end with the final Roman victory after the sacrifice of Decius Mus.[1] While much of the detail is certainly invented, as the Romans wouldn't develop a written historical tradition for more than a century after it occurred, its impact is without doubt. Indeed, while the Romans had won battles before, and acquired territory before, the period between 340 and 338 represented something a bit different. The Roman victory over the Latins and the subsequent treaties that they made with the various defeated communities and tribes represented coordinated expansion on a scale and of a nature that would have previously been unimaginable in central Italy. The number of Roman citizens, and the amount of territory held by the Romans, increased exponentially ca. 340. In these years, Rome went from a "local" to a "regional" power, virtually overnight.

By one form of reckoning then, the middle of the fourth century marked the birth of the Roman empire. In the years around 340 we can see some of the earliest evidence of a concerted push to expand and incorporate new peoples and territory into an imperial system centered on the community of Rome. While central Italians had fought battles and wars before, these had generally been focused on raiding and had rarely resulted in serious, long-term consequences for the defeated. The wars of the mid- to late fourth century were different, with defeat fundamentally altering the rights and obligations of the vanquished. Many of the practices and approaches the Romans utilized in later periods are also seen for the first time in these years, and there is increasing evidence of a coherent "Roman" identity emerging. We see new myths appearing, especially those connected with the eponymous hero Romulus, and the circulation of a new type of coinage bearing the name of "the Romans" in some parts of Italy. Foreign authors began to take notice of the growing strength of the central Italian peoples and wrote stories trying to explain their rise. This feels like the start of something special.

However, this expanding "Roman" system was still not particularly solid or well-conceived in the mid-fourth century. Looking back, from the perspective of the late Republic several centuries later, we can certainly see aspects of Rome's great empire starting to emerge in this period, but it was not yet the extension of a coherent idea, system, or approach. It was messy, ad hoc, and lacked any real planning or forethought. It is evident that the people at the head of the Roman system were largely making it up as they went along, and there was no single, guiding vision or principle shaping it beyond some vague regional ambitions and simply acquiring as much wealth and power as possible. It is doubtful that any of the people fighting in these conflicts, be they "Roman" or "Latin" or something else, would have had any idea what this system would ultimately evolve into.

It is, therefore, only retrospectively that we can pinpoint the years around 340 as a plausible "origin of empire" for the Romans—which is problematic, as it is both a bit artificial or arbitrary and opens things up for debate. Indeed, Roman authors, writing around the turn of the millennium, during the reign of the emperor Augustus, seem to have preferred a much earlier date, pushing the birth of empire back to either the late Bronze Age, with the supposed arrival of the Trojan hero Aeneas in Italy, or the eighth century, with the notional foundation of the city of Rome (this date is almost certainly wrong—it was either earlier or later, depending on how you define the "foundation" of the city). After all, if we are only looking for the beginnings of certain practices or the "seeds of greatness," why not go back to the very start? Alternatively, it is only around the year 200 BCE that contemporary Romans seem to have begun to write about a cohesive "Roman people" and empire themselves. While outsiders were evidently quite happy to label these central Italians as

Introduction

"Roman" from at least the fourth century, it was only about 200 that they fully embraced the label, narrative, and idea themselves. What should we make of this? Can we argue that a "Roman empire" existed before even the Romans themselves were aware of it?

This book will explore the rise of the Romans as an imperial power in Italy and how a motley group of central Italian families were able to come together as a single people and dominate the entirety of the Italian peninsula (and eventually the western Mediterranean)—although not necessarily in that order. As we shall see, and perhaps a bit confusingly, the emergence of the Roman people and the expansion of Roman power are two different stories that, although intertwined, are not entirely the same. Indeed, one thing that will become clear throughout this book is how powerful and effective the Romans could be, at least militarily, without being a particularly cohesive group socially, culturally, or politically. It is a paradox that seems to define much of their history, although it is particularly evident in the early periods. Throughout much of what we now call the "early Republic" (the fifth and fourth centuries), the Romans seem to have been a relatively loose federation of families that, despite the label "Roman," had a surprisingly tenuous link with the urban community of Rome, let alone each other.

The rise of the Roman empire is, therefore, not the result of a single, exceptional Roman people being released upon an unsuspecting Mediterranean world as is sometimes suggested—especially in popular media. Instead, it is the evolution and spread of a particular set of relationships, enforcing certain types of obligation in exchange for certain benefits, that were not exceptional at all. At the core of the Roman empire (and especially as it existed in Italy during the first millennium BCE) were the same, simple bonds that had connected the peoples of Italy and the wider Mediterranean world for centuries previously—bonds of family, friendship, alliance, and patronage. The Roman imperial project was not a new or unique creation, but rather a centralization and scaling up of existing relationships, networks, and power dynamics.[2] It was, fundamentally, a process of repackaging or relabeling, but in doing so, it seems to have taken on an energy of its own.

This process was deeply practical and pragmatic, and largely driven by the greed and the desire for power within a small group of elite families and their leaders. As far as we can tell, these men were not insightful founding fathers but classic Mediterranean big men, primarily interested in increasing their own—and their family's—power and prestige. They compromised when and where they had to, but were generally self-interested in nature. Some of them had been part of this Roman project from the beginning, while others joined up later, either drawn by the possibilities for power that the Roman system offered or coerced into it at the point of a sword. Over time, this centralization and scaling up were reinforced by both ritual and tradition. At its core, however, the Roman system relied on the same age-old, known, and established relationships and principles that had connected these men and their families previously. This was a profoundly Italian empire that leveraged a simple set of clan and community-based dynamics held in common across the peninsula. The basics of Rome's imperialism were clearly recognizable to, and mutually understood by, all involved—which was a key element in its success. The Romans did not have to explain their empire in Italy or rely on a newly created set of laws, institutions, or state bureaucracy (which, incidentally, did not exist). The Roman project simply utilized and leveraged the existing relationships, networks, and hierarchies that were already in place.

This more federated and relational model of early Roman society and early Roman imperialism is almost certainly a little different from what readers who are already familiar with the traditional narrative of Roman history may be used to. We do not have the spread of the Republic as a unique social or political system, or the rise of Rome as a cultural or even pseudo-nationalistic ideal. This was closer to a mafia-style takeover than it was to early modern colonization and imperialism. This is because this new model is designed to account for new, critical approaches to our ancient literary sources and the growing body of archaeological material, both of which have cast significant doubt on the overt model for Roman identity and expansion offered by our ancient literary sources. We have always known that the traditional narrative was problematic. The authors of our literary sources admit this themselves. However, it has only been in

Introduction

recent years that we have built up enough information, and developed sophisticated enough approaches, to properly challenge this narrative directly and break down the highly idealized—and indeed aspirational—histories they constructed. We are now attempting to peer behind the veil and explore what may have really happened.

Roughly charting out what is to come, the next chapter will dive into Rome's foundation myths, and particularly the community's famed founders. While most modern scholars have long assumed that these men are little more than folk heroes, their stories are intimately connected with Rome's imperial project. As suggested above, many of these foundation stories seem to have emerged alongside aspects of Rome's empire in the late fourth century. While the men they described supposedly lived in the distant past, their stories were being used to help explain a dynamic present. The Romans themselves evidently found these figures useful in this context. Some of Rome's founders were remembered as great reformers, others as great warriors, a few as great heroes (and some as great villains), but all seem to have embodied some aspect of Rome's early character—at least in the eyes of ancient authors. So, it is worth thinking about these men and the myths of early Rome, for what they can tell us about the nature of Roman society and how the Romans may have approached their early empire.

We will then move into a more chronological discussion of Roman warfare and expansion. The third chapter will begin in the fifth century, laying out the nature of Italian warfare and politics in the Archaic period (ca. 580–490) and early Republic (ca. 490–340). Despite the advances that the field of early Roman history has seen in recent years, this early period remains one of the more difficult to discuss with any certainty, so the conversation will start off quite broad and thematic. While the chapter will touch on some key moments and developments, it will generally aim to chart the rough flow of history. However, as we near the end of the fifth century, and our evidence becomes slightly more secure, a little more detail is possible. The chapter will, therefore, focus on two pivotal events—the Roman sack of Veii in 396 and the sack of Rome by Gauls in 390—which together encapsulate what seems to be happening in Rome around the turn of the fourth century. It will then carry the narrative down into the fourth century proper, looking at how the Romans responded to the sack of their city through a series of reforms, ultimately laying the foundation for their imperial system.

The fourth chapter explores the middle and late fourth century and Rome's conflicts with the Latins and the Samnites, mapping out Roman expansion in central and southern Italy. In many ways, this period is the heart of Rome's early empire-building, when the Romans established themselves as the most dominant force in Italy. They began by conquering and integrating their immediate neighbors, the Latins, and quickly moved on to include other populations, both north and south, in their growing military network. It is also a period where our information gradually improves with each passing year. We can see how the Romans adapted systems that were initially used in local governance to the processes of empire formation, and also how they continued to cling to many of their age-old practices and norms. While the Roman empire was a new creation, it was constructed to pursue some very old and traditional goals.

The final chapter covers Rome's war with the Molossian king Pyrrhus of Epirus (280–275) and the First Punic War with Carthage (264–241), illustrating how the Romans engaged with the wider Mediterranean world and major Hellenistic powers. In this period, the new issues and obstacles presented by the armies of Pyrrhus and Carthage highlight what the Roman imperial system did well and where its weaknesses were. Although the Romans were ultimately able to overcome any hurdles that were put in their way, how they approached them is both interesting and instructive. We can see what the Romans were comfortable doing, and where they struggled—and, indeed, what they were willing to sacrifice. At the end of the First Punic War, the Romans had reached a "high watermark" in their early imperialism, positioning themselves as the most important military system in the central Mediterranean. In many ways, however, this was the calm before the storm—or a brief intermission before the final act. The Carthaginians, although beaten, were far from conquered, and Rome would be at war with them again in roughly 20 years. The main narrative will end with a (very) brief discussion of the cataclysmic Second Punic War, fought between the Romans and the Carthaginian leader

Introduction

Hannibal Barca in the final decades of the third century. This conflict fundamentally reshaped both Roman society and the Roman approach to warfare, accelerating a series of trends and pushing the Romans down a new imperial course. The final section will aim to contextualize this within the broader narrative of early Rome and Roman imperialism laid out in the preceding chapters.

The book then ends with a short epilogue, summarizing the core points. After this, you will find some additional resources. These are a combination of things meant to provide a bit more depth on various arguments and to support readers who might be new to early Roman history. This includes an appendix devoted to the nature of the Roman army of the early and middle Republic for those interested in the nitty-gritty details of recruitment, tactics, and deployment in this period. This is a much more academic section, and I will admit it may not be for everyone. There will be some unavoidable Latin and Greek terms sprinkled throughout, and quite a bit more scholarly hedging and caveats as we venture into the murky depths of the ancient texts. But it will hopefully be worth the effort, for those willing to take the plunge, as it will explore some of the actual behavior of the army in the field. After the appendix, there is a basic timeline of early Roman history, a glossary of some more specific or technical terms used throughout the book, and a short discussion of Roman naming conventions. At the very back, readers will also find the "Notes" section, which offers a bit more detail on some specific points and gives an indication of the academic shoulders I am standing on while writing this narrative.

The traditional literary narrative of Rome's early empire is a bit like a childhood memory—formative but fuzzy, full of gaps, and all too often reshaped to fit the Romans' later position and self-conception. Authors like Polybius, Livy, and Dionysius of Halicarnassus were all drawn to the story of Rome's emerging empire, both for its importance and utility. It was a pan-Mediterranean creation story, as it explained the world within which they all lived. And yet, it was also amorphous and open to reinterpretation. Each of these men, and many others, retold this story, changing details and adding elements as suited their goals and needs. They were not lying about Rome's early history, as the truth was arguably unknowable—and ultimately unimportant to them. They were adapting a roughly similar story of power and growth (and perhaps, eventually, decline and fall) for their own purposes.

Until relatively recently, these later, heavily manipulated interpretations by writers like Livy and Dionysius of Halicarnassus were all that we had to work with. However, with the growth of archaeology, a more developed understanding of how societies (in general) function, and an increasingly solid grasp of the wider Mediterranean context within which the Romans and their empire were developing, some new options are available to us. Scholars have begun to reexamine the evidence with new eyes, new tools, and new contexts—and a subtly different narrative has begun to emerge as a result. This book offers that narrative.

2

SONS OF VENUS AND MARS

ROME'S FOUNDERS, FROM AENEAS TO CAMILLUS

R EADERS KEEN TO GET on to the more narrative historical action, which tracks the Romans' military conquest and political expansion across Italy in a chronological fashion, are welcome to skip this chapter and immediately jump to the next. However, for those interested in the "how" and the "why" of early Roman expansion, in addition to the "what," it may be important to begin with some context, definitions, and background. Indeed, we should probably also consider the "who" of Roman expansion—as who exactly the Romans were, especially in this early period, is not as simple and straightforward as it might seem. We could presumably call the people who lived at the site of Rome "Romans" with relative confidence. However, it turns out that the people living in Rome were only a small (and not necessarily important) part of the wider Roman community and imperial project. Much of Rome's early empire was created by people who only sometimes stayed in Rome and indeed may have only sometimes been "Roman"—even when that label is taken more flexibly and holistically.

If you find that somewhat confusing, you are in good company, as scholars have struggled with these contradictions for more than a century. But, hopefully, we can make some sense of it here. Let's begin with what later Romans thought about the matter.

In our ancient literary sources, the founders of the city of Rome were also the founders of the Roman empire, so the city and the empire were certainly linked in their minds. The city and idea of Rome were always imperial in some way. It was part of their DNA. Further, the essential nature of the empire was largely defined by the character and actions of the city's supposed founders. This was not a physical connection, but more of a psychological bond. Although the Romans knew they were not actually related to each other through blood, later Roman authors seem to have ascribed to the idea of a broadly shared, ideological lineage, which was made more flexible and inclusive by pushing it back into the mythical age of heroes in the late Bronze Age. All Romans shared a sort of symbolic link to a set of mythic founders, which gave them all a shared destiny and set of goals. The idea was captured in book 6 of the Roman poet Virgil's epic *Aeneid* and his main character Aeneas' vision of the future.[1] While the whole section is worth reading (everyone should read the *Aeneid*!), outlining the entire expanse of Roman history from Aeneas down to Augustus, and covering over a thousand years, the final lines sum it all up. To use Dryden's poetic translation of lines 6.848–53:

> But, Rome, it is thine alone, with awful sway,
> To rule mankind, and make the world obey,
> Disposing peace and war by thy own majestic way;
> To tame the proud, the fettered slave to free:
> These are imperial arts, and worthy thee.

For Virgil, writing in the late first century, Rome's empire and greatness had always been there, from the very beginning (even before the city was founded), predestined by the gods and simply waiting to come to fruition. It was not about the people necessarily, as these could (and did) change, but more the idea. One can perhaps see some resonance here with modern nationalistic myth-making, and with men like the American founding fathers serving as a cultural touchstone for later American citizens, including those whose families arrived in America long after 1776 and who have never been to cities like Philadelphia, Boston, or Washington, DC. It is less about the physical connection and more about ascribing to the same shared vision that these men were thought to embody. As a result, even though they seem to predate it, Rome's founders represent many essential features of Rome's early imperialism and are therefore worth exploring.

To be clear, though, Rome's foundation myths tell us far more about how late Republican and Imperial writers wanted to conceptualize their city, state, and empire than they do about the early periods of Roman history itself. Even with the most optimistic thinking, there is simply no way that first-century writers like Livy or Dionysius of Halicarnassus would have known much about what was happening in Italy 700 years before they were born when the city was traditionally founded, let alone in the late Bronze Age. There is no evidence that Romans, or other central Italians, were recording the sorts of details that make up the substance of these historical works and narratives. There is some limited evidence for writing in the Archaic period (short inscriptions, often religious in nature), and there was certainly a vibrant oral tradition. Indeed, it is evident that the past—and remembering the past—was vitally important to Italian peoples. But their view and use of the past was a bit different from our own. They did not seek to define events with objective, scientific accuracy, but rather viewed the past in a more relational and dynamic way. Theirs was a deeply practical form of history, which actively linked living people to their ancestors—often combining past and present, and melding belief with reality. The closest modern parallels might be the way religious texts like the Bible are sometimes used. They refer to the past but have direct relevance for the present. As a consequence of this bridging character, any attempt at "factual accuracy" (in the modern, Western sense) typically gave way to themes and principles that resonated with contemporary audiences, as this was felt to be more important.[2]

Also, we have begun to realize that the relationship between the city of Rome, the Roman people, and the Roman empire is not as simple and straightforward as we have often supposed. To put it simply, not only did most Romans not live in Rome, even in the early period, but (somewhat paradoxically) most Romans did not have a particularly strong connection with the physical city, down to at least the fourth century and possibly even later. This is true for both the poor and the elite. While the urban area of Rome certainly emerged as an important meeting point for the region's power players, and the administrative hub of their emerging imperial system, we should be careful how far we push its importance. It was not the "home" of the Romans, or typically their city of origin. It was simply the place where they usually met, and so it gave its name to the set of relationships that bound them together. It always seems to have functioned like a capital city, even in its earliest periods. Living in Rome and being "Roman" (at least as we think about this label today) were not the same thing.

This does not mean, of course, that the city of Rome's foundation stories are worthless to us today. They meant quite a bit to the Romans—who not only retold them and wrote them down but also set up shrines and statues commemorating the community's founders. They can, therefore, reveal a lot about how the Romans understood where they came from and who they were. These stories linked the Romans to each other, to the landscape, and even to the gods. While there might not be a great deal of what we might think of as objective "historical reality" in those memories, there might be a bit of "truth"; a real, remembered impression of how things were, how things changed, which moments were particularly impactful in the collective group's history, and how the Romans remembered approaching certain issues.

Rome's foundation stories and founders also help provide some context for Roman imperialism. They illustrate how Romans (of the late Republic at least) understood power as operating in different periods and the various ways in which individuals might have been able to expand the group's influence. They are suggestive of how the Romans understood their relationship with both their neighbors and the wider region. While much of this narrative was likely shaped by the practical, lived experience of Romans in the late Republic, already at the head of a vast territorial empire that had existed for over a century by that time, the way in which they talked about the city's founders is revealing. The stories of Aeneas, Romulus, and even Camillus offer an overtly idealized and mythologized version of Roman behavior and attitudes—a very particular distillation of Roman beliefs about themselves and how they came to dominate the region.[3]

Sons of Venus and Mars

THE ORIGINS OF THE ROMANS

The first thing that typically jumps out to anyone who looks at Rome's foundation narrative is that the Romans did not have a single origin story but at least two—and possibly more. Although late Republican writers worked very hard to craft a single compelling story out of the various traditions, the heterogeneous origins of the community and people were impossible to hide. Indeed, each distinct foundation story and founder seems to have played an important role in helping to define the Romans' origins. Each brought something different to the narrative and seems to have encapsulated a different facet of the Romans' identity—and perhaps a different period of their early history.

To summarize things quickly, the Romans' first founder was the Trojan hero Aeneas, who supposedly left the city of Troy after its defeat at the hands of the Greeks in the late Bronze Age, ca. 1150, and journeyed around the Mediterranean before ultimately coming to Italy.[4] Most sources do not connect Aeneas with the foundation of Rome itself, and in fact there was often said to be another, somehow unassociated, community on the site of Rome when he arrived in Italy that was ruled over by a king named Evander. Instead, Aeneas traditionally founded a distinct Roman lineage, or familial line, which supposedly included Romulus and Remus, and ultimately Julius Caesar and Augustus. Despite the obvious importance of the physical, urban center of Rome for the writers who placed Aeneas at the start of Roman history, the myth of Aeneas indicates that the origin of the Roman community was perhaps more about family than the city itself. This is an interesting distinction, which we will come back to.

The city which we now think of as Rome, on its seven hills, was traditionally founded by Romulus, the first *rex*, or "king," of Rome who lived several hundred years after Aeneas and who was also responsible for laying out the basics of the community's governance and organization.[5] He, however, did *not* establish a stable lineage. Romulus had no recorded children, and rulership of the city after his death or deification (the sources vary) was instead decided by election. Each of Rome's subsequent kings—there were six more—created new institutions and defined other aspects of the community, arguably acting as founders in their own right, albeit on a much smaller scale.[6]

The regal period in Rome traditionally came to an end in 510, after the elite families of the city rose up against the tyrannical final king of Rome, Tarquinius Superbus. In 509 the Republic was founded by Lucius Junius Brutus, with the help of others—including, perhaps awkwardly, the extended family of the deposed monarch. The nature of Rome's Republican system has often been debated, as will be discussed later in this chapter and book, and indeed seems to have been contested among the Romans themselves. The term republic, or *res publica*, means simply "the public thing" and the vagueness of the label seems quite apt. Despite its traditions and institutions, which developed over time, the Republic was always quite fluid and adaptive. At its core, however, the Republic is generally agreed to have been a power-sharing arrangement among the elite families of the region.[7] While it offered many individuals a chance at limited power, it effectively precluded anyone from rising up to the same level as the kings. Powers were limited and terms of office were typically restricted to a single year. There was only so much that an elite leader could do in that amount of time. This was recognized by later historians as well, who very quickly shifted their narratives from expansive and dramatic stories about powerful, individual rulers, to a more structured, annalistic account that emphasized the slow creep of bureaucratic change. While there were several key foundational moments that occurred in the early Republic, like the creation of Rome's first real legal code (the "Laws of the Twelve Tables") in the 450s, these were often defined by groups and institutions rather than individuals. Lucius Junius Brutus was not even considered a true founder, on the same level as Aeneas or Romulus, although his role in the creation of the *res publica* was certainly praised and remembered.

It is not until the narrative reaches the end of the fifth century that we find another founding figure: Marcus Furius Camillus. The second-century CE author Plutarch began his biography of Camillus by noting: "Turning now to Furius Camillus, among the many notable things that are told of him, this seems the most singular and strange, namely, that although in other offices of command he won many and great successes, and although he was five times chosen dictator, four times celebrated a triumph, and was styled a Second Founder of Rome, not even once was he consul."[8] The point about the consulship is technically true, although Camillus did serve as a consular tribune (another, comparable type of military command) five times and this likely reveals more about Plutarch's (mis)understanding of early Roman politics than it does about Camillus. Of relevance to us now, however, is the comment about him being styled as Rome's "Second Founder." This represents something of an inconsistency in the tradition, as Rome already had two founders by this time: Aeneas and Romulus. The suggestion that Camillus was a "Second Founder," therefore, seems to either ignore or demote Aeneas and focus exclusively on the urban center.[9] In this view, Romulus was the first founder of the city and Camillus the second, as he was remembered as being responsible for Rome's recovery from the sack of the city by Gauls in ca. 390—one of the darkest days in Rome's early history, but also an important point in Rome's development.

After that point, we have no more founders until we reach the time of the emperor Augustus, almost four centuries later. He is obviously a fascinating individual, who is remembered as the founder of the empire, the imperial family, and a new imperial Rome. According to the biographer Suetonius, Augustus famously said, "I found Rome a city of bricks, and I left it a city of marble." It is clear that Augustus, and his public relations team, were drawing heavily on the memory of Rome's early founders in constructing his image. While we will only touch on him briefly in this particular book, given our focus on earlier periods, his position in the list of founders is without doubt.

We will return to each of these early figures in turn in a moment, but woven through all of these foundation stories are some consistent threads. All of these founders were men who belonged to powerful and influential families. While some may have had a rags-to-riches element to their story—Romulus was famously abandoned and raised as a shepherd, while the sixth king of Rome, Servius Tullius, may have been a slave at one point—all were ultimately shown to be of noble blood and rose to power on the basis of their family connections. Family is central to the story of early Rome.

Second, all of these men were also military and political leaders, and indeed the two were evidently thought to go hand in hand. Even Rome's most peaceful king, Numa Pompilius, was associated with military aspects—for instance, he established a number of military priesthoods, including the *Salii* or "dancing priests," who initiated the campaigning season each year—although the famous "gates of war" (the doors to the temple of Janus in the Roman Forum, opened when the Roman state was at war) supposedly remained closed for his reign.[10] Rome, in later Roman memory at least, was founded by and through war and violence. This is important, as it suggests that the Romans understood warfare and violence to be central to their community and sense of self.

Third, virtually all of these men were either outsiders or had a strong connection with the world outside of Rome. Even Camillus, who was the latest and most "Roman" of the group, was remembered as being "exiled" at one point and had strong personal relationships with groups and families outside of the city. Rome was never remembered as being autochthonous or the product of a single, distinct ethnic or cultural group, but rather the result of immigration, negotiation, and seemingly constant growth and integration. This is something that had evidently changed by the time of Augustus (likely due to the Social War and Civil Wars of the first century), and something which he does not emphasize in his own image creation, but it is a strong theme in the earlier figures.

Fourth, the founding of Rome was a group effort. Although the narrative fixates on important individuals, there was always more than one founder, and these men worked both with and against other local elites to push the Roman enterprise forward. Even if Aeneas had sought to go and found a settlement on virgin soil, away from his past conflicts, when he arrived in Italy, he immediately found himself enmeshed in local politics and only founded his lineage through intermarriage with local families.

The rest of this chapter will explore these foundation myths in slightly more detail, focusing largely on what they tell us about the Romans' remembered past and occasionally highlighting those areas that might reveal a bit about what we might think of today as Rome's "historical reality" in these earliest periods. Many of these "real historical details" will be frustratingly vague, and there is a reason why many scholars, from the birth of the modern discipline of Roman history in the nineteenth century until today, feel that early Roman history, and particularly the monarchy, is simply unsuitable for the modern scientific discipline of history. The evidence is too late, too problematic, and indeed too mythic. Even the writers of our ancient sources themselves warn their readers to be skeptical. However, it would be unwise to discard it all too quickly. First, starting a story in the middle, when our contemporary evidence picks up ca. 200, is both confusing and unsatisfying. Second, the Romans of the late Republic evidently felt that material was important to understanding their society and the creation of their empire, and we would do well to think about why that might be. Even if it does not fit within what we consider objective, scientific history, it is clearly an important story to tell.

AENEAS

FIG 3
RRC 458. Struck silver *denarius*, 47–46 BCE. Obverse: Venus, facing right. Reverse: Aeneas, carrying the palladium in his right hand and Anchises on his left shoulder. University of Auckland Collection (UOA) inv. RR74. Image: G. Morris.[11]

Aeneas is a relatively minor character in Homer's epic poem the *Iliad*. He was a prince in the kingdom of Dardanus, located to the north of Troy, and was related to the Trojan king Priam. Aeneas' father and Priam were first cousins; both were descended from the legendary hero Ilus, who had founded Troy. Indeed, the city of Troy was also known as Ilion, named after him, which is where the title of the *Iliad* comes from. Aeneas led his people, the Dardanians, in support of their Trojan allies in the war against the Greeks. Despite his minor role in the poem, he was supposedly a demi-god; the son of the human hero Anchises and the goddess Aphrodite—the product of a union outlined in the Homeric *Hymn to Aphrodite*. According to the Greek mythic tradition, Aeneas' divine mother frequently aided him on the battlefield, although the other gods did as well, as Aeneas was famously destined for great things and so had to be protected. For instance, even Poseidon supposedly stepped in to help Aeneas in his duel with Achilles, saving him from almost certain death.[12] Following the sack of Troy by the Greeks, Aeneas heroically carried his father, Anchises, from the burning city on his shoulders and was spared by the Greeks on account of his filial piety (see Fig. 3 for a later Roman representation of this act).

After leaving Troy, Aeneas' story gets a little more complicated. Like the Greek hero Odysseus, Aeneas is remembered as one of the great travelers of this period, and there are traditions connecting him with an incredibly wide range of sites.[13] Many of these are in the central Mediterranean, from Carthage in North Africa to Sicily, and obviously Italy, although he is also recorded as visiting various locations in the eastern Mediterranean. His story is an interesting one as, despite being a minor character in Homer's works, his status as being "predestined for greatness" and the holder of the Trojan cultural legacy meant he was a useful figure for aspirational communities to attach themselves to. Claiming to be descended from Aeneas, which was possible for a shocking range of communities given his reported travels, meant a quick connection to one of the great cultural inheritances of the ancient Mediterranean world.

We know that the myth of Aeneas, including his flight from Troy and his travels in the western Mediterranean, was in circulation in Italy from a relatively early date. It has been argued that the sixth-century Sicilian poet Stesichorus of Himera connected Aeneas with Italy. This is by no means certain, as it is largely based on a later artistic depiction of his work (the late first-century *Tabula Iliacae*). However, another Augustan-era inscription, also referring to the poet's work, does mention "Aeneas and his companions setting sail for Hesperia."[14] So it is possible that at least some Greek writers were suggesting that Aeneas went west, and perhaps to Italy, not long after the *Iliad* was first written down. By the fifth century, the Sicilian community of Segesta supposedly claimed Trojan ancestry, possibly through Aeneas, when negotiating with Athens.[15] So we can certainly see a strong Sicilian connection by that date. Looking at peninsular Italy, the first-century historian Dionysius of Halicarnassus reported that at least two Greek historians writing in the fifth century—Hellanicus of Lesbos and Damastes of Sigeum—associated Aeneas with the foundation of Rome.[16] This is further supported by the accounts of two more Greek historians writing in the fourth century—Alcimus of Sicily and Dionysius of Chalcis. So the idea of Aeneas going west, to Italy and Sicily, and founding cities, including Rome, was evidently plausible.

We also have artistic representations of Aeneas, especially carrying Anchises (this is the easiest way to identify him), from central Italy and dating to the Archaic period. These include a terracotta figurine and an "intaglio," or carved gemstone, both from Etruscan contexts (north of Rome) and dating to the late sixth century.[17] Further, we have locally produced pottery depicting Aeneas and the fall of Troy from the fifth century, along with a range of imported pots bearing scenes from the myth.[18] Outside of Rome, there was evidently a strong tradition connecting Aeneas to the site of Lavinium—much stronger than that connecting him with Rome, in fact—that included the presence of a so-called *"heroon,"* or monumentalized grave of the hero, which had been the site of cult activity from at least the fourth century. Although recent archaeological work has revealed that the actual tomb only dates to the seventh century, and so several hundred years after Aeneas' supposed arrival in Italy, both the site of Lavinium and the tomb were evidently associated with Aeneas from an early date and represented a place of veneration from at least the fourth century.[19]

Scholars, when looking back at this collected evidence, have used it to support the antiquity of the myth of Aeneas and his "foundation" of Rome—or at least its royal lineage.[20] Clearly, by the late Republic and the writings of men like Virgil and Livy, there was a strong tradition linking Aeneas to the community of Rome and this had to begin somewhere.

With at least some early Greek writers suggesting a possible connection, and a smattering of art and archaeology, there was some optimism around the early relevance of this myth. However, the more we have explored the evidence, the more uncertain we have become about where it came from and when it entered Roman society. While the reported statements of some early writers indicate that at least *some* (often Greek) writers connected Aeneas to Rome from a relatively early date, it is unclear how far we should push this evidence. While it is entirely possible that these Greek writers had heard a myth that explicitly connected Aeneas and Rome, it is also possible that they were simply trying to find a believable origin story for one of the largest and most important communities in central Italy at this time. It is clear from archaeological evidence that, from the sixth century onward, the city of Rome had extensive connections with the eastern Mediterranean, and we know that Aristotle was aware of Rome being sacked by the Gauls ca. 390, suggesting the city—as a large and successful trading center—was a well-known entity. By the middle of the fourth century, Roman armies and interests were beginning to infringe on the traditional spheres of influence of various Greek communities, prompting a few more writers to take notice and try and put this emerging power in some sort of context. Making sense of an emerging Roman power, and perhaps threat, seems to be exactly what the Greek historian Timaeus of Tauromenium was doing, writing during and after the Roman war against Pyrrhus (280–275), which saw Roman hegemony spread throughout southern Italy and close to Timaeus' native Sicily. Connecting this burgeoning power with a great hero, whose descendants would have had claim to the great Trojan legacy (and a traditional rivalry with the Greeks), would have made quite a bit of sense in this context. Aeneas, as a hero known to have traveled west, may have simply fit the bill.

Beyond the passing comments of a few early Greek writers, the evidence connecting Rome and Aeneas is actually quite scant and flimsy. While Aeneas was associated with the foundation of communities in Thrace and the Peloponnese, and Cicero claimed Aeneas founded the Sicilian community of Segesta, it is noteworthy that the Romans themselves never associated him with the foundation of the city of Rome itself.[21] He supposedly founded the nearby community Lavinium, located on the Tyrrhenian coast to the south of Rome, and his son Ascanius founded the community of Alba Longa, located in the Alban hills of central Latium, but the authors of our Roman sources seem to have gone to elaborate lengths to separate him from the foundation of Rome. Further, while we have some evidence for the myth in the region, the 20 or so depictions of Aeneas represent a tiny fraction of Greek mythic iconography in central Italy. For instance, the Greek hero Herakles (the Roman "Hercules" and Etruscan "Hercle") was far more popular, with literally tens of thousands of depictions in a range of media. Theseus, Achilles, Ajax, and even minor Greek heroes like Iolaus and Triptolemos seem to have been more popular than Aeneas, even in locally produced, central Italian art. During the Archaic period, Aeneas was likely, at best, a moderately popular Latin hero—connected with Lavinium and Alba Longa, but not necessarily Rome.

Aeneas' connection with the city of Rome itself probably dates to the middle of the fourth century, when the expanding Roman military alliance fully incorporated the local region of Latium. This was a vitally important time for Rome and the Latins, especially in terms of identity. We will return to this period later in the book, when discussing the Romans' wars of expansion in Latium, but it was clearly an important period for Roman self-identity and myth-making.[22] The Romans had evidently been toying with different approaches to citizenship and community affiliation since the sixth century, when the sixth king of Rome, Servius Tullius, traditionally created the "tribal" and "centuriate" systems (something, again, we will come back to later). From that period onward, membership in the community of Rome had been under constant negotiation. As central Italy's population, and particularly its elite clans, tended to move around quite a bit, membership could never be solely tied to location, as this was never particularly stable. However, they also needed a predictable and mutually agreed way to determine who was part of the community and who was not. In this situation, the central Italians seem to have relied on two different systems.

The first system, and arguably most important, was connected to family. Individuals seem to have linked themselves to each other, and to the

Roman community, through extended family networks. While these were sometimes based on close blood ties or created through intermarriage, and so of a type we might recognize as familial today, they were also often extended—sometimes *very* extended—involving several degrees of separation and a range of different relationships. Many also relied on distant, and even clearly mythical, ancestors. This would push the limits of modern Western conceptions of "family" to their breaking points, nudging things, perhaps, into the more amorphous realm of "ethnicity."[23] In an ancient Italian context, however, the reality, or even plausibility, of the biological lineage was typically not important. In a world without DNA testing, any biological connection beyond the immediate family—and indeed, sometimes within it—would be impossible to prove anyway. Blood was usually not the most important factor—loyalty, trust, and obligation were. These networks and lineages were about creating a shared point of connection and something both sides could relate to. In a local context, this may have involved being part of a single *gens* (the Latin word for the Roman "clan") and traveling/working together, or even just acknowledging the authority of a single clan chief or *paterfamilias* ("head of household"). Some of these connections may have also been a bit looser and more sporadic. For instance, there is strong evidence for extended families returning to traditional burial grounds or *necropoleis* (singular *necropolis*, "city of the dead"), with mortuary rites perhaps acting as the impetus for what we might call a "family reunion."[24] Familial links could be quite tenuous or overlapping, and one could be connected to multiple families and lineages through different practices and relationships. But all of them helped to facilitate communication and interactions.

This set of family networks was vitally important, as Italy was quite a dynamic place. Many early Italian families seem to have traveled widely and, indeed, extended families would often disperse—big groups were hard to feed. However, they would come together at certain set times and for certain reasons—most notably religious festivals and burials—and at certain set locations. These groups operated according to a regular calendar and cycle of movement. Cities and towns often developed around these sites of meeting, particularly when the location serviced more than one group. While people did live permanently in and around many urban zones, the most successful ones were those that focused on, and catered to, these meetings of more mobile family groups. In fact, there seems to have been competition among Italy's urban communities to attract more of these groups, as they boosted the local economy, as well as the power and prestige of the families who controlled them.

What is interesting in this context is how central Italian peoples were able to utilize these family connections and push them much further than we might expect. Many families seem to have actively extended their lineages back to mythic forbearers if it suited their needs. This was usually not (or at least not *just*) a vain grasp at divine glory but rather a practical political move designed to create a connection with another group that also claimed that hero or ancestor. In this context, Aeneas, as a known traveler and founder, but with a flexible and adaptive narrative, proved quite useful, and we know that Roman families began to use Aeneas as a shared point of reference in treaties with communities in southern Italy and Sicily during the middle Republic. A shared connection with Aeneas allowed people from a wide range of communities and clans to come together as part of a single, notional, extended family, laying the foundation for other social and political connections. It did not guarantee peace, trust, and friendship, but it helped to facilitate it.

The second system was more geographic and focused on a shared awareness of law, politics, and control of land. While people seem to have been able to move across central Italy quite easily, especially in the early period, not all space was treated equally. Certain specific areas, and typically those shared sites or locations where families would come together and meet for burials, festivals, and religious reasons, were subject to an agreed set of laws and norms and a shared authority. These areas were defined by ritual boundaries and everyone who visited them agreed to operate by the accepted and shared rules. As suggested above, often these sites were (or became) towns, but they usually did not begin that way, and they clearly did not have to become urban settlements. Temple precincts, rural shrines, and even temporary festival locations also seem to have functioned in this way. However, urban centers were often preferred, as they offered a wide range of services and amenities. Families may have liked to bury their dead near stable populations, as it often meant there was someone there to take care of and protect the tombs, and urban temples and markets were often bigger and better. As time went on, and as more and more people began to settle down more permanently, the power and reach of the laws and shared authority associated with the meeting site slowly expanded to include nearby rural areas—areas which, in a Roman context, would become known as *ager Romanus* ("Roman land"). The basic principle that underpinned this, however, remained the same and was not exclusively Roman. In a region where people moved about quite a bit, there was an understanding that things operated a little differently in some areas. They couldn't always just do what they wanted, and, at least in certain contexts, they all agreed to negotiate and accommodate each other a little more—perhaps recognizing a greater authority, like that of the gods, or maybe a semi-divine ancestor who they shared, or perhaps the local clan-chief who happened to host the event or festival. Agreeing to abide by a shared set of rules that governed a particular area, for a particular length of time, seems to have made groups and individuals part of that community, at least temporarily. While this might seem quite simple, it was also quite practical and effective. This was not a land of rigid and absolute identities, but rather fluid and overlapping connections and authorities, where relationships were renegotiated every time groups met. Family and established rules over meeting places allowed for a certain degree of stability.

While both of these systems are visible in the world of Aeneas, he seems to generally embody the former—the idea of a shared lineage as a bond. Romulus, who we will discuss in a moment, seems to be the founder associated with the latter—the idea of a shared space and set of rules. Both systems, however, are key. Italy was a region full of families and clans who were in constant negotiation. Often this happened peacefully, coming together through religious rituals, trade, and intermarriage. Sometimes it was more agonistic and aggressive, with competing families engaging in raiding and rivalries. Occasionally, it resulted in outright war. Given the constant possibility of violence, understanding the nature of the underlying system and relationships was vitally important.

Sons of Venus and Mars

ROMULUS

FIG 4
Lupa Capitolina—The Capitoline She-Wolf. Capitoline Museum, Rome. Image: J. Armstrong.

While Aeneas may have been the founder of Rome's mythic lineage or family, Romulus was recognized as the founder of the *urbs* or "city" itself. Although, as with everything to do with this period, nothing is certain. Plutarch, for instance, begins his *Life of Romulus* by noting "From whom, and for what reason the great name of Rome, so famous among mankind, was given to that city, writers are not agreed." While this might strike a modern reader as a bit odd, the Romans did not seem to have minded this ambiguity. In fact, they may have even consciously worked to keep it that way, maintaining a certain flexibility within their foundation narrative. After this opening statement, Plutarch goes on to describe a series of myths known in the early Imperial period (first two centuries CE) concerning the origin of the city and its name, including that it may have come from a Greek word for strength (*rhṓmē*), or from a woman named Roma who was either a Trojan refugee, or the daughter of Italus and Leucaria, or the daughter of the Greek hero Herakles' son Telephus.

However, by the third century, one particular story had risen to prominence that connected the foundation of Rome to a man named Romulus, although even within this seemingly more accepted myth there remained significant variations.

The basic story, taking the aggregate across a wide range of sources, is that Romulus and his twin brother, Remus, were the children of the princess Rhea Silvia (also called Ilia), the daughter of King Numitor of Alba Longa, and so were supposedly descended from Aeneas (albeit separated by some 16 generations). Their grandfather, Numitor, had been denied his rightful throne by his brother Amulius, who also forced Rhea Silva to become a Vestal Virgin (a group of virginal priestesses who were dedicated to the community) to prevent any future offspring from that line. However, as Livy claimed, the Fates could not be denied, and Rhea Silvia became pregnant and gave birth to the twin boys.[25] The father of the boys is consistently left up for debate in our sources. Plutarch does not mention the father, while Livy gives this half-hearted comment: "[Rhea Silva] named Mars as their father, either because she really believed it, or because the fault might appear less heinous if a deity were the cause of it." Dionysius of Halicarnassus gives the most complete account,[26] noting:

...Ilia [Rhea Silva], after going to a grove consecrated to Mars to collect pure water for use in the sacrifices, was raped by someone in the sacred precinct. Some say that the rapist was one of the maiden's suitors, who was carried away by his passion for the girl; others say that it was Amulius himself, and that, since his purpose was to destroy her quite as much as to satisfy his passion, he had arrayed himself in armor, so as to appear more terrible and imposing, and that he also kept his features disguised. But most writers relate a fabulous story to the effect that it was a specter of the god to whom the place was consecrated; and they add that the event was accompanied by many supernatural signs, including a sudden disappearance of the sun and a darkness that spread over the sky, and that the appearance of the specter was far more marvelous than that of a man, both in stature and in beauty. And they say that the rapist, to comfort the maiden (by which it became clear that it was a god and not a mere man), commanded her not to grieve over what had happened, since she had been

Sons of Venus and Mars

united in marriage to the god of the place and as a result of her violation she should bear two sons who would far excel all men in valor and warlike achievements. And having said this, he was wrapped in a cloud and, being lifted from the earth, was carried upwards through the air.

Nine months later, Rhea Silva gave birth to the two boys, as predicted. Amulius was then put in an awkward position, as he could not let the children live but was also evidently anxious about killing the children of uncertain (and possibly divine) parentage, and so he had them put into a basket and cast it into the Tiber River, while Rhea Silva was thrown in jail. The boys obviously survived this, and the basket was carried by the river down to the site of Rome, where it was washed up by a fig tree (called the Ruminalis) and where they were found and suckled by a she-wolf (see Fig. 4 for the famous Capitoline statue) until ultimately discovered by a shepherd named Faustulus. He took the boys and raised them as his own. As they grew into manhood, the lineage (and possible divinity) of Romulus and Remus were apparently impossible to hide. As they grew and took over the flocks of their adoptive father, they began to raid other local groups, gaining some prominence. Due to their bravery and success in war, they were ultimately recognized by their grandfather Numitor and assumed their rightful positions within the family. Once in this position, the boys soon put things to right in Alba Longa by killing the treacherous Amulius and putting Numitor on the throne. Sadly, their mother, Rhea Silva, seems to have disappeared by this time, with the Augustan-era poet Ovid claiming that she, believing her boys had died as infants, had jumped into the Tiber and drowned. The boys then set off to found their own city to rule, settling on the site near the Tiber where their basket had washed up, which would become the location of Rome.

This first half of Romulus' story is full of classic Mediterranean mythic tropes: born to a virgin, possibly fathered by a god, subject of attempted murder as an infant by a jealous king, put into a basket in a river where he was saved and raised as a foundling, ultimately showing his true nature and being accepted back into his original family. There are countless heroes from around the Mediterranean who have similar origin stories. What is interesting, then, is the way in which the archetypal story is placed into a specifically Italian context. Most notably, the way the boys—and especially Romulus—demonstrated their true lineage was through success in raiding. Across all the central Italian myths and variations that concern the brothers, this is a consistent theme. As the boys grew into adulthood, they distinguished themselves through warfare and were able to set matters right through violence. They were, whether in reality or spirit, children of Mars. This was central to the Roman mythos.

This theme of violence underpinning politics is visible in the foundation of the city of Rome as well. When they arrived at the site of the new city, the brothers could neither agree on the exact site for the new settlement (Romulus favoring the Palatine hill and Remus the Aventine) nor the name of the settlement (Romulus preferring Roma while Remus supposedly wished to name it after himself, as Remonium or Remoria). The young men each took the auspices, observing aspects of nature to determine the will of the gods, although the results were inconclusive. The two men sat on different hills and watched for the flight of birds—which was evidently a standard central Italian practice when it came to divination. Remus saw six vultures flying first, which he took as a sign that his plan was favored. Romulus saw double that number flying, but later. As the young men still could not agree on who the gods actually supported, they began to build separate settlements with their followers, but tensions were rising. Ultimately there was a quarrel that resulted in Remus leaping over Romulus' half-finished wall and Romulus killing his brother for this offence—the crossing of the boundary being both a religious breach and social insult. Despite this violence, concord seems to have immediately followed. After the death of Remus, Romulus was quickly confirmed as the sole ruler of the now-unified community. He named the city after himself and set about putting in place the basic religious, political, and military institutions of the nascent state.

Our sources report that Romulus' first measures were to fortify the Palatine hill, finishing the wall that he had started, and to set up the various cults expected of a Latin community.[27] The first task is arguably understandable, given the violent context, but the second may need further explanation. Religion was vitally important to ancient Mediterranean communities on a number of levels. The presence of the gods and cults indicates, almost certainly, some attempt to grasp a cosmic order or underlying purpose to life and nature. However, one shouldn't push these mystical and metaphysical explanations too far. While many modern religions place their gods in the realm of the divine and largely beyond human comprehension, in the ancient Mediterranean basin, humans and gods seem to have co-existed on the same sociopolitical spectrum.[28] The differences between gods and men were more in terms of degree, and most gods could be considered, effectively, superhuman. They did not just take human form, they were also very human in nature. This explains the evident fluidity we often see between gods and men in both myth and at the top of the sociopolitical orders. While many modern readers might scoff at the claims of divinity made by various kings, pharaohs, and emperors in antiquity, at the time such assertions represented a much smaller movement up an established hierarchy than we might initially assume. These were not distinct categories of beings but rather different levels of power within the same system, with some mobility and, indeed, blurriness within it.

When Romulus established himself as the leader of his community, it was evidently important for him to immediately include the gods as well. This cuts to the core of what cities were in Italy at this time, and indeed the nature of urban centers across the ancient Mediterranean.[29] Communities, like archaic Rome, were not defined by stable populations or even land but were rather the hubs of communicative networks. They were places of meeting, trade, and contact, most notably among the region's elite but others as well.[30] The conversation in these hubs was typically controlled and facilitated by one or more local leaders, whose reputation and hospitality brought people together and whose authority and power guaranteed them a safe place to meet. They were places of cooperation and negotiation. Interestingly, these local, elite hosts who helped facilitate this communication almost always seemed to have included both human and divine elements, which operated in remarkably similar ways. The gods had houses (temples) and hosted banquets (festivals) where people congregated. Gods and men both occupied positions at the top of the local hierarchy, with the gods simply sitting a bit higher up and relying on their followers to manage things for them. We can see here the connection with lineages, which often included divine elements, discussed previously. Further, the fact that many communities shared the same gods meant they operated under the same divine authority and protection when participating in these activities and rites and gave them their own version of a common, divine lineage. This allowed the various groups and individuals to relinquish some of their authority, in a shared context, without a loss of prestige or dignity. Clan leaders could save face and preserve their dignity by pretending they weren't compromising with each other but bowing to the will of the gods. The gods were vitally important players within the social landscape of central Italy, and indeed the entire ancient Mediterranean basin. They acted as shared and mutually recognized leaders and patrons for communities, which encouraged and facilitated interaction and communication. This was a deeply practical religion that served an important set of social, political, and economic functions in everyday life. While small settlements may have been able to get by with a human leader, major communities needed this extra level of divine "super elites" at the top of their socioeconomic ladder—and the more the better.

In this context, one should also think a little about human elites. While the gods were important, they were also not particularly active in a practical or tangible way, and the real power of a community was obviously determined by the people who congregated there. However, while the gods, and perhaps some elite leaders, may have kept stable homes in communities, our evidence for elite habitation at sites like early Rome is quite limited. Archaic Rome was designed as a place where people *went*, but not necessarily a place where a lot of people *lived*. Indeed, while it was often useful to be close to the center of power, it was also quite unpleasant and even dangerous. With limited sewage and sanitation, disease was common in ancient cities—and especially large ones. Rome was also particularly prone to malaria due to its location near a bend in the Tiber and the marshy conditions near the foot of the hills (see Fig. 5). While communities could also be hubs of production, and it is clear that the *velabrum* in Rome (a clay bed sandwiched between the Palatine and Capitoline hills) was a bustling center of industry, this could also lead to loud and smoky conditions. As a result, most elites (and indeed the vast majority of

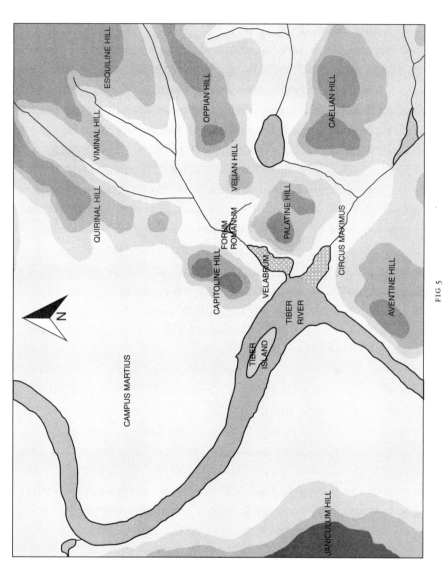

FIG 5
Map of the site of archaic Rome.

the population, as far as we can tell) lived outside of the urban area. Many of them may have been highly mobile, moving along regular transhumance routes with animals, while others may have been based in rural farms and proto-villas. The urban center of Rome was a place they visited, but only when they needed to.

However, in order to serve this bustling center and its regular flow of visitors, some people did, of course, need to live in the community as well, and Romulus is recorded as organizing them in a particular way. He established himself as a *rex*—commonly translated as "king," although that does not fully capture the essence, as will be discussed below—supposedly following Etruscan precedents. He is reported as living on the Palatine hill, in the so-called *casa Romuli* ("hut of Romulus") which was preserved down to the Empire, while his successors lived in the *regia* ("house of the king") down in the *Forum Romanum*, the political heart of the city between the hills. Romulus supposedly expanded the population of the community through a war, and subsequent treaty and alliance, with the Sabines—something which started off with seizing Sabine women at a festival and ended in a period of co-governance with the Sabine leader Titus Tatius.[31] He then divided the population into three tribes, the Tities, Ramnes, and Luceres, and also 30 *curiae* (singular *curia*, often translated as "assembly"), with 10 per tribe.[32]

The *curiae* represent one of the more important, and also enigmatic, aspects of the so-called "Romulan Constitution." The great twentieth-century historian of early Rome, Arnaldo Momigliano, famously said, "It is perhaps no exaggeration to say that we would know how the archaic Roman institutions worked if we knew what the *curiae* were," and he was surely right.[33] Frustratingly, though, despite all the advances in the field we have seen since he wrote that line over 60 years ago, we are still struggling with what *curiae* were and how they functioned—although things are, perhaps, a little clearer now.

The *curiae* are one of the few aspects of Rome's social and political organization from the regal period that is accepted by modern historians as authentically Archaic, and they evidently still existed in the late Republic and early Empire, when most of our surviving literary accounts were written. Although clearly vestigial by that later point, and relegated to a somewhat obscure religious role, the *curiae* likely represented the most important divisions of early Rome's urban community. Interestingly, given Rome's role as a hub of interaction for regional elites based outside the city (embodied by the early Senate), the *curiae* seem to have represented the population of the urban community itself, as defined by the ritual boundary of city known as the *pomerium*. The *curiae* represented the population of the city itself. They were associated with local shrines and their power did not extend beyond the limits of the urban center. This is best seen in the grant of *imperium* that the *curiae* gave to both the king and Rome's later military magistrates. *Imperium* granted these men significant power and prestige within the city, although always in negotiation with the urban political structures. Famously, *imperium*-wielding magistrates could not command military forces in Rome, except when celebrating a "triumph" (a ritual victory parade through the city). However, *imperium* gave these men the ability to act on behalf of the community outside of the *pomerium*, including giving them the power of life and death over those under their command. This sets up a tension within Roman politics, which is visible throughout much of the Republic, between the politics inside the *urbs* and politics outside its limits. The nature of Roman power and influence meant very different things in each of these contexts, and how the Romans bridged this divide was always a bit tricky.

This is also why the common translation of *rex* (plural *reges*) as "king" is not ideal. It is probably the best English translation we have but certainly doesn't capture all the nuance and complexity of the original Roman office. The *rex*, like a king, was a monarch who, once in the role, ruled for life. But the *rex*'s power operated in a very particular way. First, he was elected, usually as an adult and only after he had proven his abilities. Indeed, while family power was often hereditary, this position was explicitly not. The *rex* was, effectively, a magistrate with a life-long term. Second, the *rex* actually seemed to have more power outside of the community than he had within it. He was not the uncontested master of his community, although he did hold a privileged position there. This is probably the most significant difference between the ancient Roman office and our modern understanding of kingship. Third, in a way reminiscent of the Macedonian kingship of Philip II and Alexander the Great (at least at the start of his reign), the

Roman kings seem to have been seen as the simply "best among equals" and not inherently superior. While we do not have the same regular threat of usurpation and assassination we see in the Macedonian context, with multiple elites constantly vying for the role, the position of the Roman king was clearly negotiated and relied on keeping the goodwill of the Senate. Indeed, while the role certainly contained religious elements, Roman kings did not rule by divine right.

Romulus supposedly went on to fight various wars against other local powers, most notably the nearby communities of Veii and Fidenae, two of early Rome's most important early rivals. The *curiae*, in addition to forming Rome's first assembly, were also the basis of the army. According to our ancient sources, each *curia* supposedly contributed 100 infantrymen and 10 cavalrymen to the king, creating a total force of 3,000 infantry and 300 cavalry.[34] While most modern authors focus on the infantry, the ancient sources give more details about and place emphasis on the cavalry, which were also called the *celeres*, or "swift ones." The overall force of 300 was divided into 10 *turmae* of 30 men each, which were in turn divided into groups of 10 led by officers called *decuriones* (literally, "leaders of 10").[35] We now think most of this was invented by antiquarians writing in the late Republic, but it is an interesting set of details, as it again puts military and political power at the heart of the Roman project.

Romulus was also an active combatant himself and dedicated the first *spolia opima* ("noble spoils") of the city, which were a specific type of trophy taken during a successful duel between the commanders of opposing armies. Like so many other details of his life, the demise of Romulus is also classically enigmatic. Livy records that Romulus went out to review the army on the *Campus Martius* ("Field of Mars") outside the city when a sudden storm rose up.[36] Some stories suggest that Romulus disappeared in the storm, taken to the heavens by a whirlwind, while others suggest that he was murdered (indeed, Livy suggests "physically torn apart by hand") by some of the assembled Senators. This possible death at the hands of rival elites also sets up a theme visible throughout the Republic, famously down to Caesar, of violent tensions among the local elites. Despite his political and religious reforms, the basis of Romulus' power and life was violence.

Sons of Venus and Mars

ROME'S *REGES*

The Romans recorded that Romulus was succeeded by a series of six other kings, for seven in total, covering the almost two and a half centuries from 753 to 510. While the long reigns of modern monarchs, like the British queens Victoria and Elizabeth II, suggest that this is possible, it is surely implausible—especially given that life expectancy was lower in archaic Italy, these men always took the throne as adults, lived violent lives as warrior kings, and several are reported as dying violent deaths. Again, even our Roman sources seem to have viewed this record with a bit of skepticism. However, the nature of these kings in the Roman tradition is instructive. The first three kings—Romulus, Numa Pompilius, and Tullus Hostilius—are often considered more mythic. The fourth king, Ancus Marcius, is so frustratingly elusive that he has been argued to be either a duplication of Numa or a "placeholder" inserted into the narrative to fill things out. The final three kings—Tarquinius Priscus, Servius Tullius, and Tarquinius Superbus—are often considered slightly more historical, or at least more realistic.

While Romulus was the complete *rex*, ticking all the boxes expected of an early Roman leader, Numa and Tullus Hositilius seem to represent the two distinct sides of Roman governance—negotiation and war. Numa is often described as a religious leader or "philosopher king." Indeed, the Romans pushed this narrative so far that he became associated with some pretty incredible anecdotes—even for this somewhat mythical period. For instance, both Livy and Plutarch commented on the tradition that he was supposedly a close friend and student of the philosopher Pythagoras, known today for his mathematical theorem relating to triangles, despite the admitted fact that Pythagoras lived as many as five generations after Numa.[37] Numa also supposedly wrote a series of 24 books on divine wisdom, reportedly "rediscovered" in the second century.[38] While he would have been a rough contemporary of Homer and Hesiod, meaning that it is arguably possible for this to be true, the supposed existence of such an expansive set of literary texts in Italy at this time—miraculously preserved for 500 years, Livy suggests "not merely whole, but looking absolutely fresh"—seems to have raised eyebrows even in antiquity.

But apart from these more fantastic aspects, Numa was remembered as a negotiator. Although a Sabine, and so something of an outsider in the community (Sabines were associated with a region to the north and east of Rome), he was a consensus candidate who was elected to the position of king unanimously and held the respect of both citizens and Senators throughout his reign. As Livy suggests, "When he had thus obtained the kingship, he prepared to give the new City, founded by force of arms, a new foundation in law, statutes, and observances."[39] He did this through diplomacy and religion. He brokered treaties with local tribes, created a calendar for festivals and meetings, and established priesthoods and cults. Again, religion played many roles in ancient communities, but a key aspect was the way it brought people together in a set place, at a set time, and under known and agreed protections and conditions. Religion created the framework for the social and political interaction that defined the community. It is noteworthy that the Romans recognized this by placing a deeply religious, "philosopher king" as the community's second leader after the eponymous founder.

Tullus Hostilius, Rome's third king, represents the other side of the coin. Indeed, perhaps in an effort to emphasize this contrast with Numa, Plutarch records the tradition that Hostilius was not only *not* a consensus candidate for the position of king, but that he defeated the first *pontifex maximus*, or chief priest, in the contest for the role.[40] Livy goes on to record that not only was he unlike the peaceful negotiator Numa, but he was more warlike than even Romulus had been.[41] His reign was remembered for two major events. The first was the conquest of Alba Longa, the old home of King Numitor, now supposedly led by a Latin noble named Gaius Cluilius. This conflict evidently began over raiding for cattle and involved several famous battles as well as the creation of a couple of new institutions—most notably the fetial priests, tasked with negotiating with foreign powers and declaring war. It is, though, the conclusion of the war that is most interesting here. After defeating the Latins at Alba Longa, Tullus Hostilius famously leveled the physical city and brought the people to Rome.[42] They were not added as slaves or captives, but as citizens. Livy suggests they doubled the number of citizens in Rome, resulting in the city expanding to include the Caelian hill to allow them to settle. The prominent families of Alba Longa, including Republican powerhouses like the Julii (the family of Caesar), were also brought into the Senate at this time. Indeed, this measure brought about Tullus Hostilius' second great act, the construction of the *Curia Hostilia*, or the Senate House. He also used this influx of elites and their followers to expand the Roman army, doubling the number of cavalry and replenishing the infantry.

This is a truly fascinating development. While the community of Rome had already been established as a nexus for peaceful negotiation by Numa, and to a lesser extent Romulus, in the myth of Tullus Hostilius we can see a very different approach to politics, expansion, and imperialism brought to the fore. The religious aspects of the Roman community gave it coherence, structure, and stability, but growth, of both the army and elite, came through warfare. We can see hints of this in the life of Romulus, where his war with the Sabines resulted in an expansion of the city, but it is emphasized through the reign of Tullus Hostilius. Beyond the *pomerium* of the city, the way the Romans expanded their influence was through conquest—although of a particular type. The narrative is quite specific that this expansion did not involve territorial conquest, as the Romans were not recorded as trying to settle or control Alba Longa or its territory. In contrast, they destroyed it and brought the inhabitants to Rome, not as subjects, but as equals. This was an arrangement that was evidently accepted by both sides, even down into the more historical period of the fourth and third centuries, which will be discussed later in this book. It is also an arrangement that modern scholars have struggled to explain. Why would the Romans agree to share power equally with a people they had just conquered? Why would a conquered people agree to peacefully join a community that had just brutally conquered them? The answers to these questions lay at the heart of Roman Republican imperialism, as we will see.

Tullus Hostilius died a violent death, either at the hands of the gods or his rivals, depending on the version, and was succeeded by Ancus Marcius. As noted above, the reign of Ancus Marcius is frustrating as it lacks any of the specific traits or anecdotes that distinguish those of the kings both before and after. In general, however, he continues the trends already seen. Within the city of Rome, he continued to work toward increased structure and coherence, largely through religion. Externally, he led various campaigns against the Latins, bringing in new citizens who largely settled on the Aventine hill. He supposedly died after a reign of 24 years, leaving behind two sons, neither of whom became king.

Rome's final three kings are often associated with a period of Etruscan dominance in Rome. The first was Lucius Tarquinius Priscus, often referred to as simply "Tarquin" or "the elder Tarquin" in modern scholarship. As his name suggests, he was supposedly from the Etruscan community of Tarquinia, located about 90 km (56 miles) northwest of Rome. We should not make too much of this Etruscan origin, though. While some scholars used to see "Etruria" and "Latium" as something akin to pro-nation states, with discrete cultures and ethnic profiles (with the Etruscans being famously mysterious and perhaps eastern in origin), most scholars now understand that these are, at best, historical "mirages." Decades of archaeological work have demonstrated that all of the peoples of central Italy developed out of the same, local, broadly shared Villanovan and Apennine cultures. When this is coupled with the high levels of mobility and interaction we see across this region, it is clear we should think about all the people of central Italy as effectively part of a single population. In practical terms, the Etruscans, Latins, and even peoples like the Sabines and Umbrians, were all just "central Italians."

This does not mean, however, that all central Italians did things the same way. Individual families and communities would have had their own distinctive practices, traditions, and norms. Communities in certain regions seem to have had preferences, often shaped by the local geography. The communities of Etruria had some of the more impressive early structures, roads, and tombs—helped by the presence of easily quarried, local volcanic tuff in the region. They also seem to have preferred using a different, non-Indo-European language when writing inscriptions, although it is virtually certain that they could communicate in Latin, Greek, and a number of other languages as well. Indeed, these local preferences and norms did not stop people from regularly interacting, intermixing, and moving between communities and regions. Local differences were often variations on a theme and could perhaps be considered "branding" or conscious differentiating in order to make their own way of doing something just a little bit special. Differences were important because so much of what they did and how they lived their lives was so similar. In fact, the differences within regions in central Italy were sometimes more pronounced than those between regions.

Tarquin's father was remembered to be a man named Demaratus of Corinth, and so was likely part of a vast network of mobile Mediterranean elites that was also active across the region at this time. The dynamism and movement that scholars have increasingly identified in central Italy was not limited to this region but could be found across the Mediterranean basin. Many people were regularly on the move across this wider area as merchants, craftspeople, soldiers, raiders/pirates, migrants, and for countless other reasons—including, at least among the elite, seeking better opportunities to exert power and influence. Now, no one is suggesting that the Mediterranean was full of nomads or that there was regular mass migration. Rather, it is simply that mobility and travel were common and a regular part of life for at least a segment of ancient society, which facilitated a general level of communication, connectivity, and shared knowledge across the region. People were aware of the wider world, they knew what was happening in other communities, and movement between communities (and regions) was common. While not everyone may have traveled extensively themselves, they would not have been particularly surprised to see a foreigner or group of foreigners arrive in their settlement. Indeed, one could think about the adventures of Homer's Odysseus, and how he was able to travel widely and expect to be welcomed, following shared, accepted norms, wherever he went. Although this is obviously a fictional tale, the principles it was founded upon seem to be based on real, existing practices. While this dynamism and connectivity is evident going back to at least the Bronze Age (and likely before), there was a significant expansion in this mobility from the eighth and seventh centuries onwards.

This expansion has often been discussed under the label of "Greek colonization," although this label does not fully encapsulate the situation, as it was not only the Greeks on the move. We also have the movement of Phoenicians (and the foundation of Carthage in North Africa ca. 800) alongside the expansion of many other networks, including within Italy. Elite families from across the Mediterranean seem to have gotten more interested in not only travel itself but also establishing stable communities and bases where they could travel to and from in this period. It must be noted that the entire phenomenon and its implications are hotly debated in modern scholarship,[43] but the basic facts are largely uncontested with respect to Italy: there is clear evidence for increased movement and interaction between elites and communities from across the eastern Mediterranean and (especially southern) Italy. Tarquinia and Rome were also certainly nodes in this network of interaction, and so it would not be unusual to see men like Demaratus or Tarquin in either community.

Although much of the elder Tarquin's life, as recorded by the sources, is likely just as fictive as that of Romulus or Numa, he is a much more believable character overall. The same is generally thought to be true for the final two kings who followed him, Servius Tullius and Tarquinius Superbus. The nature of the narrative for Rome takes on a rather different tone in this period as well. The reasons for this are unclear, but it is noteworthy that it aligns roughly with the emergence of the city of Rome in archaeological terms. The elder Tarquin traditionally ruled from 616 to 578, which coincides with both the earliest archaeological evidence for the Roman Forum and a shift in the course of the Tiber which would have made Rome a much more attractive crossing point.[44] Thus, while we no longer attribute the growth of Rome in this period to exposure to a "superior Etruscan culture," the so-called "Grand Rome of the Tarquins" in the sixth century, distinguished by a spate of new public building projects, may indeed be based upon a real historical memory. From the material evidence, at least, this period saw the rise of Rome as a major urban center, and it is therefore interesting that the literature seems to change at precisely this point as well. Although it may simply be a coincidence, or the result of moving ever closer to the point when the Romans began to leave written records, the narrative for this period preserves more plausible historical details.

The elder Tarquin is perhaps the least stereotypical of Rome's kings. With a complex origin story and rise to power, all of which aligns well with what we know about the period from other sources, many details of his life and reign make sense historically. He supposedly expanded the Senate to 300 by adding 100 men from minor *gentes* ("clans" or "families"), and also doubled the number of *equites*, or "cavalry."[45] Interestingly, the Senatorial expansion did not involve warfare, as previous iterations had done, but may reflect the growing size and importance of the city during this period as a hub for elite interaction. Rome was increasingly a place people wanted to go to and associate with, and force was not needed to convince them.

This is not to say, however, that Tarquin was a peaceful king. He waged wars against all of Rome's traditional opponents, including the Latins, Etruscans, and Sabines. But, interestingly, none of these campaigns involved or culminated in integration. Instead, the sources record that Tarquin's warfare was extractive, bringing spoils and prisoners back to Rome, and using them to fund his construction projects. It is uncertain what to make of this. It is possible that, as he was recorded as a great builder, the authors of our sources assumed that his constructions were funded in the same way as those of later leaders, using the spoils of war. Alternatively, this may reflect a real historical memory, as the emergent community of Rome began to establish a discrete civic identity that sometimes militated against the inclusion of recent enemies. What is interesting, ultimately, is that it is different and highlights that the Romans envisaged another, extractive mode of warfare operating in this early period, in addition to the more integrative and expansionist model.

Rome's sixth king, Servius Tullius, was remembered as the great lawgiver of the early city. While he did engage in some limited warfare at the start of his reign, his most significant impact on the Roman community and army was through their reorganization. In a series of measures that might again align with what the archaeology suggests about the growth of Rome during the sixth century, Servius Tullius is remembered for reorganizing and rationalizing Rome's burgeoning population through the institution of a new set of tribes, which included not only the urban center (four new urban tribes, replacing Romulus' three), but also Rome's hinterland, or surrounding countryside (15 new rural tribes—which would grow to 31 over the course of the Republic). These tribes replaced the old system completely and seemed to reflect the wider catchment of the Roman community. Rome, by this period, was more than just an urban core. It was the center for a wider regional population that could be roughly categorized into 15 units, most of which bore the names of powerful families. While some scholars have attempted to firmly place these Servian tribes in the landscape as distinct geographic zones, this is likely indicative at best.[46] We should probably not imagine these tribes as having distinct territories with rigid borders in this period, but rather that they simply operated in areas of traditional influence. While they were certainly remembered as being beyond the *pomerium* of Rome and in the countryside, there is little to suggest that they were fixed or stable in this early period.

Servius Tullius also, supposedly, divided Roman society into socioeconomic groups, or "classes." By the late Republic, there were evidently seven of these divisions: the *equites* or "cavalry" (although this slowly evolved into a socioeconomic category instead of a military one), and then the first, second, third, fourth, and fifth classes, as well as the *capite censi* or "head count," each associated with a particular amount of wealth and a specific military panoply or set of equipment.[47] The fact that neither the tribal nor the centuriate systems, nor their associated assemblies, seem to have had a political role or function in the regal period has led many to suggest that these were actually innovations of the early Republic that were pushed back into the regal period by later writers to, perhaps, give them added legitimacy by virtue of greater antiquity. However, it is worth noting that these were not only political entities. The tribes and centuries formed the basis of Rome's army throughout the Republic. The tribes acted as the primary mechanism for recruitment, while the classes differentiated the troop types. Most of the rank-and-file officers of the Roman army seem to have carried titles that connected them with at least one of these institutions, most notably centurions (connected with the centuries) and military tribunes (connected to the tribes). They were also, evidently, based on clans and groups that we think might have operated in the region at this time—in other words, the Fabian tribe in the Roman system seems to be associated with the *gens Fabia* (or Fabian family) and their typical area of control. Thus, while the political aspects may have come about later, it is not unthinkable that Rome's rulers reorganized the military population in the sixth century to better capture and organize the growing strength of the community and the families that were increasingly aligned with it.

Rome's final king, Lucius Tarquinius Superbus, or "Tarquin the Proud," was in many ways the archetypal "tyrant"—in the mold of (the not coincidentally contemporary) Hippias of Athens. Although he was the latest of Rome's kings, and so one might expect him to be the one with the most reliable record, it is not clear if this is the case. The record of his reign is full of detailed and dramatic anecdotes, which give him a distinctive character—cunning but effective, cruel but efficient. However, it is likely that the vast majority of the information was passed down through the fluid oral tradition, shaped by generations of storytellers into a collection of archetypes, meaning that much of it must be taken with a rather large pinch of salt. The life of Lucius Tarquinius Superbus is a cautionary tale about the dangers of monarchy and the rationale for the creation of the Republic, and must always be seen in this light. However, this does not mean it is *entirely* made up.

For instance, Tarquinius Superbus' reign is largely defined by tensions with the region's other powerful clan leaders. This is both the reason for the fall of the monarchy, as we will see in a moment, and also seems to align with the wider picture we have constructed so far. Under Rome's first four kings, the community had expanded its population through warfare and integration, while under the elder Tarquin and Servius Tullius, Rome began to grow by attracting new members and clans peacefully. This shift in how Rome was expanding is quite important. These new arrivals were often powerful in their own right and had arrived on their own terms. They were not conquered subjects but relative equals, and many of them may not have taken kindly to being ordered around by the local ruler simply because his family had arrived first. While being in control of Rome, which was certainly one of the largest communities in the area, would have given the king a considerable amount of power and influence, it did not put him on an entirely different level from these other local elites. It is, therefore, entirely fitting that Tarquinius Superbus is associated with the "tall poppy" allegory.

The story, as preserved in the works of both Livy and Dionysius of Halicarnassus, records that Tarquinius Superbus had worked covertly to integrate his son Sextus Tarquinius, into the elite of the nearby community of Gabii—to the extent of pretending that he and his son had had a falling out, so that the Gabini did not suspect this was a plot to extend Roman power.[48] Once the young Sextus Tarquinius had won over the trust of the Gabini, he sent a messenger to his father asking for further instructions. Tarquinius Superbus did not give a verbal command. Instead, he walked to his garden with the messenger, took a stick, and struck off the heads of the tallest poppies. The messenger was then sent back to Sextus, who understood the action to mean that he should kill the chief men of Gabii and assert his own power over the community. In addition to providing a nice narrative anecdote, this story sums up the nature of elite politics in central Italy at this time. While it was applied to Gabii here, in only a few short years Tarquinius Superbus would become the "tall poppy" that was struck down at Rome. This period is defined by the rise of an expansive and competitive clan-based elite in central Italy, who increasingly interacted through, and fought over, control of the region's emerging urban centers.

THE END OF THE REGAL PERIOD

The fall of the Roman monarchy represents an interesting shift in this ongoing competition among the region's elite families, although it was certainly not the end of it. In fact, the creation of the Roman Republic seems to have consciously opened the competition up a bit more. Rather than a single family attempting to monopolize power in the community— a situation that had become increasingly untenable in a city the size of Rome in the late sixth century—the Republican system embraced open competition among the elite families, organizing and rationalizing it. It allowed a larger segment of the local elite to vie for power on a regular basis, using mutually agreed and accepted rules.

However, we shouldn't pretend that this shift was driven by noble and peaceful goals, or that it was particularly democratic in nature. Despite the popular narrative that developed over the centuries, and which played an important role in the creation of states like the modern American and French republics, this was not a popular revolt against the tyranny of "kingship" as an idea or system of government. While the increasingly cruel and oppressive actions of the Tarquins were certainly cited as a reason to remove them as leaders specifically, the change in the political system was actually reasonably subtle and motivated by the personal greed and ambitions of rival clan leaders. The shift was also shaped, first and foremost, by violence, and the events that precipitated it began with something as menial as a drunken wager between two young men.

Lucius Tarquinius Collatinus was a nephew of the king Tarquinius Superbus. One evening, while out drinking with the king's son Sextus, they began to talk about their wives and debate whose wife was the best. In order to settle the matter, they decided to head back to Rome, unannounced, and spy on the women to see what they might be up to when their husbands weren't around. When the men reached the house of Sextus, they found his wife throwing a lavish party and drinking heavily. However, when they reached the house of Collatinus, they found his wife, the virtuous Lucretia, quietly and diligently weaving by lamplight. Collatinus, therefore, won the bet, and Sextus Tarquinius was left stewing, his pride in tatters.

Sextus was not one to take a loss like this quietly, however, and he returned to the house of Collatinus several days later, while Collatinus was away. When he arrived, Lucretia welcomed the unexpected visitor warmly, prepared a fine meal for him, and offered him the guest quarters. Sextus Tarquinius waited until the servants had retired and then attacked Lucretia, attempting to rape her at sword point. Lucretia fought back valiantly until Sextus threatened to not only kill her but also disgrace her family. He said that after he killed her, he would also kill a slave and place the body next to hers. He would then claim that he had discovered her and the slave together and killed them both to save the honor of his "good friend and cousin" Collatinus. This threat was evidently too much for Lucretia, and she gave up the fight.

After Sextus left the house, Lucretia sent messengers to both her husband and her father, asking them to come home immediately and, perhaps oddly, to each bring a witness. When they arrived, she told them what had happened and made them both swear an oath, in front of their witnesses, that they would exact revenge. The men immediately swore the oath and also tried to comfort her, assuring her that clearly none of this was her fault. According to Livy, however, Lucretia could not bear the shame. Once her male family members had sworn vengeance on her behalf, she supposedly declared, "It is for you to determine what will happen to Sextus; for my own part, though I acquit myself of the sin, I do not absolve myself from punishment; never shall an unchaste woman live through the example of Lucretia."[49] She then pulled out a knife that she had hidden in her dress and stabbed herself through the heart (see Fig. 6 for Rembrandt's anachronistic depiction of this moment).

Collatinus and Lucretia's father fell to the ground in shock, wailing for their lost wife and daughter. The young Lucius Junius Brutus, however, immediately stepped forward and into action. Brutus was another member of the wider Tarquinian family (most of the characters in this narrative were related), although not a very popular or powerful one. The name Brutus was actually a nickname which meant "stupid" or "blunt"—connected to the modern English word "brute"—and he was evidently

FIG 6
Lucretia, 1669, Rembrandt.

one of the lower members of the royal family and part of the separate Junii branch. He had been brought by Collatinus merely to act as his witness, as Lucretia had requested. It was not Brutus' place or duty to right this wrong, but he clearly saw an opportunity and took it. While Collatinus and Lucretia's father wept, Brutus grabbed the knife from Lucretia's bloody hand, held it high, and declared that not only would he avenge Lucretia's honor against Sextus Tarquinius, but he would also end the entire wicked kingship of Tarquinius Superbus. For Brutus, this act was merely the final straw—one more display of cruelty and disdain for other elite families by Tarquin and his son. Brutus swore to end this tyranny. Collatinus and Lucretia's father were in no state to argue, and so Brutus led the uprising against the king.

The actual revolt, however, turned out to be quite simple and straightforward. The king was away at the time, leading an attack on a nearby settlement, and Sextus seemed to have conveniently disappeared after his attack on Lucretia. As a result, Brutus simply mobilized the remaining families and soldiers in Rome and barred the gates against the Tarquins' return. That was it. When the king returned to Rome to find the gates shut against him, he retreated to the community of Caere to the north while his son Sextus eventually ended up in Gabii. Both Tarquins supposedly fought against the Romans many times in the coming years, trying in vain to regain the throne, but this never seemed close to happening. Without a king, governance of the community was taken over jointly by Brutus and Collatinus, who were remembered as being the first consuls of the new Republic.

While much of this narrative is almost certainly invented, it offers some insight into how the Romans thought about both the monarchy and the Republic. Even in the late Republic, when popular politics were often deployed, the end of the monarchy was not remembered as a popular uprising. The common people are nowhere to be seen. Instead, this was a revolt by elites, for elites. Although the eventual overthrow of the Tarquins was clearly thought to be in response to the extreme behavior of the king and his son, it was not a reaction to the nature of their power. In fact, the system that was put in place to replace the monarchy retained almost all of the monarchy's core features and systems.

It is also important to note how the ultimate downfall of the Tarquins was shaped by the power and sacrifice of Lucretia, an elite Roman woman. Although she was obviously a victim in all of this, the fact that the deeply patriarchal Romans put a woman at the center of this story is important. While her character was written by male authors for a male audience, she was given a certain amount of agency in the narrative. She was the one who ordered her male family members to take the oath, and it was her self-sacrifice that cemented it. She was also not unique in this role, as there were other women, throughout Roman history, who performed similar actions at key moments of tension and transition. The most pivotal political moments in Rome involved the entire family, and not just the men.

THE *RES PUBLICA*

The early imperial historian Tacitus famously claimed that, in the beginning, Rome was ruled by kings but "freedom and the consulship" were established by Brutus in 509 with the creation of the Republic.[50] This is either a tremendous overstatement or a tremendous understatement, depending on your point of view. For the vast majority of people living in and around Rome, the end of the monarchy and the beginning of the Republic may have barely even registered. The closest modern comparison might be a situation where a military dictatorship is ousted through a military coup d'état, and a single "general for life" is replaced by a committee of generals, or junta, who govern more collectively. The fundamental nature of power remains the same, as does its expression. There are simply more people at the top of what is now an ever so slightly truncated pyramid. But for most people within society, life continues on as it had before.

For those generals involved in the coup, however, things are very different indeed. In late sixth-century Rome, this committee of generals would equate to the leaders of the powerful clans and families in Rome, who had previously been both competing against each other, and struggling against the monopoly on civic and community-based military power held by the king. With the removal of the king, the political playing field in Rome had

Sons of Venus and Mars

been both opened up and, with the creation of the Republic, it was levelled—at least to a certain extent.

The Republic, or *res publica* ("public thing"), is incredibly hard to define as it changed dramatically over the course of its many centuries. As suggested earlier, however, at its core it was a power-sharing agreement among a set of powerful clan leaders that had established a connection with and through the community of Rome. All our sources agree that the Republic grew out of the relationship that the community had previously developed with the king. During the regal period, the 30 *curiae* of Rome, which collectively represented the urban community, had created a special relationship with a single individual embodied by grants of *imperium* (communal power, especially in the military sphere) and *auspicium* (divine sanction).[51] These two powers gave the king the position of patron, or even an effective *paterfamilias* ("head of household") over the wider community. It allowed him to command the community's military forces as he would his own clan, conduct sacrifices, control property, make legal rulings, and speak for the community. In return, he would protect the community as he would his own family. It was a reciprocal relationship, full of ritually confirmed responsibilities. It is clear that the elites who removed Tarquinius Superbus did not want to change the nature of this relationship. Indeed, *imperium* and *auspicium* would continue to be granted throughout the entirety of the Republic, and the Republic's magistracies retained much of this symbolic, family-based character. What the elites of Rome wanted to do was share this power. Rather than being granted for life, *imperium* and *auspicium* were granted for only a year at a time, and to more than one individual.[52]

It remains unclear how it was decided who would get this power each year, or indeed how many. While Tacitus, in the opening to his *Annales* mentioned above, clearly indicates that he thought the consulship (i.e. the system of having two chief magistrates) dated to 509, our sources also admit to a tradition where the chief magistrates of the early Republic were in fact called "praetors" (literally "leaders," and the same name as a slightly lesser magistrate in later years), and there may have been more than two each year. The traditional election by the *comitia centuriata*, or centuriate assembly, has also been called into question in this early period. Although our later sources clearly assume this body was functioning as it did in the late Republic, there is a strong possibility that it did not elect consuls until at least the middle of the fifth century and possibly as late as 367. Before this point, the selection may have been similar to that of selecting the king during the regal period, where the matter was decided in the Senate, or collected elite family heads, and then sent to the *curiae* for confirmation. Of relevance for us now, though, is that the transition to the Republic seems to have changed very little, in the short term, for both the majority of Romans and, indeed, the Roman community. The Romans had effectively replaced one king with many. The nature of power remained the same, channeled through *imperium* and *auspicium*, which gave those imbued with it the power to act as a patron or *paterfamilias* for the community, but in a reciprocal manner. It was now simply more dispersed and evidently redistributed on a more regular basis.

Looking at the medium-to-long term, however, some changes do begin to emerge, even in our remembered tradition. Most notably, carving up the power of king and reallocating it every year meant that individual figures seem to have lacked the ability to impact the community in the same way as those before them. While the Roman community continued to evolve in this period, it was increasingly shaped by groups rather than individuals—if our sources are to be believed at least. For instance, we have the rise of *comitia* (political gatherings), with the tribal assembly, in particular, coming to prominence as the political voice of a group increasingly known as the "plebeians" (more about them later as well). On the other side of the coin, we have the rise of the "patricians," who seem to have represented the elite families of Rome. We also have the Senate, and then boards of *decemviri* ("10 men") who step in as lawgivers in the mid-fifth century. Internal politics in Rome were amazingly corporate in this period, at least as preserved in our sources.[53]

When it comes to warfare and activity outside of the community, however, very little seems to change. We can see a gradual shift in the aims and goals, as will be discussed in later chapters, as well as experiments with different types of military magistracies and leadership. But, despite its increasing focus on groups and bureaucracy in this period, all our evidence seems to indicate that warfare continued to operate much as it had before. A key reason behind this is that, while we often talk about "Roman warfare" and the "Roman army," there was very little that was particularly "Roman" about either in this period. In the fifth century, as in the sixth and seventh centuries before, warfare in central Italy was dominated by the region's clans. Although these extended families used communities as points of connection or alliance, or as sources for additional manpower or resources when they needed it, the armies of the period were functionally clan-based. As a result, this consistency in Roman warfare may be an authentic memory—a point arguably supported by the fact that the situation seemed to confuse ancient authors. While Rome's social and political landscape supposedly changed dramatically, in military terms Rome seems to have existed in something of an equilibrium for much of the fifth century. The Romans supposedly fought on an almost annual basis but never seemed to either accomplish or lose very much. In terms of Roman imperialism and empire then, the birth of the Republic was a nonevent.

MARCUS FURIUS CAMILLUS

Things begin to change again toward the end of the fifth century, with some subtle shifts in the nature of warfare, a monumental conflict with Rome's great rival Veii, a great defeat at the hands of the Gauls, and the emergence of Rome's next great "founder" of the city—the last, evidently, before the age of Augustus—Marcus Furius Camillus.[54]

Camillus, as Plutarch records, was known by some as the "Second Founder of Rome" after Romulus, although his legacy seems to have waned by the time of Livy and he has been largely (and sadly) forgotten by modern audiences. A key reason behind his declining popularity and status seems to be that later Romans were somewhat confused about what he had actually achieved. Although quite active—holding the office of consular tribune seven times (403, 401, 398, 394, 386, 384, and 381), dictator three times (396, 390, and 368), and the censorship once (403)—as well as being associated with every one of the key moments in Rome's history during the first half of the fourth century, the nature and ramifications of his career were contested and unclear. Not only does there seem to be an incredibly wide range of versions of his life in circulation by the late Republic, each with different details and focus, but many authors seem somewhat puzzled by Camillus' importance in the first place. While no one could doubt his popularity, given the number of times he was elected, his achievements are often uncertain. For instance, although Camillus is recorded by Livy as leading the final, victorious assault on Veii in his first dictatorship of 396, his contested settlement after the sack of Veii complicates his involvement. Although Rome defeated Veii in 396, the Romans evidently only took direct control of the community's territory years later, in 387, when it was reorganized into a number of new tribal zones. Camillus was remembered as the man in charge of the military action to capture the city, but not the political integration and ultimate acquisition of land and power. This sort of inconclusive involvement seems fairly standard for him in the surviving tradition.

Camillus is also associated with the sack of Rome by the Gauls in 390, but again in a somewhat confusing manner. The Romans clearly remembered the sack of the city by Brennus' Gauls as being one of their most humiliating military defeats. As will be discussed in more detail in the next chapter, the Gallic sack of Rome is probably one of the most important events from the city's early history, leaving an indelible mark on Roman society. However, the fact that this defeat supposedly occurred right in the middle of Camillus' illustrious military career creates something of a tension. How could Camillus have allowed this to happen? The authors of our sources resolved this by claiming that Camillus was conveniently away from Rome when the Gauls attacked, having been exiled to Ardea right before the event. Either during or after the defeat, depending on the tradition, he returned to Rome to take up the dictatorship to (perhaps) save Rome from the threat. However, when he arrived and what he did is uncertain. Both Livy and Plutarch report that Camillus arrived just in time to prevent the payment of a gold ransom to Brennus, thus saving both Rome's wealth and honor.[55] The historian Diodorus, however, suggests that Brennus had already left with the gold by the time Camillus arrived, although he notes that Camillus was later able to chase down the Gauls at Veascium and recover the money there.[56] In contrast to all of these, Polybius, who is our earliest extant source, suggests that the Gauls were able to leave with the gold and Camillus was only there to help the city rebuild.[57] So, again, our sources remember Camillus as being involved in some way, but his impact is uncertain.

Shifting to politics, in his third dictatorship Camillus supposedly oversaw the passing of the Licinio-Sextian reforms (we will discuss these in more detail in the next chapter), which ended a period of supposed political anarchy in Rome and marked the beginning of the end of the "Struggle of the Orders" and the emergence of Rome's full political system with the advent of the consulship and praetorship. This was also, certainly, a momentous episode, but Camillus' involvement is mixed—as he seems to have initially been against the measures, before helping them to pass— and it is also uncertain whether this should be seen as a "victory" or "defeat" for him. While the reforms certainly helped set Rome on the path to imperial greatness, this was only clear in hindsight. At the time, they were likely viewed as a defeat for powerful patrician elites like Camillus and his friends, as they required them to give up some of their traditional privileges to the emerging plebeian contingent.

More generally then, Camillus oversaw quite a pivotal period in Roman history, from the conquest of Veii in 396 to the passing of the Licinio-Sextian reforms in 367, although his specific involvement in each of the key moments is ambiguous. This is likely a reflection of three factors that reflect the nature of this period more generally in our sources. First, as noted above, the narrative structure of our history of the early Republic, with its annual magistracies, militates against single figures holding significant power in the narrative. This was almost certainly on purpose, and a reflection of the power-sharing arrangement at the heart of the *res publica*. Rome's collected elites and families did not want a single, powerful individual dictating matters if it could be avoided, and as a group they likely adjusted the narrative tradition so that any achievements were as corporate as possible. Indeed, another related factor to consider is the Romanocentric nature of the preserved narrative, which focuses almost exclusively on those who held political office in given years and ignores those who did not—despite their, presumed, continued importance and power in the "private" sphere. Our sources are only interested in the elites when they are explicitly and directly working within the "Roman" system. For instance, while Camillus did not hold an official office in 387, and was not mentioned by name in the narrative for that year when the Veientine tribes were created, one can still assume that he held tremendous power within the community—as he held the dictatorship only years before and the consular tribunate the year after in 386. It is unlikely that the lack of an official position within the Roman political hierarchy limited him to a great extent.

The second factor that influences our understanding of Camillus' career is, perhaps ironically, that he is truly exceptional—so much so that we struggle to find a parallel, and indeed some scholars have suggested he may be largely invented.[58] In contrast to the emphasis on groups we see in the preceding period, Camillus stands out as remarkable in his individuality. He is involved in so many important moments, and the stories which surround him are both so rich and implausible, that he feels like an archaic throwback in this period.[59] In short, Camillus defies easy categorization, either for us or the authors of our ancient sources, which likely influenced their narrative.

Third, and perhaps most importantly, it is clear that Rome's late Republican historians usually attempted to downplay innovation and change in the Republic. All three of the events discussed above, all associated with the dictatorships of Camillus, are clearly depicted as momentous events for Rome. However, Rome's historians, in their attempt to paint a relatively stable picture of Rome (Polybius claimed that Rome had only undergone "a few modifications" over its roughly 500-year history)[60] often glossed over what might be significant changes in this period. Camillus was associated with minor changes to Rome's military equipment, most notably the adoption of the *pilum* (heavy javelin) and *scutum* (oblong shield),[61] but our sources actively tried to ignore or discount any more substantive reforms.

FOUNDERS AND FOUNDING

As noted at the outset, Rome's various founders, as described in our surviving literary sources, are almost surely not historical, and so it is difficult to learn much about the true character or details of early Roman warfare or expansion from them. However, they were important to the Romans, and are therefore revealing for how the Romans thought about—or at least described—their early history. They offer both a hypothetical background for important events and institutions and key moments of remembered transition. They provide important reference points for the Roman historical schema and function as something that we can refer to when considering the totality of evidence.

To summarize things a bit, when thinking about their founders, the Romans seem to have felt that warfare was always an important facet of their identity as "Romans." All of their founders were warriors. Warfare was a tie that bound them together and was an important part of their corporate history. This is not to say, however, that ancient Rome was entirely militaristic or that the Romans were preternaturally obsessed with warfare. For most of early Roman history, warfare would have been conducted by a relatively small segment of the population—a few elite men—for limited periods of time. For most people in Rome, warfare was certainly present, but likely not an overriding concern. However, when it came to identifying as "Romans," warfare was central. Fighting, and especially fighting together, was key to what defined them as being part of that particular group and operating under that specific label. They were at their most "Roman" when they fought.

Within the stories of Rome's founders, there was also an interesting relationship between warfare and integration. In the early years, peaceful integration on equal terms was often thought to directly follow warfare. Looking particularly at figures like Romulus and Tullus Hostilius, the Romans fought and then bonded with their opponents. Under some later founders, the relationship was more complicated, but the ideas of warfare and expansion are inexorably linked throughout the narrative. This may feel a bit optimistic (and frankly unrealistic) to a modern audience, but it likely suggests something about the nature of warfare in this period—or at least how the Romans thought about it. While there were certainly two sides to each conflict, the lines between them were not thought to be either rigid or permanent. War was rarely, if ever, fought between two distinct "peoples" or "nations" in the modern sense. Rather, as an analogy, we might think of a game between two teams, where each team was picked, right before the contest, from the same pool of players. During the contest itself, the two sides would be clearly distinct, but both before and after the contest things were blurry and flexible.

Also, and perhaps surprisingly for many, the connection between founders and the actual city of Rome was not always obvious or straightforward. Aeneas, although remembered as the founder of the Roman lineage, had only a passing connection with the physical community and, while the city of Rome was always recognized as an important meeting place, its nature is not entirely consistent. There is an ongoing tension over what it meant to be "Roman" and how the urban community helped to define that. The Romans were not always, or at least not entirely, defined by the urban community. Being "Roman" did not necessarily mean coming from or living in the city. The competing importance of families and lineages also seems to regularly lurk in the background, even in accounts written in the late Republic.

Finally, it is interesting that Romans seem to have felt that their founders were vital to their identity, and attempted to push as many innovations and changes into the regal period as possible, but also felt the need to have a number of different founders and sometimes struggled to link them together into a single narrative. Rome's origin stories are complex and seem to always have been. While other communities around the Mediterranean had no trouble streamlining their origin stories and claiming a single founder and foundation story, the Romans either did not or could not. It is uncertain why this might be the case.

One possibility is that the various founders each brought something different to Rome's identity, and each was needed to explain a different facet of Rome's character. For whatever reason, Roman authors seemed to dislike change, and ascribing specific innovations to founders was preferable to gradual change over time. Alternatively, the various founders of Rome may reflect a diverse and heterogeneous origin for Roman society. By the time these myths were written down, Roman citizenship had spread across most of Italy, and so the varied founders may reflect different traditions from this wider "Roman" population—most of which had a limited connection with the city of Rome and, indeed, central Italy. A third option might be that, contrary to the seeming Roman desire for historical and social stability, Rome's various founders might reflect a recognition of Rome's regular rebirth and "reimagining." What it meant to be "Roman" may have changed over time, and Rome's regular refoundation may have been a reflection of this.

Whatever the reason, Rome's founders are certainly revealing. They highlight the centrality of warfare and elite male politics within a highly contested environment dominated by powerful clan leaders. For the authors of our sources, this is crucial to what it meant to be "Roman." It was not necessarily about a shared culture or language, although a family was evidently important, but rather a shared bond on the battlefield and in the forum and *curia*. *Romanitas* ("Roman-ness") was perhaps more limited in terms of the areas of life it influenced, but also more expansive in terms of who it could include.

The next chapter will begin to lay out how this idea or bond developed and worked in real terms, and how the elite families of Rome were able to leverage it to increase their own power and prestige. However, as often happens, this idea seems to have slowly grown beyond their control and developed a life of its own. For social animals, like humans, group identities have immense power. What may have initially been "a means to an end" for local warlords and clan chiefs slowly became something more.

3

VEII, THE GAULS, AND ROME REBORN

WARFARE IN EARLY ITALY was dominated by clans and was primarily concerned with raiding for portable wealth, as well as defending against the raids of others. Local families sometimes worked together, sometimes operated independently, and sometimes fought in larger, federated armies. However, in every instance, the basic unit and division was always the local group—the extended family, the clan, the warband, etc. Probably numbering somewhere in the region of a couple hundred men, these groups were the basis for and foundational units of Italian warfare, both tactically and organizationally. In this, early Roman warfare was no exception.

This is, of course, not at all how the authors of our surviving histories of early Rome described things. Indeed, the difference between the emerging scholarly consensus for early Roman warfare and the models offered by the ancient evidence is so great that it deserves at least a brief explanation here. To summarize a complex situation quickly, ancient authors seem to have looked back on early Rome with "rose-colored glasses," consistently describing it as a simpler and more unified time. Writing in a late Republican and early Imperial period dominated by intense civil wars and violent uprisings by powerful, independent warlords, ancient authors looked to the past for hope. The early history of city was a vision of what was possible and an idea of what they might once again become: an idyllic age with a cohesive and united community, where Romans of all types worked together and overcame their differences. Within this, they drew heavily on Greek models in describing a military system based on membership in the community, whereby a stable population of citizen-farmer-soldiers mustered individually, on an annual basis, to protect the city's farmland—or, perhaps, to increase it through calculated attacks on neighboring cities. These men were supposedly amateurs, pulled from their farms and thrust into service for the community. They fought for each other, for their families, and for the glory of Rome. This vision was then picked up and embellished by writers in the later empire, medieval, and even early modern period—shaping how we think about civic militias, even today. It was a powerful story of community identity and belonging. However, it is, and always has been, just an aspirational myth.

In reality, Rome's military system during the early and middle Republic seems to have been tribal and fairly ad hoc. Rather than recruiting individual citizen-soldiers, fighting in defense of their farmsteads, it seems to have been based on a more federated model, whereby existing warbands—typically organized by clan—were brought together for a limited time and for short-term goals. Far from being amateurs, these groups were usually made up of seasoned fighters who knew how to handle a blade far better than a plough. While they may not have fought *all* the time, war was one of their primary pursuits and a key aspect of their status and identity. This was a warrior society.

A possible, very loose analogy might be something like the system of Scottish clans in the fourteenth to seventeenth centuries. While Scottish clansmen were certainly not full-time warriors, they lived in a world where violence was common, and they were often ready for a fight if needed. Their family histories were full of blood feuds and raiding, and these activities were often key to their identity. Although some Scottish kings were able to mobilize the clans (or at least some of them) into a single army, the resultant forces were always based on the pre-existing clan groupings and the arrangements rarely lasted for long. Indeed, when they weren't fighting enemies like the English together, many clans fought among themselves and may have even switched sides in larger conflicts as suited their interests. While this obviously represents a very different historical context from archaic Italy, this sort of world and set of relationships and motivations would have almost certainly resonated with the early Romans.

This loose, federated system was not only the basis of the Roman army, but of the entire *res publica*. The Roman Republic was an agreement of mutual cooperation between its various constituent families. Individual citizens were part of this but, unlike in modern democracies, they were evidently not the most important units. Romans did not operate individually in the same way we do today. Individualism is a largely modern concept, which was only sometimes explored in antiquity—often only by philosophers and, as far as we can tell, only by elite men.[1] For most ancient people it would have been an alien concept. They were nothing without the group. In particular, the Romans emphasized the role and importance of the wider family—and especially the clan or *gens*. Everything in Roman society seems to have funneled through the extended family, which included not only immediate relatives and those bound by blood, but also a wider network of those brought together through patron-client bonds, bonds of friendship, *sodalitas* (a social and religious bond which may have been something like a "sword brother," at least in the early period), and even slavery and debt-bondage (*nexum*). This was an expansive view of "family."[2]

The Roman Republic, and the Republican system, gave clans a mechanism and framework to work together. It was, very likely, not the only such framework available to them. For instance, we certainly have other local community or civic affiliations, and the so-called "Latin League" is often presented as an early rival (and perhaps overlapping) set of relationships to the *res publica*, that may have operated similarly. But slowly, over time, the "Roman" federal framework came to dominate the local region and took on a permanence, identity, and importance of its own that surpassed that of its individual members. This is the story of Roman imperialism. While we often associate imperialism with territorial expansion, this was merely a by-product of the more important growth of the Roman relationship—a "grand bargain" between Italy's elite families that operated through Rome but was not necessarily *of* Rome.[3] Or at least not initially.

In this chapter, we will explore what caused a federation of clans based around Rome to develop into a more cohesive, expansionist, and clearly defined group, more closely resembling the state and army that we see described in accounts like that of Polybius in the second century. Again, it is noteworthy that Roman history was a relatively late development, perhaps hinting that before roughly 200 BCE there was not much of a unified Roman history to write. Much of what existed before that point could evidently be classified as individual family histories. But what caused this growing cohesion? Can we pinpoint any specific moments that can help us understand how it emerged?

FROM MONARCHY TO REPUBLIC

During the Roman regal period (eighth through sixth centuries), the Roman "state," such as it was, seems to have been based around the relatively simple idea of augmenting the existing clan-based power of the *rex*, or "king." Every Roman king was, at a basic level, simply a clan chief. As such, each king could generally depend on the support of his own extended family and followers, just like any number of other clan leaders in the region. However, what made the king of Rome (or other communities like Gabii and Praeneste) special was that, in addition to this personal clan-based power, he could—in certain specific situations—call upon the wider community to join his clan. This is what being a king, and wielding the power of *imperium*, effectively meant. It was the ability to bring members of the community into his clan, for a short period and in very specific (typically military) situations. Being king came with other perks as well, including key religious and legal roles. But, when it comes down to it, military power lay at the heart of the office.

This power did have some reciprocal benefits for the community as well. While the king obviously benefited from the extra manpower brought by the community, the community gained a dedicated protector and also benefited indirectly from any wealth or spoils that were acquired in warfare. With every victory, money would have flowed into the community—including directly into the pockets of the men involved. It might not have been an equal partnership, but there was clearly enough in it for the community that they kept electing kings and continued to support their ventures when asked. None of our evidence seems to suggest the office of king was inherently unpopular or oppressive toward the masses.

However, the Roman monarchy was not without its issues. Most notably, with the growth of Rome in the sixth century, and the rise in the number of powerful clans that seem to have come to Rome during that period, the idea of always augmenting a single family evidently bothered an increasing number of the other clan leaders. After all, why should one family get to monopolize all that community power? By the end of the sixth century, the collected leaders of Rome's many elite families had evidently had enough and decided to change the system so that each of them had equal access to the community's forces, at least in some limited way. Rather than having a single king who ruled for life, the collected clan leaders wanted multiple kingships that they could share among themselves for a year at a time. In simple terms, this is what happened at the end of the monarchy and the beginning of the Republic.

We know very little about what the wider community felt about all of this, as all of our information about this period seems to have filtered down through the elite families who ended up at the top—for whom the change would have been particularly impactful. Effectively, the ones who would have access to these new, shared kingships. However, the wider community seems to have accepted this change to the agreement and continued to support the clans of the new republican magistrates (praetors/consuls) as they had with the king. These new magistrates also seem to have kept up the same bargain as the kings and used their clans and power to protect the community. So, despite this change in government, things continued much as they had before. Warfare, for much of the fifth century, was therefore effectively clan-based, as it had been previously. It is simply that some clans (a slightly larger number than in the sixth century) sometimes had a slightly larger military force at their disposal due to their ability to supplement their usual warband with community-based troops. They continued to do this through a grant of *imperium*, which effectively extended their power as clan chief over the community troops on a temporary basis. Just like the kings before them as well, they also generally used this power for personal benefit.

This system worked quite well for much of the fifth century, and there seems to have been very little impetus to change it. Despite the traditional narrative of "crisis" in the fifth century, which readers can probably still find in many history books (and which we will discuss in a moment), if individual Roman leaders are understood to have been acting in an entirely self-interested manner, in pursuit of personal gain and wealth, Roman warfare in this period was actually reasonably successful.[4] They weren't doing much to expand the power of the Roman state overall, although they didn't really have much incentive to do so. Individual clan leaders usually only had a single year in office and likely wanted to make the most of that limited window. After that window closed, given the fluid nature of community membership in this period, these elites might even find themselves fully outside of the Roman system—and, therefore, possibly a target of Roman aggression in later years. As a result, although they wanted the state to be powerful and efficient while they were in control of it, they didn't want it to be too powerful and efficient when they weren't. This promoted a certain level of stasis in the system. The men in charge kept it functioning just well enough to accomplish their goals, but not too well, in case their rivals benefitted too much. So, the underlying principles that defined Rome's military system remained remarkably stable throughout the sixth and fifth centuries, despite the change in government. We see a gradual expansion, with more families being able to take advantage of it, but they were all using it in roughly the same way. In the early Republic, the community seems to have been little more than a resource to be exploited in order for elite clan leaders to increase their personal wealth and position.

MOUNTAINS AND PLAINS

The Romans, however, were not always on the offensive. A key feature of the literary narrative for the fifth century is an increase in the number of battles the Romans and Latins seem to have fought against the tribal peoples of the Apennines—the central mountain range that runs down Italy like a spine—including groups like the Hernici, Aequi, and Volsci. During this period, all the settlements of the central Italian lowlands, including Rome, supposedly came under increasing threat from marauding highlanders, sacking and pillaging whatever they could. Regular defensive wars against these tribes are often offered to explain Rome's lack of expected expansion and growth in this period. Effectively, the Romans would have been more expansionist and imperialist in the early Republic, if they didn't have to constantly defend the city and their farms from pesky barbarian raiders. This has become the central feature of the so-called "Crisis of the Mid-Fifth Century."

We have often assumed this increase in warfare with tribes from the Apennines was due to an increased hostility on the part of those tribes. Possibly either pushed out of the mountains by overpopulation or climatic pressures, or simply drawn to the lowlands by the desire for easy plunder, these more rustic tribes are always painted as the aggressors. However, recent work has increasingly thrown this narrative into doubt. Most notably, the archaeological evidence does not support any dramatic changes in the Apennines in the fifth century that would have encouraged the tribal peoples to change their ways and become more aggressive. As far as we can tell, they seem to have been doing what they had always done. Further, it is now clear that these highland tribes would have been well known to the lowland peoples, and vice versa, as there is ample archaeological evidence for regular interaction over the centuries.[5] It is even possible to consider the "lowland" and "highland" peoples of central Italy to be two parts of the same wider, regional population. The Hernici, Aequi, and Volsci were, effectively, Latins—but a segment of the population that was often associated with pastoralism instead of agriculture, which led to them traveling into the mountains more regularly. This complicates the picture.

Central Italy has always had shepherds, who have behaved in remarkably similar ways over the millennia—from antiquity through to the early twentieth century (less so today). They moved across the region in a regular pattern with their animals, wintering in down by the coast and summering up in the mountains, following the availability of good pasturage. As part of this, they regularly passed through the various settlements along their normal routes and may have had family and friends based in many of them. This was a known and accepted part of central Italian life. In antiquity, tribal labels, like the Sabines or Aequi, were certainly known and accepted associations, but some may have related to their position as mobile pastoralists rather than an indication of a distinct cultural or ethnic group. So the label was probably contextual. Indeed, it is worth remembering that Romulus supposedly allied with the Sabine king Titus Tatius and Rome featured a strong Sabine element in its mythic origin story. As noted, there is no real evidence to indicate a marked shift in the conditions or behavior of these groups that might explain the increased conflict visible in the record. In fact, the most significant changes we see are actually down in the lowland regions, where we see the rise of more intensive agricultural practices and permanent settlement on the landscape. While we know central Italians had been farming for centuries, the sixth and fifth centuries saw a sort of mini "agricultural revolution," with hundreds of small, permanent farmsteads suddenly appearing across the region—and particularly in the coastal plain of Latium. This has prompted another possible explanation for the "crisis." Rather than the mountain tribes becoming more warlike and aggressive, these fifth-century conflicts may have arisen from the regular transhumance routes of these pastoralists suddenly becoming more cluttered and hazardous.[6] Terrain and routes that had been open and unoccupied for millennia were, in the fifth century, suddenly full of small farms, the owners of which may have both taken offence at the sudden appearance of herds marching across their fields and also taken advantage of these passing herds and herdsmen, raiding and capturing some of this passing wealth. As a result, while the fifth century may have seen an increase in warfare between the lowland communities and the pastoral groups associated with the highlands, this was far more complex than a simple increase in raiding by highland "barbarians." It was likely the result of a change in the overall rhythm of life in the region, connected with increasingly intensive agriculture and the growth of communities in the lowland plains as much as anything else.

Despite these shifts in regional relationships, and a possible increase in warfare, the nature of Roman warfare and Roman imperialism did not change too much—or at least not quickly. Everything remained largely clan-based and clan-directed. Armies were relatively small, operated for short periods, and seemed to have engaged in targeted operations for portable wealth. They were still raiders. Although, perhaps, increasingly cohesive or cooperative raiders. In particular, regularly coming together under the banner of Rome for mutual defense—even if they were partly to blame for provoking the conflict with their neighbors—seems to have gently nudged the local clans together and more consistently aligned their interests with those of the wider community. They got used to working together and developed a mutual, if begrudging, respect for each other. It was slow going, and certainly not consistent, but Rome seems to have slowly emerged as an important point of military unity within the region—at least when they were faced with a threat. It was not just a resource to be exploited or a useful point of connection but was developing into something a bit more.

THE "STRUGGLE OF THE ORDERS"

The implications of this slowly increasing cohesion and focus on Rome were not always positive, however, as we can see from the so-called "Struggle of the Orders." This was a conflict between the "patrician" and "plebeian" groups over political power in Rome, as clan leaders sought to dominate and control the rising Roman Republic. The conflict overshadowed Roman politics for most of the fifth and fourth centuries. However, despite its central importance, scholars still aren't entirely sure exactly what to make of it. While we know the patricians and plebeians represented distinct groups of elite families in Rome, as these groups continued to exist in the late Republic, we actually don't know a great deal about who they were or how they operated in the early period. We should expect a society to change over the course of 500 years, and the fact that our authors clearly assumed that these groups functioned in a remarkably consistent way throughout the long history of the Republic, or at least described them that way, has given us cause to worry. This isn't helped by the heavily dramatized, and indeed mythologized, nature of this struggle in our literary narrative—where it is clear that the authors of our sources were embellishing extensively. This struggle for political power among elite men gave later authors the perfect opportunity to both play up the high drama and also offer useful examples for contemporary politicians.

At its core, however, and working to get past the anachronistic veneer, we can see in the "Struggle of the Orders" what amounts to "growing pains" in Rome's federation of elite families and, in fact, a continuation of the same tensions that brought about the end of the monarchy. The patricians were a group of elite clans that had become connected to Rome quite early on, had likely been instrumental in removing the final king, and had managed to monopolize power in the community in the early Republic. The plebeians were everyone else, including the (often powerful) clans and families that had joined the system and community at a slightly later date. So the difference was simply when these families put down (relatively) permanent roots in Rome. The patricians were those who got there first and helped create the republican system. The plebeians were those who arrived slightly later, presumably drawn by the allure of the system and a chance at power. From the outset, the patrician clans struggled to retain their traditional control over the system that they had helped create, while the newly arrived clans and clan leaders, lumped together under the label "plebeian," fought for a piece of the pie. In the end, just as the king had ultimately been forced out by the combined power of the patrician clans, the patrician clans were ultimately forced to cede some power to the plebeian clans. However, how and when this occurred is interesting.

In a military context, the most important development of the "Struggle of the Orders" was the creation of the consulship in 367, which officially opened the traditional military command of the community's forces to the plebeian families. But before this moment, we can see things changing, with increased tensions around the army. In the early fifth century, between 495 and 456, 12 military levies were either opposed or actively boycotted by the plebeians.[7] While the accuracy of this figure and the reasons behind the boycotts are uncertain, given the problematic nature of the evidence, it does align with the broader picture whereby a growing plebeian population—which, again, contained quite a lot of powerful clans and warbands—seems to have been increasingly disgruntled with the established patrician monopoly on military command. Again, we should not imagine these plebeians as the collected poor or the "urban mob," as they are often depicted, but simply as new arrivals to the city— and some quite powerful, wealthy, and influential—who wanted a share of the power. After all, in order to contribute men to the army in the first place (and particularly enough to make a difference to the composition of the force), they would have had to have represented members of the upper classes of Roman society. They likely did not like having to support the military endeavors of their rivals, without a chance at command themselves, simply because their rivals happened to get to Rome first. In real terms, and outside of the specific social and political setting of Rome, they were equals.

Attempts to alleviate this tension between the plebeians and patricians, and address Rome's shifting demographics, can be seen in the famous "Laws of the Twelve Tables" (451–450) and the creation of both the censorship and consular tribunate in 440s.[8] Although each of these developments arguably deserves its own chapter, they can all be understood as compromises between the heads of established elite clans and the newly arrived elites, which were meant to keep the overall Republican system functioning in the face of sustained growth.

The codification of laws in the Twelve Tables established a single set of rules that all of the powerful families agreed to abide by while operating within the confines of the community. These laws were similar to those that had existed in Rome previously, and indeed those which governed all of central Italy's urban centers and meeting places, in that they regulated relationships and applied equally to all. What made them special was that they were written down and could not be changed on a whim by those in charge of the community. They provided a greater sense of permanency and stability. Upon arriving in Rome, everyone was able to know the rules. The censorship worked to more regularly and formally catalogue who was considered a member of the community and who was not. While the census had supposedly been carried out six times previously, the creation of an office whose primary duty was regulating community membership suggests that this was increasingly a concern and likely reflects either the growth or fluidity of the community.

The consular tribunate or, more accurately, the "military tribunate with consular power" (*tribunus militum consulari potestate*) is one of the more confusing offices from early Rome, and there is no agreement among either ancient authors or modern scholars on what exactly it represented. However, skipping over the complicated details, all the evidence suggests that it also belongs within this wider set of compromises between the patricians and plebeians. It was a military office that was open to members of the plebeians as well as patricians and seems to have increased the number of available military commands, perhaps reflecting the expanding elite of Rome. It was evidently not exactly the same as the previous types of military command (the early praetorship or the dictatorship), seemingly lacking many of the religious and prestige-based elements. However, it seems to have fulfilled an important function, as the Romans used it regularly between 444 and 390, and then exclusively between 390 and 376/367, for reasons we will return to later.

THE SHIFTING NATURE OF WAR

During the course of the fifth century, we can also see a subtle evolution in the nature and goals of Roman warfare. As discussed, it seems clear that most warfare in central Italy, including Roman warfare, was dictated by the needs and desires of individual clans and clan leaders. While they would sometimes band together for mutual defense, this was a very self-interested behavior. There was no real sense of working for a collective or common good, particularly when it came to more offensive endeavors. Rome's elite were not just primarily, but seemingly only, out to improve their own individual positions. However, what those clans and clan leaders desired, and the best way to improve their positions, seemed to have gradually changed over time.

During the sixth and early fifth centuries, most of these clan leaders seemed to have sought after portable wealth, either in the form of livestock or other types of booty—armor of defeated enemies, jewelry, etc. These spoils were certainly economic and had what we would consider "monetary value," but should not be considered solely in this light, as they also brought social prestige. This was a highly competitive environment, where local clan leaders tried to accumulate as much wealth and power as they could, often explicitly at the expense of their rivals. Spoils of war were almost always publicly displayed, and this step was at least equally important, if not more, than simply possessing it. This was about claiming trophies in a highly competitive (and very violent) game. It wasn't just about getting wealth, it was about getting more wealth than others—and making sure everyone knew about it.

This all occurred as part of a wider competition among elites and elite families, which had a number of different "arenas" (e.g. politics and religion, as well as war), and where different seasons featured different contests. Some months featured political rivalries and competing for positions within communities, others may have seen more ritual displays and competitions at festivals—for instance, offering the best sacrifices or having pride of place at a ceremony. War and raiding seem to have generally occurred in the late spring (April/May), after the planting season and when the region's pastoralists were on the move with their flocks and herds, passing from the lowlands up to the summer highland pastures. This would have been a "target-rich environment" and aligns well with the traditional Roman campaign season even in later periods, which notionally began in March (named for the god of war Mars) but was focused on these late spring/early summer months.[9] While there was clearly lots of conflict between the agricultural communities and pastoralists, it is likely that everyone was actively involved—and everyone was a possible target. Clans raided clans, pastoralists and agriculturalists attacked one another and each other. Everyone seems to have been involved in the same "game." In warfare, "points" were scored by acquiring potable wealth, which was then displayed in various ways throughout the year until the next campaigning season.

The focus on portable wealth in central Italian warfare remained consistent throughout the fifth century. However, in the final decades of the century, we begin to see the first hints that at least some clans and clan leaders were starting to think about other forms of wealth—most notably land. Livy reports a marked shift in Roman behavior in the final quarter of the fifth century, when we find Roman armies engaged in conflicts with various rival Latin communities—most notably against Fidenae, Labici, and Bolae—and ultimately acquiring land as a result. The acquisition of land through warfare would have been very normal to Livy, writing in the first century BCE, and indeed seems quite natural to us today. So it is interesting that Livy both notes that the Romans were not actually seeking land initially and that these late fifth-century examples of land acquisition are actually quite exceptional. Apparently, the Romans were actually seeking portable wealth in these wars but, when that was not available, they took land from the communities as a substitute. While there are some scattered references to the acquisition of land by the Romans in the regal period and in the first years of the Republic, most notably after fighting against the Hernici, this seems to have been the exception. Italian warfare, including Roman warfare, did not usually result in the long-term control of defeated settlements or territory. An army would attack, grab what they could, and then move on, leaving the defeated opponent to pick up the pieces. But pick up the pieces they would, and the Romans, like we assume many other clans and communities, seem to have regularly fought against the same opponent year after year, suggesting that they were able to recover from a defeat relatively quickly. Military losses were important, but rarely catastrophic. However, from ca. 425, this seems to change, as defeat started to result in the long-term loss of land. The "game" was changing.

It is clear that land was conceived of as a personal spoil of war in this period, and we do not yet have the widespread use of *ager publicus* ("public land"), or even the rather vague *ager Romanus* ("Roman land," a general term often used to indicate influence in this period). So, when land was acquired through warfare, it was immediately given to individuals and not held by the state or community as a whole. It also wasn't a popular spoil as it was still widely available, it took tremendous effort and resources to exploit, and it was not something that clans felt they could accumulate or control easily. Simply put, land was acceptable, but the families of central Italy seem to have strongly preferred animals and other portable forms of wealth when engaging in warfare. However, by the late fifth century, they were at least willing to consider land if there wasn't enough portable wealth to satisfy them. Some of this likely relates to the changing economic reality of the fifth century. As noted above, as we move through the fifth century, Italians were slowly getting more and more interested in intensive agriculture and agricultural investment and the archaeology suggests that the landscape, which had previously been open, was increasingly littered with small farmsteads. While the central

Italians had a long history with agriculture and farming, from the middle of the sixth century we see new crops, techniques, and types of irrigation and infrastructure appearing in the countryside, and in increasing numbers. Farming was increasingly stable and productive, which made the land it utilized more valuable. This trend would only continue, as we move into the fourth century. It would also, slowly but inexorably, change the nature and goals of Roman warfare, moving away from the old, traditional raiding and toward something else.

THE SACKS OF VEII AND ROME

The start of the fourth century was momentous for the Romans.[10] It began, in ca. 396, with the defeat of Rome's great rival Veii, located 11 km north of Rome, across the Tiber in Etruria.[11] The defeat of Veii supposedly required an epic 10-year siege, harkening back to the siege of Troy by the Greeks described by Homer, and resulted in Rome emerging as the most important urban center within the local region. This was followed, less than a decade later, by Rome's own humiliating defeat at the hands of the Gallic chief Brennus and his warriors in ca. 390.[12] The way the Romans responded to these two events provides important details for how we should understand the community and its role in the region.

There are many reasons to explore the sack of Veii by the Romans but, in the present context, I would like to focus on only two of them: the Romans' decision to focus their attention on a single community for so long, when they had previously typically moved from target to target, and what they did after they eventually captured the community.

The decision to focus their attention on Veii over the course of 10 years is important, as it indicates an impressive degree of cooperation among the elite families of Rome. They were starting to work together, focusing more of their competitive energy (at least in the military sphere) outside of the Roman community. The war was evidently begun in 406 by the four consular tribunes of that year—two members of the Cornelii, one of the *gens Fabia* or the Fabian clan, and another of the Valeria family. While we don't know where the Valeria family was based, both the Fabii and Cornelii were associated with tribal areas to the north of Rome and so may have had interests in the area around Veii. Famously, the Fabii had engaged in a private war against Veii in the 470s, hinting that this later war was part of a long-standing feud. As a result, the initial outbreak of hostilities makes some sense given the clan-based interests of this group. Indeed, the war was also pursued by members of other clans with known interests in the region—for instance, M. Sergius Fidenas (consular tribune in 404 and 402), whose cognomen Fidenas came from his ancestor's actions at Fidenae in 437, another community to the north of Rome. So, at the outset of the conflict, everything seemed like "business as usual." We see individual families using the resources of Rome to pursue their own private initiatives. However, the war was also actively pursued by members of quite a few other clans that did *not* seem to have previous links to the area. For instance, the year 405 brought in a new group of consular tribunes, now numbering six, that included two members of the Quinctii, and one each from the Julii, Manlii, Furii, and Aemilii. Out of these, we only really know where the Aemilii were traditionally based, although this seems to have been to the south of Rome and far from Veii. Nonetheless, they evidently continued the assault on Veii, pursuing the same agenda as their predecessors.

Famously, the war against Veii was ended under the dictatorship of M. Furius Camillus in 396, whose family was also thought to be based to the south and east of Rome—again, far from Veii. Although Livy explicitly records that not every commander active in these years was focused on Veii, and in fact the Romans are reported as fighting a number of different opponents over these years alongside this war, the continued focus on Veii by such a diverse collection of clans highlights increased cooperation and unified focus in the military realm. Commanders of Roman armies were no longer simply using their year in power to enhance their personal and clan-based wealth—or at least not just that—but seemed to have begun to think and act more corporately. In a connected point, we also start to get more evidence for joint attacks on settlements in this period, with multiple Roman armies joining forces to attack and sack settlements—as at Bolae in 414. Again, in a dangerous development for the rest of the region, the Romans were starting to work together, at least in some specific situations.

We will likely never be entirely certain why the Roman elites chose to focus their attention so single-mindedly on Veii in this period, but there are a few possibilities. We know Veii was a wealthy settlement, and so the simple pursuit of wealth was likely at least one contributing factor. Livy and Plutarch's descriptions of the sack of Veii hint at the memory of the vast amount of wealth acquired—so great that the entire community of Rome joined in the plundering, not just the soldiers. As a result, it may simply be that the possible rewards outweighed their natural aversion to working together.

However, the Romans did not simply sack the community of Veii when they eventually won the war. Famously, the Romans performed a set of rituals—the *evocatio* and *devotio*—which ritually called forth the gods protecting the community and then, in their absence, condemned the settlement to "the infernal deities." This was an incredibly rare set of rituals, which were also associated with the final destruction of Carthage in 146, and represented a very particular decision to fully destroy a community. Typically, when the Romans (or really anyone else in Italy) defeated a rival community, that community was able to return to its normal strength after only a few years. "Conquest" was more of a temporary setback and was likely only intended as such. Again, Italian warfare seems to have been part of a (very violent) competition, with known "players" operating by accepted "rules," and there seems to have been the expectation that defeated "players" (clans and communities) would stay in the "game" to compete another year. What the Romans did to Veii in 396 was very different. They ritually destroyed the community and thereby stopped it from returning to power ever again—and this is one of the few times where the archaeology seems to directly support this literary narrative. Whatever happened in 396, the archaeology indicates that Veii went into a sudden and massive decline from which it never recovered. The concerted effort to destroy Veii indicates that, while the Roman clans undoubtedly wanted to acquire wealth from this war, this wasn't the only goal. They were also working together to remove a rival community and make Rome the only major urban center— the only real meeting place for local elites—within the local region.

This returns us to the question of what communities seem to have represented in archaic central Italian society.[13] Veii, like Rome, would have had a reasonably large resident population within the urban area. However, as recent archaeological work has demonstrated, most urban areas in Italy in this period contained a significant amount of open space. We shouldn't imagine communities like Rome or Veii as being densely packed with houses or huts. These early Italian communities were nothing like the bustling cities of the late Republic and Empire. While many urban centers, at least by the fifth century, had organized street grids that divided up the interior space, a surprising amount of the area inside the walls or boundaries was not developed and left clear. Archaeologists have described urban zones in early Italy as having a "leopard spot" pattern, with small clusters of buildings dotting the landscape, separated by significant amounts of open space.[14] This open space was important for many reasons, but most importantly because it was often likely filled by more transient populations—pastoralists, merchants, or just visitors. Indeed, the most important population for a community was not necessarily those who resided within its walls or confines, but those it attracted from the wider area. In this way, ancient communities might be compared to modern shopping centers, with the resident population being analogous to the retail staff that operate the stores. The size of the center is important, as is having sufficient staff to operate it, but the most important element is the collection of shoppers the center and its shops attract. Those shoppers and their relative wealth, influence, loyalty, and engagement are what determine the vitality of the shopping center.

This is precisely the situation we have with many communities in antiquity—particularly those in areas like central Italy, which had a number of urban communities located in relatively close proximity. While some clans and families were deeply invested in certain, specific communities in central Italy, many others evidently moved between them regularly, and indeed many have had relationships or associations with several concurrently. Clans regularly moved from one community to another. While this is often described in terms of "exile," it never seemed to impact their personal power or influence and often seemed to be a personal choice. These families were like shoppers who frequented a number of different stores, rather than just one, seeking the best deals at any given time.

By the late fifth century, however, it appears that communities (and the clans associated with them) had begun to realize that there might be some benefit in, perhaps violently, removing the competition. For individual clans, for centuries, it evidently suited them to both have some choice in which communities they wanted to associate with and also to have a wide range of communities available to raid if the desire took them. Freedom was quite important. But this also came with drawbacks, as it always does, as it limited the scale and scope of their endeavors. If they wanted to think a bit bigger, they needed to act in a more corporate fashion—trading some of that individual freedom for the greater resources and manpower a larger and more secure federation offered. The permanent destruction of the community of Veii, removing it as a rival nexus point for interaction, indicates that the clans of Rome were no longer thinking quite so independently. They were working together in order to ensure that "their community" was not only the most important, but really the only option available within the local region. While individual families had invested in the community of Rome before, most notably through building temples and other structures, we have never been certain whether this was the *only* place they were investing. This is one of the first times we have evidence of the elite families of Rome clearly prioritizing the community of Rome at the expense of another. The sack of Rome by the Gauls, only six years later in 390 BCE, shows the other side of the coin and the risks that came with clans focusing all their attention on a single community.[15]

The Gauls who attacked Rome were supposedly from a branch of the Seones, a group that traced their roots back to Austria and who were part of a wider movement of people from Europe into Italy during the sixth and fifth centuries. The arrival of the Senones in Italy should not be seen as some sort of "barbarian invasion," but rather was part of the regular movement of peoples between these regions. Although separated by the Alps, central Europe and northern Italy were actually quite interconnected, and their populations tightly intertwined, with strong evidence for regular interaction and movement going back to the Neolithic at least. Some periods saw more movement than others, however, and the fifth century seems to have seen quite a lot of intermixing in northern Italy—

with much of the traffic running from north to south. Throughout northern Italy, and especially down the Apennines and over on the east coast of Italy, excavations have revealed large numbers of burials full of military equipment dating to this period that has been labeled as "Gallic" or "Gallic-inspired." This is supported by (admittedly much later) literary evidence for the increased presence of Gauls and Gallic warriors. So it is likely that quite a few people were coming south into Italy from Europe in this period, and many of them seem to have been warriors, possibly drawn by the increasing demand for mercenaries in the region (see Fig. 7 below).

The specific group of Gauls that sacked Rome was led by the chieftain Brennus. We do not know exactly why he was in the vicinity of Rome, although there are several options. Livy explicitly suggests that Brennus' Gauls were seeking land to settle on, which is a possibility.[16] However, it is noteworthy that the Gauls did not try to take land from the Romans,

FIG 7
A terracotta figurine of a Gallic warrior. Egypt, 220–180 BCE. British Museum, London, 1994, 1001.2.

despite their victory. Instead, Brennus seemed to be after gold and was happy to move on once he had it. Interestingly, there is another tradition preserved by the Byzantine compiler Justin that suggests that Brennus and his Gauls were actually just passing through the region on their way south to seek mercenary service in the court of the Syracusan tyrant Dionysius I in Sicily.[17] The late fifth and fourth centuries featured a vibrant mercenary market in the ancient Mediterranean basin, largely driven by the great wars of Classical and Hellenistic Greece in the east, but embroiling the entire region. Italy was firmly enmeshed in this environment, and many soldiers from Italy were recruited into armies in the eastern Mediterranean.[18] This included many Italians from the mountainous interior of southern Italy, most notably the Samnites and Lucanians, but others as well, including quite a few Gauls from northern Italy. Brennus and his men may have been a contingent of Gallic mercenaries headed south. This explanation makes far more sense of the situation than any other.

The sack of Rome was preceded by a great defeat at the River Allia to the north of the city, whereby the full Roman army was put to flight by the Gauls, leaving Rome itself largely unprotected. Various figures are offered by the sources for the sizes of the armies, ranging from 20,000 to 40,000 each, although all are pure speculation and almost certainly far too high.[19] Somewhere in the realm of 5,000 men on each side is far more likely, particularly if Brennus was merely commanding a mercenary band. The small numbers involved do not mean the event was inconsequential though. Quite the opposite, as the men on the Roman side at least represented the unified elite of the community. While we may not be talking about a vast quantity of troops, we are talking about very high quality— likely the best they could muster at that time. However, the combined might of Rome was not enough to defeat Brennus' forces. The battle was a rout, with the Roman battle line evidently breaking very early and Rome's soldiers almost immediately running for safety. This was surely a sobering moment for the Romans, who must have realized that, however far they had come, they were still a very long way from the top of the heap in terms of Italian manpower.

Reports of the defeat and sack of the city itself are particularly conflicted. Apparently, a contingent held out on the Capitoline hill (it is

Veii, the Gauls, and Rome Reborn

unclear if it was ever defeated), in a heroic stand. Not only did this involve instances of personal bravery, enough to earn members of the Manlii family the cognomen Capitolinus, but also divine intervention. Famously, the Romans were warned of a sneak attack by the Gauls, scaling the side of the hill, by the warning honks of Juno's sacred geese who lived at a shrine there. This event was commemorated after the battle through the consecration of the temple to Juno Moneta ("Juno who warns").[20] Eventually, however, the Romans were forced to capitulate, and a somewhat one-sided truce was declared. As part of this, the Romans were required to pay a ransom of 1,000 pounds of gold to the Gauls to convince them to continue on their way. Roman honor may have been saved by the late arrival of Camillus, although most have interpreted this version of the story as a weak attempt at rewriting a humiliating episode in Rome's early history.

Despite the inconsistencies in the narrative and frustratingly inconclusive archaeological evidence for the sack (no clear evidence of a sack or city-wide fire dating to ca. 390 has ever been found), there is little doubt that the Romans were soundly defeated by a group of Gauls in the early fourth century. The sack of the city was evidently known to roughly contemporary Greek writers like Aristotle and Heracleides Ponticus, and the defeat was deeply engrained in Roman cultural memory.[21] The date of the defeat at the River Allia (July 18, the *dies Alliensis*), in particular, was always remembered as a day of bad luck and ill-omen. This was the closest the Romans had ever come to absolute destruction and one of the few moments in Rome's long history when the survival of the Roman community seemed in real doubt.

However, it obviously did not result in the end of the Roman community or, indeed, Rome's budding empire. This was not a defeat comparable to the Roman sack of Veii, as the goals of the attacking forces were very different. Although humiliating, and almost certainly both violent and destructive, the Gauls did not fully destroy the city, occupy its territory, or take the city's gods. Indeed, there is a tradition whereby the Romans were able to evacuate the gods from the city before the arrival of the Gauls, thus allowing its symbolic continuation.[22] Rather, the Gauls seem to have done to Rome what Roman armies had typically done to communities they had defeated previously: take what moveable plunder they could and move on. This was a major psychological blow, although its material impact would have been limited. Rome was still primarily a meeting place, not a population center, and so most of Rome's citizens lived outside of the community. The vast majority of their personal wealth would have, therefore, been also located outside of the urban area. What the Gauls then had access to was the wealth that was either brought to the community by those willing to pay the ransom, or (more likely) that which was located there in the temples and shrines. The defeat of Rome by the Gauls was, therefore, largely symbolic. The army had been defeated, the city had been sacked, but the majority of Rome's citizens, power, and wealth resided outside and so remained safe. This explains the Romans' relatively quick return to power after the sack.

But we should not discount the impact of this symbolic defeat, especially given the increasing cohesion of Roman clans shown in the attack on Veii less than a decade earlier. The region's clans had begun to invest a significant amount of effort and energy into the network of relationships running through Rome. They were increasingly emotionally invested in Rome, if not yet physically or economically. The city's capture and destruction was a massive shock in that context. In the years following the sack of Rome, the Romans quickly made a move to protect and secure this hub of activity from further attacks, building walls and reworking their military, resolidifying its importance and centrality in their mutual endeavor.

Further, if the Gauls of Brennus were indeed mercenaries seeking service in the army of Dionysius I of Syracuse, they would not have been alone and were likely traveling a well-worn route as they moved south. What this may indicate, then, is that Rome was being influenced by the wider military landscape of the ancient Mediterranean in the early fourth century. While the Romans had always been connected to this wider Mediterranean world, they had previously been able to engage with it largely on their own terms. The sack of Rome by Gallic mercenaries indicates that the Romans were increasingly being pushed into a Hellenistic context, with larger armies made up of more professional soldiers, whether they wanted to be or not. The sack of Rome is one of the first signs that we can see that the scale of warfare in central Italy was fundamentally changing. Even if the Roman and Latin clans had wanted to continue their traditional practice of low-level, annual raiding, outside pressures were beginning to make that untenable.

TRIBUTUM, STIPENDIUM, AND PAYING FOR WAR

Given the changing scale of warfare, and the increasing presence and importance of mercenaries, it is not a coincidence that this period also saw the introduction of both a "war tax" on Roman citizens (*tributum*) and payment to soldiers (*stipendium*) in Rome. As the introduction of *tributum* and *stipendium* occurs in the wider context of the siege of Veii, it has often been assumed that this tax/payment system was implemented so that the Romans could keep the army in the field for longer in order to support the purported "siege."[23] However, it is highly unlikely that the siege was the archetypal full investment of a community, designed to cut off reinforcements or supplies. The Romans did not camp outside the gates of Veii for years on end. A far more comparable situation is, perhaps, the Spartan siege of Athens at roughly the same time. It was more about consistent pressure than full envelopment.

During the Peloponnesian War in Greece (431–404), fought between Sparta and Athens in Greece, the Spartans invaded Attica regularly during the 10 years between 431 and 421. During these periods, the Spartans limited the Athenians' access to the rest of Attica, drove citizens within the city walls (leading to a plague), and generally caused quite a bit of trouble. It is, therefore, often talked about as a siege. However, the Spartans did not, during these invasions, ever attempt to fully cut the city off—an impossibility, in any case, due to the "long walls" linking the city to the harbor of Piraeus—and returned home at the end of each campaigning season.[24] Later, in 413, the Spartans fortified and permanently occupied the site of Decelea in Attica, making the siege more permanent, although it was still not a complete encirclement. Decelea is actually more than 21 km (ca. 14 miles) from Athens.

It is likely that the Roman siege of Veii operated along similar lines. It may have simply represented regular annual warfare against a single target, which would have been an anomaly at the time. At most, it may have represented the establishment of a permanent military camp in the region to keep pressure on the Veientines year-round. However, it is not entirely clear why this would have been needed given the evidently close proximity of clans like the Fabii to Veii, and indeed Rome itself was only located 11 km away—less than a day's walk. The distance between Decelea and Athens (21 km) is almost twice this distance, hinting that the army could have used Rome itself as an effective base. This is without even accounting for the fact that the extremely limited funds that Roman *tributum* and *stipendium* represented were almost certainly not enough to supply an army for any significant length of time.

Contrary to the common arguments, our main source on the matter, Livy, actually says that *tributum* and *stipendium* were introduced to deal with a completely different military situation that just happened to occur at the same time as the siege of Veii: the capture of the city of Anxur in southern Latium.[25] Although nowhere near as big and powerful as Veii, Anxur was a tough nut to crack, and in order to take it the Romans were forced to bring together three rather large armies. However, after sacking the city, the Romans discovered that the spoils were not enough to adequately recompense the massed troops. As a result, members of the Senate donated funds to pay the soldiers, which became the first *tributum* and *stipendium*. As this proved very effective in motivating the troops, this was soon taken up as a regular tax and payment.

So *tributum* and *stipendium* were not established to pay soldiers going into the field, but rather soldiers returning from it. It was not a support payment (at least in this period), meant to buy supplies or other material to allow them to conduct a siege, but a guaranteed payment by the community at the end of a campaign. In this way, *tributum* and *stipendium* were actually very similar to the taxation and payment that formed a key part of Hellenistic military systems and that allowed them to field their large mercenary armies. It was almost certainly a far smaller amount than soldiers fighting for Hellenistic armies would have been used to, although, given the fact that Rome's economy was not monetized or based on coinage at this time, this is quite difficult to quantify. But the core principle seems to have been the same. Rome's soldiers were already what we might call "professional," even in this period, as part of a local warrior elite. Fighting was an important part of their status and identity. But regular payment did change things slightly, offering greater stability and less personal risk. Even if the war went poorly, provided they survived, they would come out with something.

This was also a community payment in return for military service, putting the community as a whole—for perhaps the first time—within the great patronage networks that bound Roman armies together. Traditionally, Rome's generals would have always been the most important entity in the distribution of wealth to soldiers. The portable wealth acquired by the army in raids passed directly through the general's hands and was personally given to the soldiers by the general both after battles and at the end of their service through gifts called donatives.[26] This is true even in the late Republic and Empire. *Tributum* and *stipendium* did not upset this longstanding relationship but added another element to it. Now, it was not only the general who gave wealth to the soldiers at the end of the war, but the wider community as well. And with that wealth came obligation. It bound the soldiers not only to their general but to the wider community. *Tributum* and *stipendium* indicate that the unified Roman elite—or even the nascent Roman "state"—was, albeit on a small scale, stepping into the military realm more directly.

However, if *tributum* and *stipendium* were not intended to fund ongoing warfare in this period, how did the Romans support their wars? The short version is that they funded warfare as they had always done: privately. The soldiers—as wealthy men in their own right—generally supported themselves. Warfare in this period was relatively limited and likely did not last longer than a couple of weeks at most. We can imagine it as something like an expensive (and violent) hobby. Men would have purchased their own equipment and brought their own supplies. Once a year, they joined up with their friends and family to engage in a raid— competing against other groups of friends and family. Although not everyone on the battlefield was high status, as each of the soldiers likely brought along followers, clients, and slaves to support them, this would all be considered part of the cost for those engaging in war. For longer wars, the general or overall commander would leverage his greater

networks and clout to support those beneath him, as part of a wider pyramid of obligation and power. Just as heads of family provided for their
children and followers, clan chiefs provided for the lesser heads of families beneath them, and in the Roman system the general or consul at the
head of the army was considered the top of the patronage ladder. This was
not done out of simple good will though. This was an investment, which
they hoped would be repaid through spoils gained by successful action. It
may have also served to limit how often and how regularly individuals
and clans held high office in this period. While holding office in Rome
opened up many opportunities for advancement, it was often an expensive and exhausting endeavor. This is likely why kings did not fight every
year, but why the Roman Republic was able to field multiple armies year
after year. There was always a new clan chief, waiting in the wings, ready
for his turn. War was paid for by the elite of Rome, largely individually,
but increasingly in a corporate fashion as well.

THE CONSULSHIP, THE PRAETORSHIP,
AND MILITARY LEADERSHIP

As Rome entered the fourth century, its traditional clan-based military
system also started to have problems—perhaps showing its age, and
unsuitability in this new, Hellenistic context. Up until this time, Rome
had been reasonably successful due to being one of the most attractive
options for regional clans to exercise community-based power. Many of
central Italy's clans were able to wield quite a bit of power individually,
simply by virtue of their size, strength, and wealth, but were limited by
the nature of the clan structure. They did not necessarily need Rome, or
any other community, to do most of what they wanted to do. However,
while clans (with their associated followers) could evidently number in
the low thousands, this would have paled in comparison to the tens or
even hundreds of thousands of men who were counted as citizens of
Rome in this period. Italian chiefs would have been also aware of the ever
increasing scale of warfare across the Mediterranean, with ever larger
armies being deployed in the east, in particular, during this period. The

tremendous resources that were able to be mobilized by and through communities like Rome make their appeal obvious, and the inclusive early Republican system allowed Rome's roughly 50 patrician families to split power and rotate through the high offices.

The problem was that Rome's 50 patrician families were not the only clans in the region, and their (arguably natural) desire to monopolize power within Rome had started to limit and strangle its growth. In the middle of the fifth century, Rome's patrician elite had closed their ranks and refused to let anyone else into the ruling class. It was around this time that this group of families formally adopted the label "patrician," with everyone else grouped together as "plebeians." As a result of this closing of the patriciate, Rome was no longer a viable destination for newcomers who wanted to access that power themselves. While the community may have still been attractive for small, independent families, many of the more powerful clans that had not made the mid-fifth-century cut-off seem to have either stayed away or only loosely aligned. The so-called "secessions of the plebs," which marked the fifth century, may have represented very real threats by plebeian families, both powerful and not, to leave and align with a different community if the patricians did not make concessions.

The "Struggle of the Orders" did ultimately end with something like plebeian parity, but this took almost two centuries to achieve. The patrician families tried long and hard to hold on to power, which often meant keeping things as they were. Had politics and warfare in central Italy continued on in the fourth century as it had before, this may not have been an issue. However, the context was changing, as the sacks of Veii and Rome had made clear. The sack of Veii had removed one of the other options for local clans to operate through and was not the only such community to be captured and controlled by Rome. Although of less importance, and certainly less dramatically, we can see similar things occurring at Fidenae and elsewhere. So, not only were Rome's patrician families monopolizing power in the city of Rome, they were also removing alternative options outside of it. Further, the sack of Rome by the Gauls had highlighted that warfare was beginning to operate on a larger scale in this period. The world was changing, and the Romans needed to change with it.

The first step that the Romans took after their defeat by the Gauls was to expand their tribal system for the first time since the start of the Republic, adding four new tribes that incorporated the land and population of Veii. A central Italian clan on its own was likely able to muster 300–500 warriors. While we should not assume that clans can be rigidly equated to Rome's tribal units in this period, multiplying 500 by Rome's 21 tribes in the period ca. 390 gives us a total of 10,500. This is, obviously, a far cry from Rome's reported census figures, for instance the 152,373 citizens in 392 reported by Pliny,[27] but is perhaps an accurate approximation of the total available armed forces for Rome in this period—when only the top socioeconomic levels of society (the *equites* and single *classis*) usually fought.

Indeed, we can perhaps say the proof is in the results. Rome's loss at the River Allia, and the subsequent defeat/ransom at Rome, suggests that Rome's existing system, which was evidently very well suited to dominating the local region, was unable to defeat the equivalent of a single mercenary contingent within a larger Hellenistic army. Rome's fifth-century system had allowed Rome's clans to defeat and destroy their local rival Veii, but the Romans were simply not equipped to defeat the larger armies beginning to operate in the fourth-century Mediterranean world. Even as early as the battle of Platea in Greece in 479, during the Persian War, the allied Greeks had been able to mobilize a force of at least 70,000, and the kingdom of Macedon seemed to be able to field a force of roughly comparable size by the 330s. While Rome's clans could come together to field forces in the thousands, leaders elsewhere in the Mediterranean—and even Italy—were fielding forces in the tens of thousands. Manpower was, therefore, a key concern, and evidently enough of one to force Rome's patrician families into making some changes.

The expansion of Rome's tribal system by four would have increased their military manpower by a couple thousand men, which was a step in the right direction, but not enough to change the overall situation on its own. Rome also evidently began to build fortifications around the city, the great circuit walls known as the "Servian Walls" which are still visible in sections of the city today (see fig. 8). This suggests an increased focus and investment in the community by the wider population, and perhaps a recognition that the

Veii, the Gauls, and Rome Reborn

FIG 8

Rome's fourth-century "Servian Walls." Semi-extant section located near the modern Termini Station in Rome. Photo: J. Armstrong.

physical city of Rome was far more important to them than they previously realized.[28] While it seems clear that individual clans and families retained their distinct identities, and competition between the clans remained high, the fourth century saw the community emerge as the primary (and relatively peaceful) venue for that competition. While previously clans would have competed on a regional playing field, often raiding each other and engaging in a quite violent form of competition, from the fourth century onward we start to see competition for political positions within the community playing a much larger role, as well as competitive building and other forms of urban, elite display. Violence was increasingly directed outward, toward communities and entities not in the Roman system.

As part of this wider set of developments, we also have a shake-up within Rome's military leadership. In 376 the plebian tribunes

Gaius Licinius Stolo and Lucius Sextius Lateranus introduced a series of three measures that shook the Roman system from top to bottom.[29] These supposedly worked to alleviate debt, restricted access to public land (*ager publicus*), and also introduced the consulship. While seemingly innocuous to us today, these measures were evidently so controversial at the time that they brought Roman politics to a standstill for almost a decade, and the situation ultimately required the help of a dictator (the great man, Camillus, now at the end of his long career) in 367.[30] The land and debt issues have a sort of universality to them—we can, arguably, all empathize with the stress of debt and desire to own property—although it is difficult to understand why these might have been so controversial in this period. Indeed, the narrative for these has long been assumed to be heavily influenced by later social struggles, especially from the second century. As a result, the consulship has emerged as the likely crux of the matter and why the proposal of this particular set of laws seems to have stopped Rome in its tracks.[31]

Entering the fourth century, the Romans seem to have had two distinct military systems and irregularly alternated between them in different years, depending on what people wanted to do and the perceived needs and goals for the coming year. The first system was the traditional one, based on the *curiae*. This was effectively the same system that had been put in place at the start of the Republic by Brutus and his friends, repurposing Rome's regal institutions. Its commanders (in the early Republic, known as "praetors") held *imperium*, which was a very strong and prestigious form of command that was tightly connected to their role as clan chiefs.[32] However, by the final decades of the fifth century, it is clear that this system was showing its age and unsuitability for the changing military context. Most notably, the traditional system seems to have been limited by the size and nature of the *curiae*, which were focused on the urban community itself and so only included a fraction of Rome's expanding population. While Rome's wider tribal system included tens of thousands of individuals spread across the wider region, the *curiae* likely contained only a part of this. Recruiting an army from the *curiae* would still allow leaders to augment their clans, as the kings had done, to raid or pursue a feud, but wouldn't be appropriate for a major endeavor or assault. So, in terms of pros and cons, it provided a high level of control and prestige, but a low number of soldiers.

The second system the Romans utilized in this period was based on the tribes. Brought in during the second half of the fifth century, it evidently leveraged the wider citizen population included in Rome's new tribal structure and seems to have utilized a new set of tribal military leaders, known as military tribunes (in this period known as "military tribunes with consular power," to differentiate them from the "military tribunes" of the late Republic). This system was clearly designed with Rome's changing military context in mind, as it offered a dramatic increase in manpower. However, in its early incarnation, it was seemingly limited by both the nature of the leadership (lacking *imperium*) and its dispersed nature, with up to six men holding the office at a time. This was likely a more explicitly federated army, and with a weaker central command, as perhaps reflected in their rather mixed record in battle. Despite their ability to put more soldiers in the field, under more commanders, this new tribal system was evidently only marginally more capable than the previous model between the 440s and 360s. So, thinking again in terms of pros and cons, this second system provided a high level of manpower, but a much lower level of command and control.

Both of the existing systems were compromises between Rome's elite families, and with the community, that reflected a careful balancing of competitive instincts and interests. The elite clans recognized that they could do more, especially in the wider regional context, when working together. However, they were also deeply concerned with their local and internal competitions over community power and prestige. The period ca. 367 represents a renegotiation of the compromise, which accounts of the changing situation in Latium and the wider Mediterranean. Everyone realized that they needed larger armies in the fourth century. However, they also needed better and stronger command systems to make appropriate use of this increased manpower. The consulship, which was brought in as a result of the Licinio-Sextian reforms, seems to have combined these two pre-existing systems—granting the power of *imperium* over the full tribal structure—attempting (largely successfully) to take the best parts of each. The later consulship of the middle and late Republic bears all the hallmarks of this marriage. Consuls commanded an army that was evidently recruited using the tribal system, as Polybius indicates, but was also imbued with *imperium* through the *curiae* and exercised that incredibly potent form of command. It also focused command into the hands of two men, which likely worked to consolidate forces and decision-making, although this did not stop the regular appointment of dictators throughout the period. So the consuls seem to have represented the culmination of 150 years of development in military leadership in Rome, as they combined the best elements of the Roman community's expanded manpower and resources with the strong leadership of the traditional clan-based leaders.

THE NEW ROMAN CITIZENSHIP

While we will talk quite a bit about both Roman citizenship and Roman allies in the next chapter, it is worth introducing the topic here as well—as, alongside the changes to military leadership, there is evidence that the Romans also began to think quite carefully about community membership in the early fourth century. It is likely, from the somewhat halting and piecemeal changes that the Roman community enacted in this area, that the Romans did not have a pre-existing grand strategy for expansion. Rather, the changing situation the clans and community faced in this period provoked a series of ad hoc responses, encouraging development in certain areas and curtailing it in others. The totality of these changes, however, would have significant repercussions for both the nature of their military and their relationships with other communities in the wider region.

As with virtually every aspect of Roman history, none of these developments happened suddenly or in isolation. The Romans had been thinking about who was a part of the community, and who was not, at least as early as the sixth century when we had the traditional creation of Rome's tribal system by Servius Tullius. While previously membership may have simply included whoever happened to be in the community at a given point in time, the tribal system explicitly, and at least semi-permanently, included people outside of the urban community as well—and sometimes quite a distance outside. While there have always been doubts about the reliability of this material and early date, this sort of system fits broadly with everything else we know about central Italian society in the sixth century. Rome was not the only community dealing with these issues, and this aligns with what other communities were doing as well. While it is likely that Rome's early tribal system was more of an "opt in" system for the families, rather than the community formally prescribing things, it hints that these ideas were circulating.

While the tribal assembly seems to have grown in power during the early Republic, it is noteworthy that the number of tribes themselves did not expand between 495 and 387. While various *gentes* may have moved in or through the community of Rome, they were not recognized with a new tribal designation or voting contingent and would have presumably needed to incorporate themselves into an existing tribe if they wished to permanently associate. The creation of the censorship and the consular tribunes in the 440s is an indication that tribal affiliation was increasingly important in this period, but little changed beyond that.

In the early fourth century, however, there was a new focus on, and expansion of, Roman citizenship. The most significant change is the addition of the four new tribes based in the traditional territory of Veii, incorporating that population. Roughly 30 years later, in 358, another two tribes were added, the Poblilia and Pomptina, to the south and east of Rome. This dramatic expansion of Rome's tribes, increasing the number by almost 30 percent from 21 to 27 in less than 30 years, would have had significant implications for Rome's military system. One can imagine that this was similar to the dramatic growth of the United States in the middle of the nineteenth century, or the European Union more recently. Politically, the new tribes had the potential to alter the power balance, although it is unlikely they would have shifted things significantly. While each tribe would have had an equal vote in the assembly, the new tribes would have been outnumbered by the existing ones. The new tribes would have represented a significant addition to Rome's army though. Six new tribes would have added a large number of new soldiers and would have spread the military load more widely, taking pressure off the existing families.

It is also worth considering what being a Roman citizen meant in this period. While the authors of our sources, writing during the late Republic and Empire, often assumed that Roman citizenship was always a great honor and privilege, it is clear that this was not always the case. During the early Republic, and indeed down to the early second century, Roman citizenship was arguably more about obligation—especially with regard to military service and taxation—than it was about rights and privileges. Being a Roman citizen would have meant you were able to vote in the assemblies, although this required being in Rome on the appropriate days, which would have been difficult for most, and what or who a citizen could vote for would have been controlled tightly by the elite clans anyway. Citizens would have been able to use Roman legal systems, although this was both limited and of uncertain value in this early period, when Roman power did not extend particularly far beyond the *pomerium* of the city itself. From the start of the fourth century, being a citizen would have granted someone access to *ager publicus*, although this was also quite limited and was already dominated by a few elite clans. The fact that many people turned down Roman citizenship in the fourth and early third centuries, and so many defeated opponents were "granted" it in this period—for instance the Capenates and Falisci in 388, the people of Veii in 387, the people of Tusculum in 381, and Velitrae in 380—is suggestive of its true nature. Being a Roman citizen meant, first and foremost, supporting the expanding military system through either active service or paying taxes. The very fact that the Romans experimented with a type of citizenship that did not have the right to vote (*cives sine suffragio*) during the fourth century further demonstrates that the core meaning of citizenship in Rome in this period was not political participation and engagement but rather military obligation. The political aspects were secondary and indeed optional.

In contrast to modern conceptions of citizenship (and indeed later Roman varieties), fourth-century Roman citizenship was generally extended to communities and not individuals. Citizenship was corporate. This is important given the high levels of mobility that seem to have been present in Italy during this period. If a family or individual was unhappy with their citizenship status in relation to Rome, they could theoretically move to a different community, or alter their affiliation, in order to change it.[33] In fact, this seems to have happened enough that the Romans were forced to pass laws attempting to limit this movement, although this did not happen until more than a century later. Granting citizenship to a particular community laid the obligation for military service and taxation on the community as a whole. People could move, and indeed often did, but the obligation remained. The community, as represented and embodied by the stable urban center, was required to contribute to Rome's military system. Further, and especially in this early period, it is likely that tribal affiliation was relational as well as geographic. To fully separate from a tribe, a family likely had to do more than move. They would need to sever their relationships and find a new social, economic, and political network to be a part of. While this was evidently possible, the difficulties involved likely explain why Rome's extension of tribal status was successful, even in areas that might not have been particularly excited about acquiring it.

In the first half of the fourth century, we can see a subtle reinterpretation of the nature of Roman citizenship, and particularly the role of the tribes. When the tribes were initially created, very possibly in the sixth century, they seemed to be a representation of Rome's expanding community and the various families that were a part of it. This is why they were almost all named after powerful clans and likely represented those clans and their followers. However, during the fifth century, the tribes slowly came to represent the wider citizen body in a social and political sense. While still individually dominated by specific families, together they represented the voice of the assembled community. By the second half of the fifth century, the tribes seem to have slowly taken on a more important military role in the community, associated with the creation of the enigmatic consular tribunes and likely the censorship as well. It is likely in this period as well that, at least in years with consular tribunes, recruitment was regularly funneled through the tribes. The advent of *tributum*, which funded war, was also managed by the tribes (and men known as tribunes) and introduced in this period.

By the early fourth century, the Romans seem to have moved toward a fundamentally tribal army. Between the Gallic sack (390) and the Licinio-Sextian reforms (367) the Romans only used consular tribunes to lead their armies, and it is clear that the later consular system also relied on the tribes and military tribunes (although in this later system, the tribunes were subordinate to the consuls and praetors). The Romans also used new tribes, and adding new citizens to existing tribes, to expand their military resources, regularly doing so during the first half of the century. Tribes became one of the first expressions of Roman military expansion (and perhaps "imperialism"), permanently incorporating new peoples and groups within a Roman system that was geared around extraction— primarily of military manpower.

The increased importance and expansion of the Roman tribal system is important for two reasons. First, it was evidently very effective in its goal of increasing Rome's military resources. Although only recently emerging from a humiliating defeat, Rome quickly went from strength to strength in this period, regularly defeating large, allied armies from across central Italy—including increasing numbers of Gauls. As the record of victories attests, Rome's military system after 367 was vastly superior to whatever had come before. Second, this new approach to citizenship, which was fundamentally extractive and able to be applied easily across new territories, increasingly put the Romans at odds with their neighbors.

The sack and destruction of Veii had demonstrated that the powerful clans of Rome were increasingly seeking to monopolize power within the region, funneling influence, wealth, and communication through a single community, Rome, that they controlled. It is likely that Rome's neighbors had noted (and perhaps raised their eyebrows at) this rising monopoly and the exceptional steps that the Romans had taken in destroying the rival city of Veii. However, Veii would have seemed like a singular exception, being both very close to Rome and quite large, and there was little indication, at least initially, that the Romans were planning on pursuing similar practices elsewhere. But in the early fourth century, the Romans' rapid centralization of military power through tribal citizenship seems to have put their neighbors, both north and south, on edge. The Romans had begun to change the nature of the great game they all played, increasingly hoarding resources, and removing options for advancement and power for clans and families outside of the Roman elite. This growing tension would turn into an outright war in the decades that followed.

ROME REBORN

To try and summarize things a bit then, in 367 Rome emerged from a tumultuous two decades as a resurgent power. The sack of Veii in 396 had removed a local, rival base of power and demonstrated that Rome and its collected clans and elites were the dominant network within the wider region. The sack of Veii could be considered the culmination of a century of warfare and work to increase the local significance of the Roman community and network. However, less than a decade later, the limited and local nature of this success was revealed by Rome's defeat at the hands of the Gauls. While Rome may have been the most important local center of power, the Roman military network was clearly just that—a local one. Rome's collected elites and traditional mode of operating were simply not functioning on the same level or scale as other powers and networks in the Mediterranean basin. Whether or not Brennus' Gauls were actually mercenaries traveling to serve in the army of Dionysius I of Syracuse or not, they seem to be indicative of that type of group. From the middle of the fifth century, the entire Mediterranean (and especially Italy) was increasingly full of both mercenary units and the ever larger armies that incorporated them. While Rome had emerged victorious from her previous local struggles, this new, larger context presented new challenges.

The Romans' response to the Gallic disaster is revealing. Perhaps unsurprisingly, in the aftermath of the defeat, the Romans immediately worked to expand their military capacity. Specifically, they added a number of new tribes to the existing tribal system, emphasizing their fundamentally military nature in this period. While we often associate the tribal assembly with plebeian agitation and popular legislation by the late Republic, in this period the tribes were closely linked to the military. The Romans also fortified the site of Rome and chose to only utilize consular tribunes as military leaders—completely forgoing the archaic praetors and *imperium*-based system. While the first two measures, the tribes and fortifications, seemed to be a success, the third was not. The consular tribunate was ultimately deemed to not be up to the task, and the Romans entered a period of political turmoil, resulting in the creation of a new magistracy—the consulship of 367. Livy clearly paints the conflict around the new consulship as an internal and political one, and there is almost certainly some truth in this. Both the early consulship/praetorship and the post-367 variety clearly came with an increased level of prestige when compared with the consular tribunate, and this community-based prestige was increasingly important for Rome's elite clan leaders in this period. However, this explanation has never made sense on its own, and possibly not even to Livy himself, whose narrative of events is famously confused and somewhat contradictory. Looking at the nature of military power, and the way in which the consulship seems to combine the power of both the curiate and tribal structures through the mechanism of Rome's emerging centuriate system, it is likely that this magistracy represented a fundamentally new type of command that unlocked the full potential of Rome's manpower reserves.

Overall, this period saw an intense centralization of power and authority in Rome. Although likely not yet a unified "Roman people," there was a clear movement in that direction. While many clans had previously at least attempted to operate independently as they had always done, by the beginning of the fourth century the writing was on the wall that this was no longer a viable approach. The competition was getting bigger, and in order to compete the people of Rome needed to band together more tightly. The clans of Rome started pool their resources, both in terms of portable wealth (*tributum* and *stipendium*) and land (*ager publicus*, or "public land," which emerges in this period). There was also an increased focus on community membership. In some ways the fortifications of Rome were a symbol of this, a clear physical demarcation of "us" and "them" with access strictly controlled—a marked change from the relatively open community that had existed before. In addition, we have the rise of censorship in Rome, which recorded who was a citizen and who was not, as well as how much wealth they had (and so what military roles they could perform). Although supposedly created in 443, it was remembered as being a somewhat menial office in the early years. The office only came to real prominence ca. 367, and by the late fourth century was one of the most important offices in the Roman political system. The Romans also began to think seriously about what citizenship meant in this period, creating levels of obligation (most of which seem to have been military in nature) that extended beyond the limits of the tribes. Much of this represented amalgamation, extension, or scaling up of existing systems, rather than something wholly new, although the combined resultant change was still substantial.

This period, therefore, marks the birth of Rome as an increasingly centralized, and possibly "imperial," military power. To be clear, this "imperialist" Roman entity was still in its infancy, if it existed at all in this period. The Romans did not immediately begin to conquer vast swathes of territory or dominate the region. Indeed, many of the measures put in place seem to have been defensively minded. They ensured that the clans of Rome were sufficiently prepared to protect themselves against another force of Gauls or mercenaries. It was also not, necessarily, yet a "state" in the way we might recognize one today. While military power was increasingly focused through the community, the community is unlikely to have exercised a total monopoly upon it. There was almost certainly, still, quite a bit of low-level warfare occurring in the region. Individual clans continued to raid each other, and many parts of life and war continued as they always had. However, the systems had been put in place to allow Rome to compete on the emerging Hellenistic stage, not only defensively, but offensively as well.

4

THE ROMANS, THE LATINS,

AND THE SAMNITES

THE SECOND HALF OF the fourth century was defined by ever larger conflicts for the Romans, as they began to operate on a regional scale. Part of this may have been due to the changing character of the Roman federation and the ambitions of its clans and members. Not only were the elite families of Rome becoming more cohesive and working together to expand the system; they were also becoming more effective and efficient as they focused their efforts on joint goals. Additionally, while Rome's warrior elite had always been keen to pursue military glory, by the middle of the fourth century Rome seems to have become one of *the* places to be if you had military ambitions within Italy. With the reforms of 367, military command was (at least theoretically) open to anyone. The stranglehold of the patricians had been broken, and Rome was once again open and accepting of powerful, new arrivals and we see a flood of new names and families appearing in the records. This was a system and a context that favored the bold, and it is clear from the actions of plebeian commanders in particular that many families in central Italy were keen to make use of it.

The increasing scale of warfare in Italy was not only due to these internal developments, however, and may have also been the result of changes in the wider region. The fourth century was an "Age of Empires," where larger and larger armies began to operate farther and farther from home, all across the Mediterranean basin. Alexander the Great's 10-year march east through the Persian empire, with tens of thousands of men at his back, is perhaps the most extreme example, but it is one of many. This increase in the scale of warfare also drove military innovation. When locally sourced troops and supplies were not enough to feed the demand of these more expansive military ambitions, armies increasingly relied on mercenary units and purchased goods, acquired with the now ubiquitous coinage (introduced to the Mediterranean in the sixth century).[1] This greater scale also required greater centralization and control of resources, which in turn increased the scale as states competed for resources, creating a feedback cycle that pumped ever more energy into the system.

Despite this rapidly changing context, the emerging Roman state was reasonably well situated. It had experienced a painful (re)birth after 390, but by 350, the measures the Romans had put in place were bearing fruit. By 387, Rome's tribes were the most important institutions for Roman military power, allowing Rome to leverage an expanding citizen body.[2] The Romans had also created a new set of military magistrates to command this army, which centralized and focused Roman military power.[3] While some tensions remained within the social and political systems of Rome, the elite families had evidently settled on a new compromise, providing a degree of equality for newcomers and exchanging a little more of their independence for at least the possibility of much more power—assuming they could win election to one of the top offices.

These changes in Rome brought about some unintended consequences. The expansion of Rome's citizen body would have exponentially increased not only the state's military manpower, but also the number of powerful elites present within the system. When the Romans added new tribes, they were not simply adding rank-and-file soldiers, but the powerful clan leaders who had traditionally led them. They were integrating clans and communities, with their local hierarchies intact. The traditional patrician elite of Rome that had managed to dominate Rome's early Republican system would have been confronted with a growing group of powerful plebeian clans and clan leaders. These new men would not accept being left out of the power-sharing arrangement of the *res publica* for long.[4] While patrician families would continue to wield outsized influence within the system, and indeed they continued to monopolize the praetorship after

367, the "grand bargain" at the core of the Roman system required the active buy-in of the wider group of clans and elites within Rome's military system. Allowing the plebeian elite into the highest offices of this new system was almost certainly a natural result of Rome's expanding military systems. The ending of the "Struggle of the Orders" was the by-product of Rome's growing population, which was funneled exclusively, and somewhat by definition, into the plebeian segment of society. So, by the middle of the fourth century, Rome and her military were doing well. It had required some tough choices and compromises by those in power, prompted by some real threats and issues, but the end result was an innovative, effective, and expansive system that allowed the Romans to spread their influence across the region. Nevertheless, this expansion brought still further issues—as well as opportunities.

The highly competitive game that the families and clans associated with Rome were playing was slowly changing its character. Internally, it became more political and focused on winning magistracies. Elites struggled against each other, but in a more social and political context. They resorted less and less to violence, at least when engaging with other "Romans," although the threat of violence remained in the background and indeed would rear its head in the late Republic. Externally, however, the Roman system became even more violent, as these magistrates led ever larger armies against anyone who was not part of their system. Raiding and warfare seems to have increased and spread across an ever larger area. This was a worrying development for the rest of the region.[5] Indeed, the emergence of this powerful military federation in the first half of the fourth century, based in and through the community of Rome, seems to have upset the regional balance of power and quickly alienated and antagonized those clans and communities in Latium that had previously stayed out of the Roman network. Many of these groups seem to have realized that the situation was quickly reaching a point of no return, wherein Roman military expansion either had to be stopped or they would be forced to become a part of it—whether they wanted to or not, and likely as a junior partner. This led to the so-called "Great Latin War" in 340, when the Roman alliance faced off against a confederation of the remaining, unaffiliated Latins, defeating them in relatively short order. As we shall see, the Romans were able to incorporate these peoples into their system, too, adding them to the tribal structure through both their inclusion into existing tribes and the creation of a few more.

One could also include Rome's wars with the Etruscans, who were often supported by Gauls (perhaps as mercenaries or perhaps as allies—the difference is arguably negligible), in this same struggle. Although the Etruscans were traditionally recognized as a distinct culture, it is clear that both Latium and Etruria's clans and communities existed within the same regional network. People and groups moved easily between the regions, and operated in essentially the same way. The way in which the Romans defeated and incorporated these populations is vital to understanding the nature of their emerging empire in this period. Most notably, the Romans seem to have utilized a slightly different system in the north, often incorporating clans and communities as allies (called "*socii*" or "companions") instead of citizens. While the end result was arguably the same, with an expansion of Rome's armed forces, the mechanism is important, as we shall see.

Rome's wars against the Samnites represent a third, slightly different situation. While the Latins and Etruscans were Rome's immediate neighbors and seem to have operated using effectively the same social, political, religious, and military systems, the peoples and communities of Campania and Samnium represented a certain, slightly further degree of difference. To be clear, and in contrast to how they are often described in modern histories, the Campanians and Samnites were certainly not foreign or unknown to the Romans in the fourth century. Quite the reverse, in fact, as it is likely that many Roman and Latin families had strong connections with the peoples and places of these regions. However, Campania and Samnium, located to the south and east of Rome and Latium, were more firmly integrated into the wider Hellenistic social, economic, and military landscape. The region of Campania had been colonized by Greeks in the eighth century and was dominated by major settlements like Capua and Neapolis, with social and economic networks that may have exceeded Rome's own—particularly when it came to the eastern Mediterranean. Samnium, located in the mountainous interior of Italy to the east of Campania, had very few permanent settlements and was populated by more mobile, pastoral groups. It was, however, far from an isolated backwater, as its tribes—along with those of Lucania—were well-connected and often recruited as mercenaries by both local and foreign powers. Although sometimes described and depicted as barbarians, by both ancient and modern authors, they were an important and respected part of many Hellenistic militaries.[6] The peoples of these regions, while sharing many of the same social, economic, and military networks as central Italy, also had some of their own—with many of them extending well beyond the edges of Italy. As the Romans expanded into these regions, they seemed to use a mixture of grants of citizenship and alliances, showing both an awareness of the complex situation on the ground—they did not apply a one-size-fits-all model—and the variability which their federated system allowed for.

However, the fact that the peoples of Campania and Samnium seem to have had stronger connections with the wider Mediterranean meant that warfare in this area took on a different flavor. The peoples and communities in this region had more options for military alliances available to them and were not afraid to use them—even after the Romans had supposedly conquered the area. Famously, some Samnites joined the forces of Pyrrhus against Rome, and some joined Hannibal when he invaded Italy almost a century later. As they moved into this area, the Roman system had to compete with others and occasionally seemed to struggle in this context. As a result, the Roman approach to the Samnites and Campanians is, in many ways, indicative of what their approach would be to the wider Mediterranean world. The Romans deployed both a "carrot" and "stick" in these contexts, actively (and often violently) negotiating to cement their power and influence.

Rome's wars with the Samnites take us down to 290 and, at their conclusion, the Romans were effectively the masters of most of peninsular Italy. Some areas and conflicts remained, most notably with the Greek communities of southern Italy and their allies from across the Hellenistic Mediterranean (discussed in the next chapter), but the core of Rome's Italian empire was in place by this point and, perhaps more importantly, the key systems had been established. We can see how the Romans adapted and tweaked the imperial systems established in the early fourth century to deal with new situations and peoples, and also gain insight into the motivations and goals behind their expansion. Indeed, a question that has plagued scholars, both ancient and modern, is *why* the Romans expanded during this period. Were they bloodthirsty imperialists, set on world domination? Were they defensive imperialists, merely protecting their interests in a proactive manner? Were they accidental imperialists, stumbling into an empire, when they were simply trying to acquire wealth? Or something else entirely?

Our interpretations of events in this period will always be tainted by our knowledge of the outcome—we know that the Romans will win these wars and eventually construct a Mediterranean-wide empire. The ultimate trajectory of Roman power shapes our understanding and all too often hides the multitude of potential futures—and failures—that were possible. When considering Roman actions, we should always bear in mind that the end result was never set, and they had a virtually infinite range of options to choose from. Further, it is worth remembering that we are dealing with a moving target, and that with every victory, and every new population integrated, the nature of the Roman system and Roman society changed. But despite this dynamic context, or indeed perhaps because of the trends visible within Roman decision-making, some plausible answers might be attainable.

ROME AND THE LATINS

Rome's most significant conflict in the second half of the fourth century was with the Latins. While the "First Samnite War" technically predates the "Great Latin War," and the conflicts with the Samnites lasted longer (over 50 years, all told), the war with the Latins had a more profound impact on Roman society as a whole.[7] This conflict had been simmering for decades, and its conclusion resulted in a massive expansion of Rome's military system—possibly doubling the size of Rome's citizen body and military capacity, if Roman census data are to be believed.

The region of Latium (see fig. 9) is defined as that bordered by the Tyrrhenian Sea in the west, the Tiber in the north, the Apennine Mountains

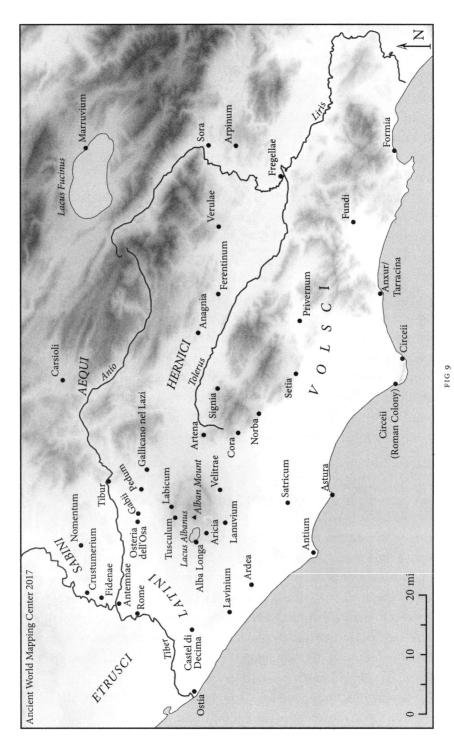

FIG 9

Map of Latium and the Tyrrhenian coast. Produced by the Ancient World Mapping Center.

in the east, and includes the marshy region of the Pontine plains in the south, ending roughly at the Circeian promontory and the coastal town of Anxur/Tarracina. The area of the Monti Lepini, with Formia and Fundi, was something of a liminal zone between Latium and Campania. The core of the Latin region, known as *Latium vetus* ("old Latium") was the coastal plain that wrapped around the Alban hills—a volcanic spur of the Apennines. The word Latium is likely derived from the Latin word *latus*, which means "flat"—so Latium meant "the flat land" or plain that spread out from these hills. Rome was situated at the northern edge of this territory, bordering the region of Etruria. The peoples of *Latium vetus* were remembered as the Romans' closest relations and traditional allies, as well as rivals. These people were thought to share a common mythic lineage with the Romans through the kings and kingdom of Alba Longa (and possibly Aeneas), as well as a shared language and set of ritual customs and beliefs. While archaeology has indicated that cultural divisions in central Italy are blurry at best, the region of Latium does seem to exhibit enough common traits to plausibly call it home to a distinct "material culture"—which makes some sense given its relatively closed geography.[8] The region, bordered by rivers and mountains, certainly did not cut off communication with the rest of the peninsula, although it did encourage internal movement and connections. A further strip of land to the east and south, including some of the mountainous land of the interior as well as several important river valleys (especially the Tolerus, Liris, and Anio), was known as *Latium adjectum* ("attached Latium" or "added Latium"). This area was traditionally thought to be dominated by more pastoral peoples, like the Volsci and Hernici, although it is increasingly uncertain whether we should think about them as discrete cultures. While the differing geography of this land was conducive to different rhythms and practices, we now think these groups were actually part of the same, wider regional culture.

As with the label "Roman," especially in the early periods, who "the Latins" were, as a people, is quite difficult to pin down.[9] The label seems to be somewhat contextual. Although broadly referring to people and communities in the region Latium, it is likely one of several labels that might apply to individuals or groups living there, and it is of uncertain importance in the day-to-day life of most people. Certainly, the most important label for anyone in the region would have been family affiliation, and it is likely many families moved within and across Latium and central Italy on a regular basis. Being Latin was a choice. Urban communities, as more stable entities, would have presumably retained a Latin affiliation more easily, but our evidence is not entirely clear on this. Communities seem to have been able to change their affiliation too.

That being said, our sources do discuss the "old Latins" and people of the "Latin name," implying some form of shared history and identity, reinforced by shared festivals and cults like that of Jupiter Latiaris at the Lucus Ferentinae near Alba Longa. It required the choice to be backed up with actions, at least sometimes. Our sources even hint that there was something akin to a "Latin League" or federation. Whether this was ever a formal league or alliance comparable to the Athenian Delian League or the Spartan Peloponnesian League is highly unlikely—although this does seem to be what the authors of our sources thought. This traditional Latin grouping usually contained 30 members, although exactly who these members were seems to vary, and it evidently included both clans and communities as well as (at least sometimes) Rome.[10]

But while the peoples and clans of Latium seem to have regularly come together for shared festivals and may have even mobilized allied armies for joint ventures, this was evidently only one of many networks in which the clans and communities of the region engaged. It clearly did not preclude them from operating independently, through a single community, or even within a rival network or league—for instance that of the Etruscans, or indeed of the Romans themselves. A group might be "Roman" one day and "Latin" the next (or, indeed, "Sabine," "Volscian," and "Etruscan," among others) depending on how they wanted to affiliate and the context in which they found themselves. Although the peoples shared some basic cultural norms, there is little to suggest that these were fixed, absolute, or expected for much of their long history.[11] This was a very flexible and fluid association.

As should be clear from the discussion so far, however, things were clearly changing by the fourth century. This is visible across a range of different areas but is perhaps best attested in law. For instance, we have the so-called "Latin rights" (*ius Latini*), which were supposedly shared among all the people of Latium and included the rights to trade, intermarry, migrate, and become a citizen. These were likely traditional customs shared by everyone within the region for centuries that never needed to be put in a legal context. However, as the Roman network and identity expanded, it put these customary practices in jeopardy. Indeed, as we will see, one of the measures the Romans introduced after the war with the Latins in 338 was the curtailment of some of these rights for some conquered communities. The "Latin rights" may have only become an established set of legal principles when the Romans started to regulate them and take some of them away. You only need to list things out formally when they become contested. Indeed, by the late Republic, "Latin rights" were increasingly granted to communities across the Mediterranean as a step toward full Roman citizenship. Being "Latin," in this later period, was little more than a political and legal step toward being "Roman" and completely divorced from its original cultural and geographic context. Their core meaning, in a legal sense, was to delineate a specific relationship to Rome.

In the middle of the fourth century, an appropriate analogy or metaphor for understanding the early "Roman" and "Latin" relationship might be to understand them as members of a family. They were, in many ways, siblings, and for several centuries they had co-existed in the same context. They lived and played together. They argued, fought, and made up. They grew up together. However, beginning in the late fifth century, the "Roman" network had begun to grow a bit faster, and largely at the expense of the wider "Latin" association. What had been a relatively equal and fluid relationship became not only unequal but a little more antagonistic. The Romans were like a large and increasingly overbearing brother, bullying younger siblings into doing what they wanted. This only increased as time went on, getting worse and worse, straining relationships and familial bonds. By the middle of the fourth century, the Latins seem to have had enough of their pushy "siblings" in Rome.

This is obviously a very loose metaphor, but it is possible that the Romans themselves viewed the relationship in this way, as the myth of Romulus and Remus—which first seems to emerge in this period (the first clear evidence is a statue group erected in Rome by the Ogulnii brothers ca. 300)—can easily be read as the story of the Romans and the Latins. While Romulus is obviously associated with Rome, Remus was actually known as a Latin hero, and Dionysius of Halicarnassus reported that he was associated with the foundation of a number of Latin communities.[12] Reading the myth as an (admittedly Romano-centric) explanation for the conflict between Rome and the Latins helps to make sense of the wider situation, and particularly the way in which the twinned birth and later fratricide can work together within a single narrative. From the Roman perspective, Remus, as a proxy for the Latins, attacked Romulus out of jealousy. Remus was defeated, and Romulus (and the Romans) then unified the population under his sole rule.

In reality, we don't know why the Latins ultimately rose up against the Romans. It is possible that the peoples of Latium, who had yet to be brought into the Roman system (either forcefully or peacefully), were fighting against the very idea of the expansive system of obligation that the Romans were increasingly rolling out across the region. However, taking the myth of Romulus and Remus as a guide, it is perhaps more likely that, for many Latin elites, this was a disagreement over *how*, and not *whether*, the peoples of the region should unify, and under whose leadership. While the communities and clans of Latium had not necessarily faced the same Gallic threat as the Romans, and indeed some may have used Gallic mercenaries or otherwise allied with them, they would have all realized the situation had changed—the military context was evolving, getting ever larger, and they needed to band together to survive within it. However, simply joining up with the Roman system would not have been the first choice of many Latin clan leaders. While the "Struggle of the Orders" had slowly opened up the positions of power, the process was still ongoing, and the entire apparatus was still dominated by a small handful of patrician clans who had been in charge of Rome from the late sixth century. New arrivals, many of whom commanded powerful clans and vast resources, were still classified as plebeian and forced to compete for less than half of the available positions. They were also still locked out of many of the non-military offices, including most of the priesthoods and other positions of honor. Most of the powerful clans of Latium would not have willingly accepted this situation if there was the possibility of them establishing a partnership on more equal terms. Thus, one might consider the Latin War as something like "aggressive negotiation."

Open war between the Romans and Latins broke out in 340 and was closely connected to the actions of the Romans in Samnium and Campania, which will be discussed slightly later in this chapter. The exact details of the leadup are uncertain, but there seems to have been consistent warfare and raiding between the peoples of southern Latium, Campania, and north-eastern Samnium, running through the territory of the Sidinici. This area, not far from Fregellae and between the Liris and Volturnus rivers, was evidently a hotbed of military activity. At the junction of three larger social, economic, and perhaps cultural zones, it featured a number of ongoing conflicts, most of which likely stretched back centuries, but which were slowly growing in scale and importance due to the expanding alliances and federations involved. Just like Europe before World War I, the ever increasing web of alliances meant that even small conflicts could quickly flare up to engulf a larger region.

The historian Livy provides our only surviving account of the conflict, and he has a frustrating tendency to use broad labels like "Roman," "Latin," "Campanian," and "Samnite" for the forces involved, which we know conceal a tremendous diversity. It is clear that none of these groups, including the Romans, were fully unified or operated with a consistent and coherent foreign policy. In reality, we are talking about collections of individual clans and communities that were attempting to use their broader connections, and perhaps new allies, to pursue traditional grudges. Locals, at the time, may not have even understood these battles and events would be later understood and described as part of a wider conflict between two "sides" or opposing forces. This organization and rationalization would largely come later. However, as Livy likely also recognized, trying to describe events using individual family groups would make things hopelessly complex and confusing. Although certainly more accurate, the fickle and fluid nature of these families is not conducive to a coherent narrative. As a result, we will also use those broad regional labels here (see fig. 10), but with the important caveat that what they represent was likely fluid and they should be taken as indicative of a broad set of goals and not a discrete social, cultural, or ethnic group.

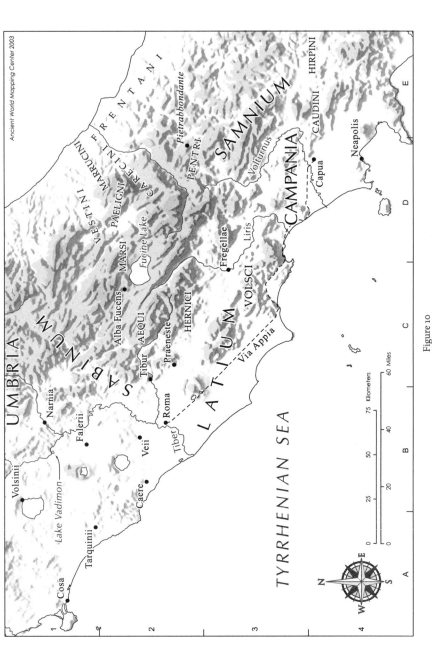

Figure 10
Map of central Italy, including Campania and northern Samnium. Produced by the Ancient World Mapping Center for *The Romans: From Village to Empire: A History of Rome from Earliest Times to the End of the Western Empire*. Used with permission.

The Romans had established relationships with some of the families and communities in the region around Fregellae and had inserted themselves into this series of local disputes, seemingly to dictate terms to those involved—and especially the Latins, who had most recently been the aggressors. The Latin leaders involved did not take kindly to this intrusion and mobilized their forces and allies for war against Rome. The Romans, evidently allied with at least some of the local Samnite tribes, mobilized in return. The two sides fought a famous battle at the Veseris River, near Mount Vesuvius in Campania, which was won in 340 by the Roman consuls Publius Decius Mus and Titus Manlius Torquatus. This is the battle mentioned at the start of Chapter One of this book and its description is one of the richest that we have for the period—despite seeming somewhat routine. Within this account is where we find Livy's description of the manipular legion and also the heroic sacrifice of Decius Mus and the execution by Manlius Torquatus of his own son for breaking ranks. This collection of dramatic and important stories really stands out in Livy's wider narrative. Although there are obviously a number of possible reasons for this sudden richness, it is likely that it is indicative of a change in the available source tradition, with this conflict featuring more evidence. In other words, the Romans (and Latins) seem to have remembered this conflict well. The war continued into 339, with the Battle of Trifanum (another victory for the Romans). It ended in 338 after the Roman victory at the Battle of Pedum.

These battles were fought across Latium, Samnium, and Campania and very likely involved a number of clans and communities from across this region, fighting on either side. Alliances, labels, and relationships were evidently fluid and overlapping, and each battle likely featured a new constellation of "Romans" and "Latins." Indeed, it is worth considering how regional this war was, despite its notional "Latin" character. The first battle was fought down in central Campania, not far from Neapolis (modern-day Naples), the second was between Campania and Latium, near the mouth of the Liris River, while the third was not too far from Rome itself. While this conflict seems to have originated in a certain region, it was not focused on a particular piece of territory. We should not think in terms of a fight over borders or boundaries, but rather a fluid series of engagements between well-connected local powers and their allies. Indeed, the war involved Samnites and Campanians fighting on both sides, highlighting how all of these groups were operating within the same sphere and likely subject to a complex network of alliances and relationships. While many modern maps depicting this conflict attempt to show concrete zones of control, with clearly defined limits, the situation on the ground was evidently far messier. The "First Samnite War" and "Great Latin War" occurred between and across at least four regional associations—Roman, Latin, Samnite, and Campanian—which we can only loosely connect to the physical landscape. This was not a war about land, but rather power and influence over people.

The regional nature of the Latin War is also revealed in the settlement that concluded it. It seems clear that the Romans had decided to use the situation to lay down some new ground rules for interaction within the region. Following the conclusion of the war, the Romans established new relationships with almost all of the major Latin communities, whether they were directly involved or not. They gave full citizenship status to seven of the communities (the Lanuvini, Aricini, Nomentani, Pedani, Tusculani, Veliterni, and Antiantes), and a new type of citizenship without the right to vote to a further five (the Campani, Fundani, Formiani, Cumani, and Suessulani).[13] Although the relative importance of the right to vote and the difference between these types of citizenship has been long debated, the most important point for this book, and for our understanding of Roman imperialism in general, is that the Romans added these 12 communities to the number committed to supporting its military—either through direct military service or the contribution of *tributum*. Interestingly, two of the strongest Latin communities at the time, Tibur and Praeneste, were not incorporated as citizens—either with the right to vote or without it. They were clearly defeated, as land was taken away from both, but they were not brought fully into the system.[14] Instead, they remained in a sort of liminal zone as "allies." They were required to contribute troops to the Roman cause, but as part of a slightly different relationship that we will discuss in a moment.

These are all major political changes that would have had a dramatic impact on how each community engaged in warfare. However, the

Romans did not stop there. As commented on earlier, another thing the Romans did in this period was to begin to regulate the so-called "Latin Rights," highlighting how all of this related to (and, indeed, was supported by) the social and economic relationships that crisscrossed the region. "Latin Rights" were traditional practices and norms of behavior, broadly shared by those within the region, that had been present for generations. As a result, even attempting to change or limit them would have been a big deal. Indeed, many of the suggested regulations introduced in the aftermath of 338 would have been largely unenforceable in real terms. But still, several Latin communities were evidently deprived of the right to trade, intermarry, and hold communal councils. This sort of policy, even if never actually enforced, would have encouraged people to move to communities with full citizenship, where full legal rights could be enjoyed. As a result, it likely represents a Roman attempt to shift attention and activity away from these communities and toward those that were within the Roman network after 338. So, in a way, it may have been a less extreme version of what the Romans did with Veii. Rather than killing these communities off with a religious ritual, they slowly strangled them with legal, economic, social, and political restrictions. Indeed, it is noteworthy that the right of migration was the one right that Livy suggests was not revoked. People were still allowed to move and change their affiliation if they wished, and this is likely the behavior that the Romans were subtly encouraging. For those who stayed in these communities, it is likely that they were not let off the hook entirely, as they were presumably made into "allies." So they would have had to contribute to the Roman war effort anyway as part of that relationship. Although Livy does not comment on this explicitly in his narrative, these remaining "Latin" communities are regularly mentioned as a specific subset of Rome's allies and possibly carried an official designation within the *socii* as well—at least in later times.[15]

The result of the war with the Latins was that the Romans added 12 major communities to their tribal manpower pool through two different types of citizenship and, perhaps equally importantly, made communities within the Roman network vastly more appealing to local Latins. Clans and individuals could stay in local communities that had not been given citizen status if they wished, but the Romans had put restrictions on what they were able to do. Some communities were given the full set of "Latin rights," although this may have simply indicated things that could be taken away from them if they misbehaved. Members of other communities were barred from trading or intermarrying with Romans, and their local laws would not be respected or acknowledged in Roman courts or contexts. Given the increasing Roman dominance of the region, and how many communities would now have identified as "Roman," staying in these non-Roman communities would have amounted to ostracism. The result of the war was, therefore, a significant, short-term gain in manpower, evidently adding Latin communities and clans that the Romans felt they could trust in a military context, and long-term control over the region, focusing all local activity on communities that were within their network.

THE ROMANS AND THEIR ALLIES

The Roman approach to military expansion in Latium focused on citizenship, but this was not the only option that they explored. The Romans also made treaties that were then used to recruit allies—which the Romans called *socii* (singular *socius*). *Socii* were common throughout Italy and were not an exclusively Roman phenomenon. The term *socius* meant "companion" or "colleague," and is where we get the English word "social." In Latin, it has a wide range of associations, including in business and law (meaning a partner or associate). Indeed, by the late Republic, these more peaceful definitions seem to have predominated. But in the early and middle Republic its most important usage—and most common in a historical context—is as a military ally of some sort.

Seeking allies was standard practice, and was supposedly one of the first things that Romulus did upon founding his new city, way back at the start of the regal period:

> Rome was now strong enough to hold her own in war with any of the neighboring communities; but due to a lack of women the community's greatness might only last a single generation, since they had neither hope

of offspring at home nor the right of intermarriage with their neighbors. So, on the advice of the senate, Romulus sent envoys around to all the neighboring peoples to ask for the right of alliance (*societatem*) and of intermarriage.[16]

This is obviously a mythic context, but it shows the centrality of allies to the ancient community. Rome's other kings continued this tradition and supposedly made a number of alliances, although Tarquinius Superbus, Rome's final king, was the most prolific in this sphere. All of this detail from the regal period is almost certainly either invented or heavily reinterpreted within a late Republican context, but the vital importance of alliances in extending and securing the power of the community is consistently reinforced. No community stood alone, it seems, especially in war.

Entering the Republic, mentions of *socii* take on a slightly different tone. In the early fifth century, the most common mention of *socii* is in reference to the Hernici and typically focuses on the composition of armies in the field. The Hernici were a people associated with *Latium adjectum*, toward the mountainous interior of Latium. They had fought against the Romans in the 490s and 480s, alongside the Volsci, but were defeated in 487/6. After the war, the Romans confiscated two-thirds of their territory and made them into *socii*. This is an interesting arrangement, as while the confiscation of land (a rare, and indeed singular, occurrence in this period) indicates that they are being punished, the designation as *socii* indicates an alliance with at least a semblance of equality and respect. *Socii* were partners, not clients or followers. While they might follow a foreign leader, they did not do so blindly. It was likely a decision born out of practicality and pragmatism based on who would be the most effective in that role in a given situation.

Dionysius suggests that this treaty between the Hernici and the Romans was very similar to that signed between Rome and the Latins almost a decade earlier, in 493, known as the *foedus Cassianum* (the "treaty of Cassius" named after the Roman consul, Spurius Cassius Vecellinus, who was responsible for it).[17] Dionysius gives a relatively detailed account the treaty of Cassius—hinting that he may have actually seen a version of it—which includes the clause: "Let the Romans and Latins assist one another, when warred upon, with all their forces, and let each have an equal share of the spoils and booty taken in their common wars."[18] The Romans and at least some Latins were back at war roughly 50 years later, which suggests that either the treaty did not cover all of the Latins, or that, comparable to contemporary treaties in the Greek world, it may have expired after a set amount of time. The first point, at least, is almost certainly true. As we have discussed already, "the Latins" was evidently quite a fuzzy label at the best of times, and this is particularly true when we look back this far. We only occasionally get more detail on the nature of Rome's Latin allies, as when the army of the Latin community of Tusculum was labelled as *socii* when coming to the aid of Rome in 460 or when the Etruscan community of Sutrium is listed as a *socius* of Rome in 389. On the second point, the duration of Italian treaties, it is uncertain. For instance, despite the changing nature of Roman-Latin relations, Livy evidently assumed that the alliance with Hernici lasted into the fourth century, although they were at war again by 362.

One thing that is clear from the ancient evidence, though, is that the *socii* were military allies who operated on roughly equal terms with the Romans. Although allied forces were typically described as being led by Romans, as one might expect them to be, this was not always the case and they seem to have had significant agency in the relationship. Indeed, one must not forget that the Romans would have also fulfilled the role of a *socius* to their allies. From the perspective of Tusculum, they would have been aided by Roman allies in 460. *Socii* were companions, who fought together and protected each other, shared equally in spoils, and seemingly lacked the strong sense of obligation that citizenship carried. While there was evidently an agreement to defend each other when attacked, which the Romans invoked when criticizing the Latins and Hernici in 386, there was not necessarily the same commitment to join an offensive action—at least at the outset.[19] By the late third century, this had evidently changed, as indicated by the so-called *formula togatorum* (the "list of toga wearers") that was published in this period.[20] The "formula" was a list, kept in Rome, which seems to have listed the obligations of Rome's various allies and was evidently not restricted to defensive actions. The allied obligation to fight on demand for the Romans was therefore evidently in place by the late third century, although how early we should push it is uncertain.[21]

While it is possible that the Romans had always exerted some informal pressure on allies to fight "on demand," there is a strong likelihood that the more rigid and one-sided principles outlined in the so-called *formula togatorum* originated in the dark days of the Second Punic War (218–201). This is the context where it is first mentioned in our sources and also when Rome's reliance on the allies would have been at its greatest. Before this point, allied support for Roman armies was likely more variable. It is possible that individual leaders could leverage their personal connections and networks to "strongly encourage" allied engagement, and an equal share in any spoils gained would have surely made aggressive warfare and raiding profitable—we have numerous mentions of allied volunteers in our narrative. However, the formal expectation to contribute troops to all Roman wars probably did not exist until the late third century. Indeed, it probably wouldn't have even been feasible, given the huge number of allies the Romans had by the end of the fourth century. Mobilizing them all would have been a massive undertaking and probably overkill for the types of activities they were engaging in—generally still just localized raids. Intriguingly as well, alliances could be made either peacefully or after warfare, evidently without significant changes to the terms. As noted, the Hernici, although supposedly made allies after their defeat, operated on equal terms with other *socii* who had allied willingly. This would continue to hold true in later periods.

While the Romans expanded citizenship and tribal structures within Latium in the fourth century, they also fought a series of wars in the north against various Etruscan communities. This included engagements around Tarquinia, in the immediate aftermath of the Gallic sack, which ended with a Roman victory and the acquisition of two allied settlements, Sutrium and Nepete, in 386.[22] Interestingly, despite the fact that this territory was reasonably close to the new tribes created on the land of Veii (both communities would have easily fit within the proposed location of the *tribus Sabatina*), which were created the previous year, the Romans did not make the communities or people part of this arrangement. Instead, they made them (or retained them as) *socii*, indicating that this was a conscious decision based on their assessment of the specific situation. Indeed, the arrangements at Sutrium and Nepete were far from exceptional. As the Romans campaigned farther north, and also south and east, during the course of the fourth century, they seem to have begun to make more varied decisions around how to deal with defeated populations. Some were made citizens, others were made *socii*, and others were evidently left to their own devices.[23]

Elsewhere in Italy, and even the wider Mediterranean, the Romans were also active diplomatically. We know the Romans signed a treaty with Carthage in 348, although that evidently did not involve promises of military support. The Romans were evidently allied with at least some Samnite tribes when the First Samnite War broke out in 343. There is also mention of treaties with the Lucanians and Apulians in 326, although the details are hazy at best. For most alliances in this period, though, and especially those in Etruria and the north, we can only hypothesize on their nature and date based on reports of Roman military success and later references to allied forces from those regions serving for Rome. For instance, by the second century we have references to the "cohort from Perusia"[24] in the Roman army, as well as mentions of cohorts of Marsi, Paelignians, Marrucini, Camerinians, and Umbrians. These were important Italian peoples, from across Italy, with strong military backgrounds who seem to have been defeated in this period. In addition, we have named cohorts from Placentina, Samnium, Aesernina, Firmana, Vestina, and Cremona. These were regions and communities across Italy that the Romans fought in during the fourth century.[25] All of these cohorts would have been allied forces and were likely the result of alliances formed sometime during the fourth century, just based on when the Romans seem to have been active in these areas.

We also have some additional evidence from the foundation of colonies. While Roman colonies would have contained Roman citizens, subject to levy through the tribal system, those given "Latin rights" are presumed to have been integrated under the same type of treaty as the Latin *socii* after 338. There were also the "maritime colonies," called this due to their location on the coast, which were small Roman citizen colonies but not subject to either the levy or *tributum* in the same way as others.

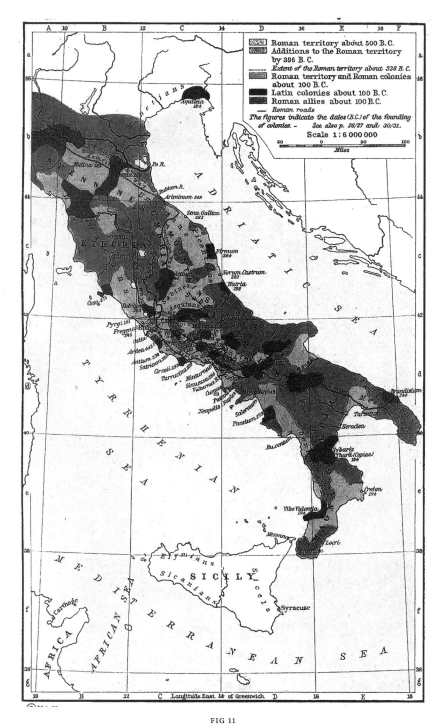

FIG 11
Indicative map of Roman and allied territory by ca. 100 BCE. Map courtesy of the United States Military Academy at West Point, Department of History. Used with permission.

Instead, these communities seem to have been tasked with defending their local coastal area and maritime routes and indeed may have even been given funds by the state to support this work—as hoards of early Roman bronze coinage have been found at some of them.

This complex and patchy evidence for Rome's citizen and allied networks has been used to create some quite speculative maps, like the one in fig. 11, which are almost certainly incorrect in many, if not most, of their details. In particular, their attempts to show Rome's varied influence and networks by shading territory in different tones is almost certainly incorrect, as Roman power did not operate in this way at this time. While land was increasingly important economically, Roman imperialism was focused on people and communities. However, this point aside, these types of maps do still manage to show the diverse set of relationships that the Romans seem to have created across the Italian landscape, and how the Roman approach to local communities seems to have changed every few miles.

MEN FOR THE LEGIONS

There is still quite a bit of debate around why the Romans might have utilized one type of relationship for one group or community and a different type for another. Our sources do not offer a clear rationale behind the choices, in no small part because the authors of our late Republican and Imperial sources were likely uncertain themselves. Given that neither the category of Italian *socius* nor that of "citizens without the right to vote" existed by the time Livy and Dionysius were writing (both disappeared in the aftermath of the Social War of the early first century), it is no wonder they were confused about why the Romans might have deployed them centuries before.

It is possible that choice was based on culture, and that the Romans only brought peoples who were relatively close to them culturally or linguistically in as full citizens.[26] In short, they integrated those who could be integrated easily, but were happy to keep others at arm's length. Incorporation as "citizens without the right to vote" or as allies may have

The Romans, the Latins, and the Samnites

indicate varying levels of social and cultural distance—or so the argument goes. And yet, of course, we have Latin communities, located very near to Rome, that were brought in as *socii* and "citizens without the right to vote." Additionally, we have Roman colonies and Roman citizens dotted throughout the Italian peninsula, many in areas that seem to be quite distant—both geographically and culturally. While one could make the argument that these were perhaps "transplants" in these regions, with citizens moving from Rome to take over the local communities, the archaeology suggests that, if this happened, it was not enough to change the patterns of daily life. Roman expansion in Italy, even utilizing Roman citizen colonies, does not always, or indeed typically, result in a marked shift in material culture.[27] Romans who ventured out to these colonies seem to have integrated and conformed to local norms and networks. People could also "become Roman" politically and legally without changing their way of life. The cultural argument has therefore increasingly been shown to be a weak one, at least on its own. If we focus our gaze more directly on the military, however, it may yet have some merit.

The central aspect of both Rome's citizen and allied expansion seems to have been military, and it is possible that the nature of the local military forces played a significant role in determining how a community or group was integrated. Citizen soldiers, both with and without the right to vote, would have been mobilized through the tribal system. While the various classes and classifications of soldiers within this system evidently allowed for quite a bit of diversity—the Romans could find a place for virtually any type of solider in their armies—there seems to have been an expectation that communities with citizen status would send their own citizens to fight. They would be recruited by local military tribunes, through the tribal structures, and would follow the commands of their local tribal leaders. Allied communities, however, may not have had this expectation. Allied forces were raised, and evidently operated, as a distinct group within the Roman military system, utilizing their own recruitment systems and command structure—although obviously following the overall leadership of the Roman consul or praetor when in the field. We have very little information about the internal structures of allied contingents, except for the fact that they typically provided most of the Romans' cavalry forces and were divided into "cohorts" of infantry (here, cohort is evidently a generic term for "unit") and *turmae* for cavalry. But there is no indication that they were raised in a comparable way to the Roman citizen forces, which opens up a range of possibilities.

It is possible that the Romans utilized alliances in instances where the local military organization was not conducive to their own tribal structure or for recruiting local citizen soldiers. This unsuitability may have been as simple as having different command structures or norms, different troop types, or something as fundamental as a different military tradition altogether. For instance, it is noteworthy that the Romans generally used alliances and *socii* in areas of Italy that typically relied on mercenaries instead of local troops. It would not make sense for the Romans to try and integrate the citizens of a community that had traditionally contracted out for their military needs. Rather, they could make an alliance and simply request that the allied community send forces, of whatever type they wished, when required. This may explain why the community of Neapolis, a great center of mercenary activity in the fourth century, was not given citizenship when incorporated in the 320s, while other nearby communities were. It was not about social or cultural bonds, or at least not strictly, but rather the nature of their existing military system. Indeed, we may even have hints of this in the Roman treatment of Tibur and Praeneste in 338 noted above. Livy suggests they were made into allies instead of citizens "because they had once, in weariness at the military power (*imperium*) of Rome, united in arms with the Gauls."[28] This has often been taken to mean simply that the people of Tibur and Praeneste had allied with Rome's natural enemies, which had naturally irked the Romans, although there is the possibility that it indicates something more substantial. Gauls were often employed as mercenaries in Italy during this period, and it is possible that this indicates the communities of Tibur and Praeneste had begun to transition to a mercenary-based military system which would not have been conducive to the Roman tribal structure.

Either way, in terms of Roman warfare and Roman imperialism, the difference between allies and citizens may not have been as significant as often supposed—at least at this time. Both systems expanded the manpower of the Roman army. Indeed, initially, many communities may have preferred being labelled as *socii* instead of citizens, as this both implied a more equal relationship and may not have been particularly onerous as it seems to have simply involved promising to not attack the ally and to help defend if the ally was attacked, while also opening the door for joint actions. Citizens, conversely, would have been obligated to either serve in the army or pay tax (*tributum*) every year. As the benefits of citizenship were likely limited in this period, many may have grumbled at being saddled with this obligation. It was only in the second and first centuries that the balance shifted in the other direction.

CAMPANIA AND SAMNIUM

The Romans' involvement, and subsequent wars, in Campania and Samnium are closely linked to the events that occurred in Latium. While modern histories often try to separate these regions out as distinct zones (and the wars into discrete sets of actions), it is clear that the people within them considered themselves to be part of the same interconnected region. There were no rigid borders. Labels like "Greek" or "Samnite" should be treated with the same sort of skepticism we have generally adopted for "Roman" and "Latin." Indeed, although we may start to see greater diversity in culture and connections the farther we travel from Rome, the regions were still dominated by powerful families and clans, just like in Latium. This was not a "new world." Indeed, the wars the Romans fought seem to have been for and about many of the same things. Although, this is not to say that it did not offer up both new problems and new opportunities.

The Romans had been actively engaging in the regions we know as Campania and Samnium since the 350s. In 357 the Roman consul Gaius Marcius led an unprovoked raid on the community of Privernum, on the southern edge of Latium, a town that Livy suggests had previously enjoyed a long period of peace.[29] Gaius Marcius was a major figure in this period, holding the Roman consulship three times as well as being the first plebeian dictator (356), and he seems to have had particular interests in this area of Italy. In addition to his attack in 357, he was also consul in 344, during a period of conflict with Aurunci in south-eastern Latium, and two years later he was active in Campania.[30] As a result, rather than a broadly held Roman policy, there is a strong possibility that much of the "Roman" activity in this area was still driven by the individual interests of specific Roman clans and military leaders.

However, while individual families continued to influence the specific goals and targets of warfare, there does seem to be a wider movement among Rome's elites to pursue military actions farther from the city. This is due to several related factors. First, the growth of Rome's citizen and allied networks had limited opportunities for local warfare. Rome's elite clans were simply not allowed to campaign in the same areas they used to, as the areas were now controlled by "Romans" and their allies. This was the, perhaps unforeseen, byproduct of Rome's imperial expansion—it limited warfare, at least internally. The Romans had to look elsewhere, and slightly farther afield, for viable targets. Second, Rome's expansive network had brought in a number of new families, many of which likely had existing interests and connections (as well as feuds and targets) outside of Latium that would have drawn their attention—and Rome's forces, when they happened to have them at their command. It is likely not a coincidence that the admission of plebeians into the consulship coincided with a dramatic expansion in the nature and spread of Roman warfare. Most plebeians were, after all, simply from families that had been integrated into the Roman system at a slightly later date than their patrician counterparts. Many of them may have arrived in the fourth century from regions like southern Latium, Samnium, and Campania and seem to have been keen to utilize the Roman system to pursue their traditional goals and grudges. Third, the ever increasing size of Rome's armed forces allowed for greater ambitions. During this period, the Romans were able to compete with other large and established powers in a new way. The Romans no longer needed to worry about angering the great powers of southern Italy, with their allies from around the Mediterranean.

For instance, and as mentioned previously, in 348 Rome famously made a treaty with Carthage.[31] As with other alliances, this one seems to indicate roughly equal standing between the two parties and set limits on raiding, trade, and settlement foundations. It notably did not include the usual mutual defense clauses, although this may have been brought in as part of a third (or possibly fourth) treaty in 279. While scholars have debated the details of this treaty for more than a century, one thing it clearly indicates is that the Romans, as a recognized group or federation, were understood to have both interests and control stretching across a wide swathe of territory. The treaty stipulates that the Romans should not "raid or trade or found a city on the farther side of Kale Akte, Mastia, and Tarseum." While Tarseum has yet to be solidly identified, Kale Akte (or "the Fair Promontory") is in Sicily, and Mastia is in Spain. The assumption that the Romans would be able to control activity across such a wide area suggests the strength and extent of their network in this period, extending south and west into the Tyrrhenian Sea.[32] Rome had come a long way in 50 years.

The Romans also seem to have been engaging in raids and warfare to the south and east of Latium. In 345 the Romans captured the community of Sora in the mountains near Samnium and also defeated the Aurunci in the same area. Given this activity and their connections in the regions, it is not a surprise that the Romans are recorded as coming into conflict with Samnite tribes beginning in 343. Open warfare was supposedly initiated by a raid by Samnite tribes against the Sidicini, a tribe we have already mentioned that seemed to have resided in this contentious zone. The Sidicini called on their allies in the Campanian community of Capua for assistance, which led to the Samnites attacking Capua, evidently overwhelming their forces easily. The people of Capua then sent envoys to Rome asking for an alliance and their help against the Samnites. The Senate of Rome initially refused, as it seems they already had a treaty with the Samnite tribes involved.

Livy (our main ancient source for these events), uses the label "Samnites" as a generic, undifferentiated umbrella term for all the peoples living in the south-central Apennines, and particularly those that fought against the Romans. This has long created an artificial sense of homogeneity for this group, and an equally artificial sense of difference between them and the Romans (and Latins), which is still found in many textbooks. However, this is just a historiographical mirage. The archaeological record suggests that the area featured quite a few distinct tribes, and it is virtually certain that they did not negotiate, operate, or identify as a single group in this period. Indeed, many may have felt they had more in common with people we would call "Latins" or "Campanians" than others within their region.[33] Peoples across the region, especially in the northern parts of Samnium, seemed to be pursuing similar aims and fighting the same opponents as the Romans. It is perhaps not surprising then that the Romans had negotiated a treaty with some of the local tribes in the region and, indeed, may have fought alongside them against the Aurunci, Volsci, and even other Latins. As with elsewhere, we should consider the "Samnites," at least in the northern sections of the region, as simply "central Italian clans" that seem to have operated a roughly similar way to the clans that made up the "Roman" and "Latin" confederations.

Faced with a somewhat awkward situation, where a prospective ally was seeking help against an existing ally, the Roman Senate offered to send envoys to help negotiate but would not violate the treaty they had made with the Samnite tribes. In response to this, the messengers from Capua performed one of the more interesting diplomatic maneuvers in the long history of the Republic. They performed an action known as the *deditio*, or "complete surrender." They had come to Rome initially asking for an alliance, or to become *socii*. Again, this was a common military agreement in ancient Italy, which varied in nature, but usually involved mutual protection and roughly equal status. When this proved impossible, the Capuans changed the offer and gave themselves over fully to the Romans. Rather than asking to be equals, they were asking to become Roman clients—or perhaps citizens, which may have been the same thing in this period.[34] And indeed, they seem to have been given citizenship without the right to vote by 338, once again hinting that this status was not necessarily an honor. The *deditio* changed the equation for the Romans, as rather than breaking their treaty with the Samnites by agreeing to a new one with Capua, this meant that the Samnites would be breaking their treaty by continuing to attack the (now Roman) client community of Capua.

The Samnites evidently did not see things the same way as the Romans, perhaps (and arguably rightly) feeling that this move by Capua was a bit deceitful and not really in keeping with how these relationships were supposed to work. This sparked the so-called, and short-lived, "First Samnite War," from 343 to 340. In general, we should understand the war as being simply a continuation of previous actions. The Romans fought several battles in northern Campania in 343 and 342 against a series of local Samnite tribes. In 341 they were back to fighting around Privernum and southern Latium, once again highlighting how fluid warfare and identity were in this period and region, and the Romans evidently agreed to peace with the Samnites at the end of the year. 340 saw the start of the Latin War discussed above, although this again largely took place in southern Latium and Campania, at Vesuvius and Trifanum. It must surely be considered part of the same overall action.

The "Second Samnite War" or "Great Samnite War," to use the modern labels, supposedly occurred between 326 and 304. However, the seeming gap between this conflict and the "First" is largely a modern construction. While the Romans rarely officially fought against the Samnites between 340 and 326, they were certainly active in the same area and engaging with many of the same peoples in roughly the same manner. They are simply not referred to as Samnites, explicitly, in the sources. In the period from 337 to 335, the Romans fought against the Sidicini and ultimately captured the nearby community of Cales, which was made a citizen colony in 334. The Romans also, in this year, gave various Campanian and Samnite communities citizenship without the vote.[35] As usual, this is painted in a very positive light, but hints that the Romans were fighting more widely—and against various Samnite tribes directly—without Livy recording it. In 332 the community of Acerrae near Neapolis was also given citizenship without the vote. In 330–329 the Romans were once again fighting near Privernum in southern Latium, ultimately integrating it as a citizen community.

Again, there is very little to separate this series of conflicts from those of 343–340, apart from the general absence of "Samnites" in the narrative. However, even this is uncertain, as it is entirely possible that the Samnites were there, most notably in 334 (if Velleius Paterculus is to be believed), or perhaps in the years 337 to 335 as well, when the Romans fought against the Sidicini. Indeed, it would be somewhat surprising if they were not, given the location on the edge of Samnium. Further, although much of this period between 338 and 326 has been depicted as subtle and largely peaceful strategic maneuvering by the Romans, given both the ongoing warfare throughout the region and aggressive expansion of Roman citizenship (and military obligation), it is difficult to understand this as being all that different from the Latin War of 340–338.[36] The overall goals of the Romans seem consistent, with the expansion of military obligation, and the specific goals and aims of generals (when they are mentioned) are also constant, generally raiding for wealth and portable spoils. The middle of the fourth century saw a glut of triumphs celebrated, with 18 between the years 360 and 329—which is more than one every two years.[37] While the collective Roman system was gaining in resources, the individual leaders were also gaining in wealth, which they paraded through the streets of Rome.

The Romans supposedly only came into direct conflict with the Samnite peoples again in 326. The clear connection between this "new" conflict and the wider picture of Roman warfare during the period again hints that the Samnites were always involved, even if indirectly. In 328 the Campanian community of Palaeopolis (literally "old city," which was near Neapolis, or "the new city," modern Naples) attacked some nearby "Romans." It is uncertain which "Romans" they attacked exactly, as by this point it could have been any number of different communities in the region. This action prompted the Roman Senate to send two consular armies into the region in 327. Although this was technically the wider Roman federation protecting its own members, the spread of Roman citizens and allies across the region over the previous decades meant that it was increasingly difficult to avoid antagonizing the Romans in some way—even if pursuing old, traditional grudges.

The paired communities of Palaeopolis and Neapolis both prepared for war against the Romans, evidently recruiting men from the nearby community of Nola as well as from Samnium. While it is possible that the Samnites who were recruited were allies, it is likely that at least some were serving as mercenaries. After the arrival of the two Roman armies, the people of Neapolis had a change of heart and decided to ally with the Romans instead—leaving Palaeopolis on its own. The city of Palaeopolis was then taken by the Romans in short order, and the communities of Allifae, Callifae,

The Romans, the Latins, and the Samnites

and Rufrium in Samnium were also sacked by Roman forces. We can plausibly assume that these communities were allied to Palaeopolis, although it isn't entirely clear, and they may have just represented convenient targets for aggressive Roman generals.

This is all quite messy, which is standard for Italian politics of the time, and shows how fluid many of these relationships were. When everyone is a rival, it is hard to know who your true friends are. The Romans continued to raid Samnium in 325 and extended their attacks over to the Adriatic coast and the communities of the Vestini. The Romans continued to raid the territory of the Samnites year after year, rejecting a proposed peace in 321. This warfare seems to have been entirely extractive. Roman commanders celebrated triumphs in 326, 324, and two in 322, but did not make any permanent gains and there are no mentions of alliances or grants of citizenship in the sources.

In 321, however, the Romans suffered a setback. The two consuls for that year, Veturius Calvinus and Postumius Albinus, were camped in Campania near the community of Capua. A "Samnite" force, under the command of a man named Gaius Pontius, occupied a narrow pass through the Apennines near the community of Beneventum known as the Caudine Forks. He had spies inform the Romans that his army was attacking the Apulian community of Lucera (a Roman ally) on the other side of the pass, over on the east coast of Italy, prompting the consuls to march to its aid. When the Romans were in the narrow pass, the Samnites struck, blocking both sides of the pass and trapping them in the narrow defile. Livy offers a vivid account of the action, including the surely fictitious debate among the Samnites over what to do with the trapped Romans.[38] Indeed, his entire account is likely heavily embellished, as there is no pass in the area of Beneventum that even remotely matches his description of the action, although it is clear that the Romans did remember suffering a major defeat around this time. In the end, it was decided that the Roman army would be set free, but the men were stripped of their clothes and armor and forced to "pass under the yoke" in a humiliating fashion (see fig. 12 for an early modern depiction of what this may have looked like). The consuls were also forced to agree to a treaty, although the wider Senate evidently repudiated this upon their return to Rome.

FIG 12
Les Romains passant sous le joug ("The Romans passing under the yoke"), 1858, Marc Charles Gabriel Gleyre.

While the Roman defeat is interesting, and the story quite dramatic, it is actually the supposed treaty that followed that is the most revealing. Traditionally, elected leaders of the Roman army had been allowed to negotiate treaties on behalf of the wider group.[39] Obviously, this had generally been to the group's advantage, as they had often been negotiating from a position of strength after a victory, but the precedent was clear going back to the regal period. Roman generals, imbued with *imperium*, could act on behalf of the Roman community beyond the *pomerium*. It is likely that the consuls felt within their rights to negotiate with the Samnites on behalf of the Roman Senate and people. However, it is clear that not every member of the expanding Roman federation felt as if they wanted to be bound by this treaty, made in a moment of defeat. What had worked in the sixth and fifth centuries was no longer appropriate in the late fourth century. In the end, the Senate decided that the agreement made was a personal one by those men and clans who had been there at the time and was not binding on the wider alliance. In a fascinating and somewhat shocking move, in 320 those who had made a pledge at Caudium were actually handed over to the Samnites, as they had made a promise on behalf of the community that they could not keep.[40] While ancient communities (and, indeed, modern ones) do have a tendency to mutually bask in victories but blame individual leaders for defeats, this is, perhaps, slightly different. The Roman commanders were not necessarily blamed for the defeat. It is rather that the implications of the defeat were to be borne personally. Just as individual commanders were able to claim personal possession of the spoils of war, so were they responsible for the losses.

Although the period between 321 and 316 is often described as a lull in the "Samnite War," the Romans were far from peaceful in this period. The Romans were active at Ferentinum in 319, located in southern Latium (again, near the Sidinici), and were fighting in Apulia, on the eastern side of Samnium, in 318. They also extended their military network in this year, establishing two new tribes (Falerna and Oufentina), with the *tribus* Falerna covering part of the regions of Campania and Samnium. Further, in this year, they added Roman colonies in the region of Apulia. In 317 they were active in both Lucania and Apulia. So the Romans were operating around, and likely through, the region of Samnium in these years, and actively incorporated communities and peoples that could plausibly be considered "Samnite"—although whether they were ever considered or labeled as such is unknown. Again, the Romans are simply not explicitly recorded as raiding or attacking Samnite sites directly in this period. In 316 the Romans once again began to raid Samnite communities, attacking the community of Saticula (near the newly founded tribe of Falerna). Between 316 and 304 the Romans regularly raided and captured settlements throughout Samnium and Campania, celebrating triumphs and establishing a number of colonies. From 312 there was also regular activity in Etruria and Umbria to the north, but this did not amount to much. In 304 Livy reports that the Romans "restored the ancient treaty" with the Samnites (again, it is unclear exactly which peoples or communities this referred to) and established a new treaty with the Marrucini, Marsi, Paerligni, and Frentani—all local tribes from the same broad region.[41] In 303 colonies were established at Sora and Alba Fucens in the regions of Samnium and Campania, and citizenship extended to Trebulanum and Arpinum in the same area. These moves by the Romans did not, however, mark the end of hostilities in the region, as regular warfare resumed only a few years later.

The so-called "Third Samnite War" (traditionally 298–290) has a frustratingly misleading modern name. Although the Romans supposedly restored a treaty with the Samnites in 304, it is clear that this treaty did not include all of the various Samnite tribes and peoples. Livy's description of the situation, although likely embellished, indicates that the Romans did not think that the region was particularly peaceful—at the very least, they were clearly on their guard. As a result, the actions of the "Third Samnite War" should really be considered a continuation of the "Second" and seem to be considered as such by some ancient authors. Both the definition of and division between these conflicts (i.e. "first," "second," and "third" Samnite Wars) are largely modern conventions.[42] Additionally, although this conflict evidently involved at least some Samnites, it was certainly not defined by them. While this war was fought across Italy, including in Samnium, much of it was focused on Etruria to the north of Rome and the most important actions—like the battle of Sentinum in 295—took place in Etruria. Indeed, it is not entirely clear whether we should really consider it a single war at all, as it seems to represent a wide-ranging series of military actions against a number of different opponents.

Perhaps the best way to understand the events of the period from 298 to ca. 290 (and very likely after) is that the Romans seem to have been targeting the remaining peoples and communities within the wider region of central Italy who had not yet agreed to an alliance or citizenship arrangement with them. While one could imagine this as the strategic "mopping up" of any remaining pockets of resistance, this presupposes that the Romans desired peace and imperial control. That is certainly possible, although it is equally possible that the Romans were quite happy to continue raiding in this period and may have wanted to have at least some local targets available for this sort of activity. Active warfare seems to have been more profitable and often more desirable than extending imperial control in this period. As a result, the Romans continued to fight against various Samnite tribes and communities, as well as Etruscans, Lucanians, Gauls, and several others. Livy suggests that these peoples began to ally with each other, which makes some sense given the wider context. In the face of this belligerent Roman military federation, the remaining independent actors may have sought to join forces. However, any alliances that were formed were evidently short-lived and seemingly ad hoc. Indeed, it is possible that many of the Gauls, Samnites, Lucanians, and other groups mentioned in our sources and battle descriptions were not traditional allies but, yet again, serving as mercenaries.

The details of the war are also a little confusing. Livy records that Romans conducted raids in both Etruria and Samnium between 298 and 296, supposedly fighting key battles at Volterrae in Etruria in 298 and Tifernum in Samnium in 297. On the face of it, this appears straightforward. However, we actually have another source for Roman warfare in this period that complicates things. One of the consuls in 298 was Lucius Cornelius Scipio Barbatus, whose sarcophagus (fig. 13) is one of our earliest extant pieces of solid "Roman" evidence. And, somewhat frustratingly, the inscription on the sarcophagus does not align particularly well with Livy's account of this period. In his record for 298, Livy suggests that Scipio Barbatus was given command in Etruria while his co-consul, Gnaeus Fulvius, was given Samnium.[43] The year began with the Lucanians peacefully asking for Roman assistance against the Samnites and offering hostages in exchange for support. The Romans accepted this offer and Gnaeus Fulvius marched south, winning a battle against the Samnites before capturing the communities of Bovianum and Aufidena. Scipio Barbatus marched north and won a great victory at Volterrae against the

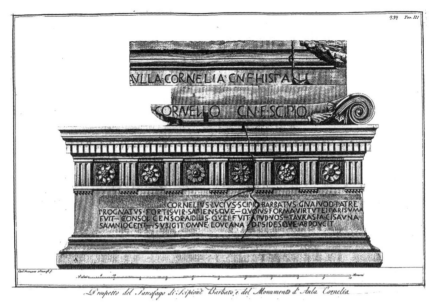

FIG 13

Sketch by Giovanni Battista Piranesi (1756–57) of the sarcophagus of L. Cornelius Scipio Barbatus, cos. 298 BCE. Original sarcophagus is now in the Vatican Museum. The lower half bears the honorific inscription detailing his career and achievements (CONSOL · CENSOR · AIDILIS · QVEI · FVIT · APVD · VOS—TAVRASIA · CISAVNA/SAMNIO · CEPIT—SVBIGIT · OMNE · LOVCANA · OPSIDESQVE · ABDOVCIT) and is one of the earliest pieces of contemporary evidence we have for Roman magistrates and warfare. Sketch held by the University of Tokyo General Library; courtesy of the Internet Archive.

Etruscans in a battle that lasted all day and into the evening. He is then reported to have gone into Faliscan land, where he raided widely.

The inscription found upon Scipio Barbatus' sarcophagus (*CIL* VI 1285) offers a slightly different version of events. It records that "[Scipio Barbatus] was consul, censor, and aedile among you, he captured Taurasia Cisauna in Samnium and subjugated all of Lucania and led off hostages." In the inscription, there is no mention of victories in Etruria (e.g. Volterrae), but rather Scipio Barbatus claims to have captured a community in Samnium and suggests that Lucania was subjugated militarily and any hostages were prisoners of war. This seeming conflict between Livy's account and the sarcophagus inscription has confused scholars. It is possible that either Livy or his sources were mistaken about the events of 298 and not only switched the actions of the two consuls but also misinterpreted the situation in Lucania. This period is generally accepted to have

The Romans, the Latins, and the Samnites

more reliable records, and indeed Livy indicates in his narrative for 296 that he had four different accounts he could use as source material.[44] However, this does not necessarily mean that the resultant narrative is any more secure. Livy may have selected an incorrect version of events to transmit or simply changed the events himself. Alternatively, it is possible that the inscription on the sarcophagus is incorrect or misleading. Although the sarcophagus itself dates to the middle of the third century, as Scipio Barbatus died in 270, the inscription we see today is not the original one. The first inscription was erased and replaced by a new one ca. 200, possibly to enhance or clarify certain family achievements.[45] As a result, it is possible that later Scipiones either reworked or "misremembered" their family history when updating the wording. Finally, a third option is that the military achievements listed were never intended to match up with what the Roman magistracies attained. Most scholars have assumed that the military actions recorded on the sarcophagus are supposed to relate to the year 298, as this was the only year when Scipio Barbatus held *imperium* as one of the two elected Roman consuls. However, as discussed, powerful clan leaders could, and often did, lead independent military actions using their own clan-based forces. It is possible that the capture of Taurasia Cisauna in Samnium, and his actions in Lucania, were meant to be understood as the successful actions of a private warlord, occurring in a different year or years from his consulship, celebrated in the context of a private family tomb. They may not have represented "Roman" warfare at all.

Moving beyond the details (about which we can only speculate), the wider picture of warfare in this period is thankfully roughly consistent. The Romans evidently continued to raid across both northern and southern Italy during the 290s, generally winning the battles they fought—although it is clear that successful raiding was occurring on both sides. The last great battle of this conflict, at least for which we have any detail, was fought at Sentinum in 295. This is in the region of Marche, located on the Adriatic coast of Italy, north of Abruzzo and east of Umbria. It is, therefore, quite far from the region of Samnium and, indeed, slightly north and east of the main Etruscan centers as well. Our sources remember the battle as a desperate last stand against the rise of Rome by the remaining independent powers within the region, including the Etruscans, Gauls, Umbrians, and Samnites. The Romans sent both of the consuls for that year north, the very experienced Quintus Fabius Maximus Rullianus and Publius Decius Mus, to fight against the amassing army. They went with a full levy of four legions, along with allied contingents, with the total force supposedly numbering roughly 40,000 men. The Romans were also supported by two additional armies, under the command of praetors, one of which stayed near Rome while the other was active in the central Apennines. The difference in scale between the forces here and that which seemed to be available to them a century earlier at the River Allia is noteworthy and shows how much things had changed.

The battle was an epic event.[46] The Romans were able to weaken the opposing army by attacking various cities on their way north, drawing away the Etruscan and Umbrian contingents in defense of their home communities.[47] When the two armies faced off at Sentinum, the Romans supposedly faced a force composed of only Gauls and Samnites—although it still, evidently, outnumbered their own. For two full days, the armies encamped on the plain across from each other before the Romans finally engaged. On the day of the battle, Fabius Maximus commanded the right side of the Roman line, across from the Gallic contingent, while Publius Decius Mus was on the left, across from the Samnites. Livy also provides detailed commentary on the tactics deployed, which included a *devotio* or self-sacrifice by Publius Decius Mus (just like his father, in 340, and later his son, in 279) and one of the only reported instances of the *testudo* or "tortoise" formation being used in open combat—albeit performed here by the Gauls, and not the Romans. In the end, the Romans were victorious, supposedly killing 20,000 enemies and losing slightly less than 9,000 themselves—although this was still a very high casualty rate, between 10 and 20 per cent.

The surviving Roman consul, Quintus Fabius Maximus Rullianus, celebrated a triumph after the battle. However, this still did not mark the end of warfare in the region. Immediately following the battle of Sentinum, the army of Decius Mus was given to the praetor Appius Claudius, who went south to fight in Samnium, while Fabius Maximus returned to fight in Etruria. Both commanders, along with the pro-consul Lucius Volumnius, supposedly won further significant battles (and acquired significant booty) in that year. Indeed, regular warfare against the same opponents continued until at least 292.[48]

It is not clear when, or indeed if, the "Third Samnite War" ended. Many scholars, following the later Roman chronicler Eutropius, have taken the year 290 as the notional end of the war.[49] As noted above, we know the war continued on after 292 and into Livy's eleventh book as, although we lack the text for the book itself, a surviving summary of the text opens with the Roman consul of 292, Fabius Gurges, fighting unsuccessfully in Samnium.[50] The summary goes on to suggest the young Fabius was then joined by his father, the venerable Fabius Maximus, and won a great victory against the Samnites, defeating the general Gaius Pontius and celebrating a triumph. The consul for 291, Lucius Postumius also celebrated a triumph against the Samnites, while the consul of 290, Curius Dentatus, celebrated two triumphs—one against the Samnites and another against the Sabines. It was during Dentatus' term as consul that the treaty with the Samnites was supposedly renewed for a fourth time, and new colonies were established at Castrum, Sena, and Hadria in the modern regions of Marche and Abruzzo.[51] This aligns with Eutropius' claim that the war ended in 290, and there is also an absence of evidence for any further triumphs or victories over these opponents in our sources, providing a plausible ending point. However, the fact that the Romans reportedly faced off against Samnite, Etruscan, Umbrian, and Gallic contingents in their war against Pyrrhus (280–275), and indeed saw both Samnites and Gauls across the battlefield in their war against Hannibal in the final years of the third century, hints at the ongoing nature of these conflicts.[52] Indeed, even apart from these specific instances, there is ample evidence for continued raiding and military activity in this area throughout the third century.

While much has been made of the Samnite Wars, and particularly the "Second Samnite War," as a turning point or "watershed moment" in Roman history, this is not evident in the warfare of the period. While there were certainly important events and changes happening in Roman politics across the period, and Roman society more widely, the Roman approach to warfare and imperialism seems to have remained remarkably consistent. Roman armies continued to raid across the Italian peninsula, as they had done before, targeting communities and groups that were not yet within their military network. The Romans also continually sought to expand this network through various means, adding four citizen tribes across southern Latium, Campania, and Samnium, as well as a series of colonies, and myriad alliances. None of this was new. It continued the same set of systems that the Romans had been using since the Gallic sack of Rome back in 390.

While there seems to be a memory of gradual equipment change in this period, shifting from the traditional circular shield (*aspis*) and thrusting spear (*hasta*) to the oblong shield (*scutum*) and heavy javelin (*pilum*), this was likely a gradual change brought about by two broad developments. The first is a gradual shift in military equipment across the entire Italian peninsula, which saw the slow adoption of Gallic equipment types— including the *pilum*, *scutum*, and so-called Montefortino-style ("jockey cap") helmet—from north or south. This equipment was likely initially carried south and popularized by Gallic mercenaries, who were recruited through southern Italy to serve across the wider Mediterranean, and it was soon being produced locally across Italy in various versions and iterations. So the Romans and central Italians were simply being carried along with this trend. Additionally, Roman equipment likely shifted because the composition of the army was changing. During the course of the fourth century, the Romans added a total of eight new tribes, four to the north of the city and four in southern Latium and Campania. They also added a huge number of allies from across Italy. It is likely that many of the men in these new tribes, colonies, and allied communities fought in new ways, and many seem to have favored these new equipment types—especially those in Campania and Samnium. The Romans were not changing their own equipment so much as adding new soldiers who were equipped in a slightly different way.

ROME'S ITALIAN EMPIRE

The Romans' wars in the late fourth century highlight the nature of the Roman imperial system in this period. As emphasized throughout this book, the emerging Roman empire, like the Republic itself, was a federated, power-sharing arrangement, designed by and for powerful clan leaders. Being part of the Roman system granted these leaders access to a tremendous body of manpower and resources that they could use, provided they were elected, to pursue glory, power, and wealth for themselves and their clan. This seems to have been the initial intention and remained the primary aim. However, as we enter the fourth century, the clan leaders who met together as the Senate recognized that there was significant benefit for all in expanding the system and its resources. Indeed, it is likely that they recognized that their horizons might be limited if they did not expand, as the wider military context was changing—a point vividly brought home by the Gallic sack of the city in 390. As a result, while most warfare conducted by the Romans was still dictated by very personal goals and ambitions, as a group they also slowly worked to expand the federation by extending military obligation through citizenship and expanding the group's military alliances.

While later sources usually depict the extension of citizenship as a positive thing, and indeed a sign of Roman generosity, this was not always, or indeed usually, the case. The benefits of citizenship were often quite limited in the fourth century, while the burdens could be onerous. Previously, central Italian peoples may have only had to contribute to warfare, either personally or through payments/support, every once in a while, but under the Roman system it became an annual burden. Alliances were also quite mixed. While being an ally meant you were generally safe from predation by other parts of the Roman system, it would have also created a more limited form of obligation to support the Romans if they were attacked. The expanding alliance network of the Romans would have also limited opportunities for independent warfare, as there were an increasing number of communities protected by it. As a result, any men and clans that actively wanted to engage in warfare had only a few options available to them. They could, as many evidently did, serve as mercenaries in armies elsewhere— either in Italy, beyond the Roman sphere, or somewhere farther afield. Alternatively, they could serve as part of the Roman army, which was evidently a popular choice. While the *formula togatorum* suggests that the Romans may have required allied service by the late third century, in the fourth century it was likely more flexible—and often more desirable.

Within all of this, however, the Roman label and affiliation were evidently quite loose. While we start to get hints of the Romans developing corporate myths and talking about themselves as "Romans," this is all surprisingly late. Indeed, the first solid evidence we have for the term "Romans" being used is from currency produced in the final decades of the fourth century—and likely not by the Romans themselves. Rome's imperial state and federation was a practical and pragmatic agreement, not a deeply patriotic one. In the midst of this tremendous expansion of *Romanitas*, or "Roman-ness," it is difficult to imagine many of the newly enfranchised individuals and families feeling a particularly strong connection to that affiliation. What the Roman system did was leverage existing connections and relationships and direct them toward this emerging military federation. Clans and communities were already used to mobilizing their members for warfare, and military alliances had been common across the region for centuries. All the Roman imperial system did was organize these existing relationships and unify them under a single banner. It did this through a combination of the threat of violence and the appeal of opportunity—especially for community and clan leaders. In a Mediterranean context where increasingly large and expansive federations and armies were operating, the Roman system offered a chance for Italian elites to compete. While power in the Roman system was still dominated by the patrician clans who had helped create it back in the late sixth century, it was increasingly open to the new arrivals (who would have arrived under the "plebeian" label) with the ending of the so-called "Struggle of the Orders." Indeed, this inclusion of the plebeians was almost certainly a precondition of Rome's expansion in these years.

5

ROME AND THE MEDITERRANEAN

THE MEDITERRANEAN WORLD WAS in a state of rapid and dynamic change as it entered the third century. This was one of those surprisingly rare moments in human history where the world was being transformed before peoples' very eyes. We have grown so used to the idea of rapid progress in the modern day that we forget how exceptional it is for our species. Most humans, at most points in time, would have lived, worked, and loved following the same basic norms as their parents, grandparents, and great-grandparents before them. Change occurred slowly, often imperceptibly, and any form of rapid change was typically catastrophic or violent—almost certainly negative. The period around the end of the fourth century, however, was a bit different for those in the Mediterranean basin. The conquests of Alexander the Great, followed by the wars of his successors, fundamentally altered the social, political, and economic landscape of the eastern Mediterranean. While the region had had its share of major, regional conflicts since the start of the fifth century (e.g. the Persian Wars and the Peloponnesian War), this activity had grown in scale over time, with a smaller number of ever larger military powers vying for supremacy. Although individual communities obviously remained, politics and warfare were increasingly dictated by leagues and kingdoms.[1] Indeed, for a brief period at least, the eastern Mediterranean had been dominated by only two great powers—Alexander's Macedonian kingdom and the Persian empire. By 300, it had devolved and was slightly more diverse, but power still operated at a regional level. For some, this rapid change was certainly catastrophic, as wars destroyed families and fortunes. But for others, it was merely worrying, and perhaps even exciting.

In the central and western Mediterranean, the social, political, and economic landscape was also shifting, with the rise of both the Roman and Carthaginian confederations. This was not a coincidence. The ancient Mediterranean was closely interconnected, especially among the elite, and both clan and community leaders in Italy, North Africa, Sicily, Iberia, and southern Gaul would have been very aware of what was happening to the east. Indeed, it is likely they and their families were closely involved with the events there. The Hellenistic kingdoms that emerged after Alexander's death recruited heavily from the central and western Mediterranean areas. There were Italians in the army of Alexander that marched into Babylon, and Gauls and Celts in the Ptolemaic army in Egypt.[2] The Mediterranean world must be considered a single military context in this period, and it seems clear that the Romans and Carthaginians understood this when considering their own empires and ambitions. In order to compete and engage as equals, they also needed to be able to operate on a regional level, mobilizing ever larger armies and negotiating on behalf of ever larger confederations.

The Romans' wars in the early third century offer intriguing insights into how their unique, Italian system matched up with those of both the eastern Mediterranean and North Africa. Although mutually comprehensible, and competing in the same sphere, no two kingdoms or confederations were exactly alike. The wars the Romans fought against the other major Mediterranean powers in this period highlight the advantages that the Roman approach brought, most notably in terms of quickly and easily bringing large numbers of infantry together, and also its disadvantages, specifically the lack of centralization which limited their ability to pursue long-term strategies. This chapter will discuss two of the most important engagements in this period, the Romans' war against Pyrrhus (280–275) and the first war against Carthage (264–241), and explore what they might be able to reveal about the Romans' emerging empire as well as what the Romans seem to have learned from each war.

Rome and the Mediterranean

THE EMERGING HELLENISTIC CONTEXT

Before discussing Rome's conflicts, it is worth laying out the context the Romans were operating within. While Polybius, followed by many modern historians, seems to suggest that the Romans suddenly emerged out of the darkness and isolation of central Italy about this time, to the surprise of everyone, this is simply not true. Rome, and the Romans, were anything but isolated and disconnected at the start of the third century.

While it was always recognized that people moved about from time to time, we used to think that this movement was limited and only associated with very specific motivations and contexts—the movement of armies, the regular routes of merchants, or the occasional mass migration. It was assumed that, for the vast majority of people, sedentary agriculture was the dominant way of life. Models were based on the premise that most people stayed put, and didn't know or think about life beyond the edges of their small farms. However, the more we have learned, and the more the archaeological record has revealed, the more we have begun to understand that regular movement was not only common but perhaps an important and even necessary part of life for many.[3]

As discussed earlier in this book, scholars have increasingly recognized that the ancient Mediterranean was far more dynamic and connected than traditionally thought. In this context, we know Rome was a powerful trading community, with extensive connections around the eastern Mediterranean, as early as the sixth century—if not earlier. The archaeological record, in particular, has demonstrated how the urban community served as an important hub of communication, both locally and regionally. While some families may have lived on and worked the same rural farmstead for generations, others (including members of those same farming families) moved from location to location within a region, or from region to region, on a regular basis—and often through sites like Rome.

Intermarriage facilitated movement, as did warfare. Festivals and religious events also encouraged at least some regular trips or pilgrimages. Further, populations were not homogenous, and many seem to have contained both stable and more mobile elements, with pastoralists in particular moving about with the seasons, along with merchants and craftspeople. This is all without considering the much higher levels of mobility visible among the Mediterranean's elites (the wealthy have always liked to travel!), where evidence abounds, and hospitality for guests was an established and seemingly universally understood principle. Greeks, Iberians, Italians, North Africans, Phoenicians, and others all traveled and interacted regularly from the Bronze Age onward. In Rome specifically, we know Greeks visited, and perhaps migrated, from within Italy and Sicily and from as far away as Asia Minor (modern-day Turkey), and Rome's treaties with the Carthaginians (among other types of evidence) suggest that people from Rome traveled widely as well.

Rome's military system ca. 300 was a product of this wider, interconnected, pan-Mediterranean context, and it is, therefore, no surprise that it bears some striking resemblances to what we see elsewhere in the Mediterranean basin at this time. From the middle of the sixth century, the region had experienced something of an "arms race," arguably instigated, or at least catalyzed, by the tremendous success of Cyrus the Great (ruled ca. 550–530) and the rise of the Achaemenid empire in Persia.

While the Near East had seen a number of great empires, including those of the Egyptians, the Hittites, the Neo-Babylonians, and others, the Achaemenid approach to military power seems to have represented a marked evolution. Like many Near Eastern leaders before him, Cyrus the Great had relied heavily on military might and the threat of violence to exert influence, and utilized both alliances and simple coercion, following traditional practices in the region established by expansive "states" and "empires" going back to the Neolithic. Cyrus and his successors could evidently summon forces from client states and communities that were under their control, as part of his imperial system, which both augmented his army and served as a visible symbol of power and control. However, Cyrus also sought to innovate and, in particular, made use of the recent invention of coinage. This technology first emerged in Asia Minor in the sixth century, and Cyrus made extensive use of it to both encourage and cement a new set of military relationships. This resulted in an army we might label as "mercenary"—although this label, as used in modern times, hardly does justice to the ancient institution.[4]

The rise of coinage-supported mercenary service shifted the nature of military power across the Mediterranean region. Although mercenaries themselves were not a new phenomenon in the Mediterranean in the fifth century, with evidence for them going back to the start of the Iron Age at least, the spread of coinage seems to have revolutionized the relationship between states, elites, and those who fought for them. It added a new element that regularized relationships and facilitated transactions. While ancient mercenary service typically did involve payment of some type, this was not the only, or indeed primary, bond that connected mercenary units to their leader. Ancient mercenary service was always based on pre-existing social and political relationships. The line between "mercenaries" and "allies" was, therefore, a fuzzy one, as we will see. However, coinage allowed for the easy quantification of the social capital needed to support this relationship, in a portable and transferable form. It was a tangible symbol of their service, which they could then exchange for goods and resources.

While the technology of coinage obviously spread quickly after its introduction, it was almost always linked with military service in the ancient Mediterranean region. This seems to have been the primary reason why it was minted, and access to coinage was one of the key factors required for engaging in ever-larger wars.[5] Cyrus the Great dramatically expanded the use of coinage for soldiers in his army, allowing him to field armies that were far larger than his rivals. This model was gradually picked up by other communities around the Mediterranean seeking ways to expand their military forces beyond those who were able to be mobilized internally. Even communities renowned for their citizen forces, like Sparta or Athens, began to rely heavily on paid soldiers by the fifth century. This is particularly true for navies, which required large numbers of men (a single trireme required roughly 200 men). The Athenian expedition to Sicily in 415 included 134 triremes, which would have necessitated almost 27,000 sailors. While it is likely that this contained a large number of Athenian citizens, the find spots of Athenian coinage from this period hint that many of the sailors were actually recruited from Ionia, on the Anatolian coast—as this is where the coinage ended up. By the fourth century, coinage-based mercenary service was common in the Mediterranean and almost certainly formed a part of every large army.

To reiterate the point, though, men in Hellenistic armies were not simply "soldiers for hire" who served whoever was able to pay them the most, or indeed whoever offered to pay them first. As noted above, ancient mercenary service seems to have been based, first and foremost, on social bonds. Payment was important, but this is arguably the case in virtually any military context. Even in today's state-based armies, soldiers expect to be paid. Ancient military leaders were typically always responsible for supporting their soldiers and distributing booty, whether it was a private warband or Hellenistic army. War was an economic operation. For mercenaries, rather than being the primary reason why men served, payment in coinage seems to have cemented the bond in a symbolic sense. This was a special relationship, whereby individuals and groups were bound together in a very specific way. It was a distinct type of alliance, which seems to have been defined by being both temporary and between groups from different communities but was not any less potent or important for that. This type of bond allowed powerful leaders and states to mobilize large numbers of men, from a wide area, for a specific purpose, and at a specific time. It was also, evidently, mutually understood by men and groups across the Mediterranean region. Alexander's army included Greeks, Macedonians, Italians, and Persians to name but a few. Indeed, DNA analysis from the graves associated with the battle of Himera in Sicily in the early fifth century indicates that armies may have contained men from as far away as Latvia and Ukraine, as well as Spain, North Africa, Greece, and, of course, Italy.[6] These men would have come from a wide range of economic contexts, and coinage would have functioned very differently within each, but they all seem to have understood the nature of the military relationship and what coinage symbolized within that.

Apart from the still limited use of coinage, Rome's army ca. 300 would not have looked out of place on a Hellenistic battlefield alongside the armies of Alexander and his successors, or indeed the forces of Carthage or Syracuse. Rome's forces were also composed of a mix of different groups, many of whom may have had experience serving as mercenaries in other Hellenistic forces. Recruited via tribes and communities, pulled from a wide area, and often only loosely linked to the polity of Rome, the

Roman army shared many similarities with those of its Hellenistic rivals. Indeed, although the Romans did not mint their own coinage until ca. 300— a point we will return to later—it must be remembered the Romans did support their soldiers financially through the *stipendium* (paid for by the war tax known as *tributum*), and through the distribution of spoils. Notwithstanding the utilization of the specific medium of coinage and the more regularized pay scales adopted by many Hellenistic armies, there was little functional difference between these systems.

The specific character and equipment of the Roman army would also have not been out of place. While much has been made of the *sarissa-pike* phalanx of the armies of Alexander the Great and his successors, Hellenistic armies were actually quite diverse. For instance, Polybius gives this description of the army of Ptolemy IV at the battle of Raphia in 217.[7] The army was composed of 70,000 infantry and 5,000 cavalry, along with 73 elephants. The cavalry contained 3,000 Libyans and 2,000 Greeks, supplemented by 700 members of the royal guard. The infantry was highly varied, as one might expect given the army's size. There were 3,000 members of the royal guard, a phalanx of 25,000 Egyptian troops, 3,000 Libyan phalangites (soldiers in the phalanx), 8,000 Greek mercenaries, 2,000 peltasts (light infantry), 3,000 Cretans, 6,000 Celts (Thracians and Galatians), and another 20,000 troops of unknown types. Within this body, the Greeks, Thracians, and Galatians represented the mainstays of Macedonian armies since the time of Philip II and Alexander the Great and could be found in most armies of the region. Peltasts were defined more by equipment than origin, but would have been common, and Cretans were also widely used as mercenaries in the region. So, roughly a third of Ptolemy's army was composed of troops, and troop types, that would have been common across the armies of the wider eastern Mediterranean. His army also contained 25,000 Egyptians and 5,000 Libyans, which may not have been exclusive to his kingdom but were obviously locally recruited. The nature of the remaining troops is unknown, but they were presumably also locally raised and likely represented some form of light infantry. The army of Ptolemy IV is, therefore, a fairly standard Hellenistic force: large and diverse, mobilized through a range of different mechanisms, clearly pulling heavily from the wider region but with a strong local character.

Rome's army would have had a broadly similar character. It, too, was large and diverse and was mobilized through a range of different mechanisms, pulling from the wider region—although perhaps not quite as wide as the army of Ptolemy. Here, the Romans had an advantage over some of their Hellenistic rivals, as their local area, Italy, featured a strong martial tradition and was full of warriors of different types. In northern Italy, there were Gauls, who were widely used as light to medium infantry in Hellenistic armies and were likely making an appearance in Roman armies from the start of the third century as the Romans incorporated the region into its sphere of influence. Cavalrymen could be recruited from Campania and southern Italy, and evidently were by the fourth century. Military equipment finds suggest that other types of infantry, from peltasts to phalangites, could be found in the varied clans and communities of the peninsula. Indeed, if we are to take anything away from Livy and Polybius' descriptions of Rome's Republican army (see the Appendix for detailed discussion), even when presenting idealized and systemized versions of the army, they cannot help but highlight its diversity.

Further, the units of the Roman army seem to have behaved in a remarkably similar way to the mercenary forces of Hellenistic armies. The soldiers of Italy's clans and communities equipped themselves and likely showed up at the Roman muster in a wide variety of equipment, relying on their leaders to find an appropriate place for them. They also seem to have featured many types of internal organization. In the fifth and fourth centuries, it is almost certain that the varied organization of Rome's armies, with *manipuli* ("maniples"), *ordines* (more rigid blocks of troops), *vexilla* (units following a banner), and cohorts, was simply a reflection of the diversity of entities, clans, and communities that the Romans could summon to their cause. It would make no sense, from a tactical perspective, to take thousands of individual Italians, with no previous connection, throw them into new formations, and expect them to fight in an effective manner after only a couple of days or weeks. The units of the Roman army instead reflected pre-existing units within Italian society, in exactly the same way as Hellenistic armies.

The Roman army was also recruited using a range of different mechanisms, like Hellenistic armies. Looking again at the army of Ptolemy, we have roughly half of the army being recruited from allies (esp. Libyans) and mercenaries, and the other half seemingly composed of locally raised Egyptian troops. The 20,000 troops included in Polybius' overall count, but not specifically described, obviously creates a rather large margin of error. But taking that as a rough model, it is noteworthy that a similar ratio is suggested for the split between citizens and allies within Roman forces of this period. All of these troops would have been financially and logistically supported in some way, although the mechanisms and relationships would have been different.

All of this is to say that when the Romans began to face off against the great powers of the Hellenistic Mediterranean ca. 300, they did so with an army that was both comparable and mutually comprehensible. This was not a great clash of cultures, or a contest between forces which were previously unknown to each other, but rather a competition between groups that were well aware of, and connected to, each other, and were consciously operating within a shared military context. They were using similar troops, recruited in similar ways, and using similar systems. Each army was its own unique construction, but we can consider this little more than "variation on a theme" or making the most of local resources and advantages. Given this context, the Romans' success is perhaps all that much more impressive, particularly since they evidently lacked the cohesion, organization, and centralized control of resources that many of their eastern rivals had already developed.

THE BIRTH OF *ROMANITAS*

As we near the end of the fourth century, it is likely that the Roman military system continued to leverage existing social and military relationships in a federated manner, with surprisingly little bureaucracy at the center. While they had created the system of *tributum* and *stipendium* at the start of the fourth century to help support warfare, this seems to have operated in a devolved manner. The tribes would not physically send money to a central Roman treasury, as indeed there was no single Roman currency in use and even the existence of the *Aerarium* ("public treasury") in this period is uncertain. While there was an agreed weight standard in place, using bronze, it is highly unlikely that this was either used universally or consistently for the *tributum* and *stipendium*. Instead, it is likely that *tributum* was collected and *stipendium* distributed entirely at the tribal level, managed by local *tribuni aerarii*, and likely delivered "in kind"—or, more accurately, in whatever supplies the tribal unit required for warfare.[8] This was likely little more than a standardization and rationalization of the earlier practices of local people supporting local troops. Even as late as the second century, the Roman antiquarian writer Varro reports that soldiers often had to chase individual *tribuni aerarii* for reimbursement for their wages.[9] The tribes were, therefore, able to handle their own needs without funneling everything through a central state apparatus. This same devolved approach is visible throughout the Roman military system, which is a key reason why it was so easily expandable. The families, clans, and communities that made up Rome's military continued to function as they had before, but unified in a broad strategic way under this new federation. They simply directed their efforts toward new, and increasingly "Roman," goals.

However, the Romans' military network also had limitations. While it was tremendously effective at scaling up existing systems and bringing together hundreds of smaller warbands on a single battlefield year after year, it was also confined by the nature of those existing structures. It could not easily do things that required more, different, or larger structures. It would always be a mosaic or patchwork of smaller units, made up of the various distinct groups and entities within its network. It also lacked the centralized resources and bureaucracy required for major military expenses. While the potential of the devolved approach is clearly evidenced by the construction of Rome's great fortifications in the early fourth century, possessing a large, state-based navy may have been a step too far. Although many Romans were evidently seafarers, and the treaties with Carthage hint at an extended influence over naval matters in the western Mediterranean, they did not exercise this influence through a traditional state-based navy, but rather through individual and privately owned ships. It is only in the period around 300 that we can see the Roman system slowly developing many of the attributes and features common in other Hellenistic "states."[10] This included an increasingly cohesive, centralized bureaucracy, a(n admittedly small) navy by 311, and an emerging community ethos and identity that bound the wider population together in a way not seen—and indeed, perhaps, not possible—earlier. In the military realm, this is visible in two key areas: roads and coinage.

In 312 Appius Claudius Caecus was elected to the censorship and initiated one of the more active and important periods of censorial activity in Rome's history. The censorship had been created as a relatively minor magistracy in 443 but had gradually grown in importance alongside Rome's tribal system. By the middle of the fourth century, it had come to real prominence, helping to shape the army of the new consuls through both census classifications and the addition of new tribes. However, the office only developed into the pinnacle of Roman politics in the final decades of the fourth century, when a law, known as the *lex Ovinia*, gave it control over membership within the Senate, and when Appius Claudius Caecus demonstrated its power over state finances and construction.

Once elected to the office, Appius Claudius Caecus commissioned the great *Via Appia* (named after himself), a newly paved road that stretched 211 km (131 miles) from Rome down to Capua in Campania. Although the road obviously served as an important route for trade and communication, given Rome's ongoing military activity in the region during this period it is assumed that warfare played a driving role in its construction. He also built the Claudian aqueduct in Rome, changed the composition of the Senate, and gave landless citizens full citizen rights, among several other measures. However, he is most remembered for the *Via Appia*, which not only represented one of Rome's largest building projects and but also one of the first community-based projects that was not focused on the urban zone itself.

For the Romans, the construction of the *Via Appia* was revolutionary, and a fundamentally new expression of their imperialism—it was a state-based infrastructure project that supported (perhaps, among other things) military action. Now, this was not Rome's first great building project. The massive temple to Jupiter Optimus Maximus on the Capitoline, built in the sixth century and the foundations of which are still visible in the lower levels of the Musei Capitolini, highlight what the Romans could do even at that early date. We also have, of course, Rome's great Servian Walls of the early fourth century, whose 11 km (7 miles) circuit (measuring up to 10 m high and 3.6 m wide) would have represented a huge investment. However, both of these earlier projects were located in the city itself, where the Romans were used to focusing their attention and resources. The *Via Appia* was different, extending into contested territory and, while still visually impressive, serving a more practical purpose.

This sort of project had a long history in the Mediterranean, which the Romans would have been aware of. The Persian "Royal Road" had famously linked Sardis, near the Aegean coast in modern-day Turkey, to the Persian heartland, in modern-day Iran. This was in place since at least the start of the fifth century, facilitating the movement of troops. Although not an engineering feat on the same level as the *Via Appia*—the "Royal Road" was often little more than a beaten dirt track—its scale and scope were renowned. It is worth stopping, however, to really consider what building a road meant. Today, in an era dominated by motor vehicles, we think of roads as a natural precursor to communication and connectivity. However, in the ancient Mediterranean, travel by sea was often far more efficient than by land. Land travel was slow, often dangerous, and roads were costly to build and maintain. As a result, Hellenistic powers typically invested more in harbors and navies than they did in roads—sometimes explicitly refocusing attention on maritime transport at the expense of the land-based options. Indeed, while Rome obviously invested in roads as well, the community also built harbors in this period, planting a series of citizen colonies down the Tyrrhenian coast in this period, known as *coloniae maritimae*, seemingly designed to encourage and protect maritime transport. So why would anyone build a road like the *Via Appia*? In short, roads were recognized as important to expansion and power. Diodorus suggests that Alexander had even proposed to build a road across North Africa, from Egypt to Gibraltar, to facilitate the conquest of the west. This idea was never carried out, evidently nixed by Alexander's successor, Perdiccas, after his death (if we believe the story at all), but the idea of building a road to extend one's military control and influence was evidently accepted. Rome's *Via Appia* would surely have been seen in this context.[11]

Building a road outside of the community was not revolutionary in and of itself. Italians had been doing this for centuries for economic reasons, and regions like Etruria, in particular, were crisscrossed with advanced road networks. The technology was not new. Indeed, the Romans themselves had evidently built roads to connect *coloniae* and communities previously—for instance, the *Via Amerina*, which connected Rome to Nepi—and the existence of a *Via Latina* of some sort is often assumed, linking Rome to the interior of Latium. What was revolutionary about the *Via Appia* was the scale of investment, evident purpose, and the fact it was evidently built by "the Romans" as a whole. This was the first time that the Romans had mobilized resources, as a group, to construct a major piece of infrastructure outside the city—and with, evidently, a military function. As has been argued, the Roman military model up to this period was based on bringing *men* together, for a short period of time, for a specific and usually short-term goal. It was not designed to centralize *resources*, or work toward longer-term projects outside the limits of the city. We only start to see this here, at the end of the fourth century.

Although indicative of a new, more corporate ethos in Rome, it is worth noting that the *Via Appia* was something of a "one-off" in this period, and we do not see any similar constructions for almost half a century. The *Via Appia* was extended farther south in 268 and then again in 241, following Rome's increased military interests there. We have the construction of the *Via Aurelia* also in 241, connecting Rome to the communities of coastal Etruria, and a flurry of roadbuilding in the late third century connecting Rome to other areas in the north and east—for instance, the *Via Flaminia* of 220 connecting to Arminium on the northern Adriatic coast—but this early expression was somewhat singular. It highlights what the Romans were capable of, but also perhaps the limits of their comfort.

In a connected development, at this same time (ca. 310) we also have the first appearance of coinage bearing the Roman name. Indeed, the timing is so convenient that scholars have often suggested that Roman coinage was likely introduced to help pay for the *Via Appia*. This is a possibility,

FIG 14

RRC 1. The first "Roman" coin. Minted in the late fourth century BCE. Struck bronze. Obverse: laureate head of Apollo, facing right. Reverse: man-headed bull walking right; PΩMAIΩN (Greek for "of the Romans") above. ACANS inv.07GS16. Image: M. Rampe.

although the fact that these initial coinage issues were tiny indicates they could not have financed the entire project on their own. Interestingly as well, the coinage, although bearing the name of the Romans, was almost certainly not minted in Rome but down in Campania—likely by the community of Neapolis and/or one of its neighbors. The first Roman coin (RRC 1 – see fig. 14) is of the same type, style, and weight as an existing Neapolitan type, with a man-headed bull on one side and youthful Apollo on the other. The only real difference between this issue and previous Neapolitan ones was that the Roman coin bore the Greek word PΩMAIΩN ("of the Romans") on the reverse.[12] Scholars continue to argue over how to interpret this first Roman coin, but at the very least it shows that the Romans were getting interested in coinage and were presumably using it in a way comparable to the rest of the Mediterranean world: for military expenses. Although we are unsure what those expenses might have been, and indeed who was commissioning them, it links the Roman system into this wider military economy and the gradual centralization of resources, in this instance metal, under a Roman label.

However, as with the *Via Appia*, this use of coinage was evidently limited and exceptional. There is no evidence that the Romans minted any further coinage for several decades, and they certainly did not do so in any great numbers until the First Punic War—which we will discuss later on in this chapter. So, again, we have hints at what the Roman military system was capable of, and their knowledge of the wider, Hellenistic, military landscape, but also a seeming lack of desire to fully engage. They could mint coinage or build state roads if they wanted, and they did so on occasion, but only rarely.

This lack of desire to regularly centralize resources and grant power to the state can be traced back to the nature of the Roman military system— and, indeed, the basic Republican system. As emphasized throughout this book, the Roman Republic was a federation of elite families who worked together for mutual benefit, but in a highly competitive environment. While they clearly recognized that a stronger and more expansive Republic benefited them all—"a rising tide lifts all boats"—their approach to the system was deeply self-interested. The Roman elite wanted to increase the power of the Republic so that, when they came to power themselves, they had more resources at their disposal. But they were also quite wary of competitors gaining too much power, which limited the types of long-term strategy they tended to pursue. No one likes to do the "dirty work" while someone else gets the glory, and the entire Roman system was set up to avoid this. Military campaigns in this period were typically intended to be single-year ventures, and usually only lasted a couple weeks. It is noteworthy that when the Romans began to regularly engage in warfare that pushed beyond this limit, also in this period, they also introduced the concept of prorogation—allowing a magistrate to stay in command beyond his year, to finish up his military activity.[13] Specific campaigns were, at least in this period, closely tied to specific commanders.

The wider community was only loosely involved in warfare, evidently supplying *stipendium* and supporting recruitment, but once the army was in the field it was under the *imperium* and *auspicium* of the individual general and, effectively, an independent entity. The wider Roman elite, embodied by the Senate, and the Roman community both seemed able to support warfare further if required, and some exceptional examples show what was possible. However, the severely limited and ad hoc nature of these instances illustrates how they did not align with the core nature of the Roman system at this time. Although operating in a Hellenistic context, the Romans did not focus on a single powerful family or dynasty, but rather a collection of them. The Romans had no problem with kings, provided they could have more than one.

PYRRHUS OF EPIRUS

Rome's war against Pyrrhus (280–275) highlights everything the Roman military did well and why the Romans, as a group, may not have felt the need to move further down the path toward greater centralization taken by many of their Hellenistic rivals. The war began in Tarentum, in the far south of Italy. As discussed earlier, during the late fourth and early third centuries, the Romans had pushed their interests deep into southern Italy, incorporating parts of Campania and Samnium as citizen tribes and establishing military alliances and systems of obligation throughout the region. This brought a whole new population under the Roman label, which in turn brought a whole new set of interests and relationships—extending the Romans' social, political, and economic network farther south.

This brought the Romans into conflict with one of the other major hubs of elite activity in Italy: the community of Tarentum. Located in Apulia, on the inside of the "heel" of Italy, Tarentum was one of the only colonies associated with Sparta and was supposedly founded in the eighth century. With excellent harbors and in a prime location to influence both east-west Mediterranean and north-south Adriatic trade and movement, coupled with access to the Italian interior (especially Bruttium and Lucania), Tarentum was one of the more important communities in southern Italy, and its network represented a clear rival to Roman power in the region. A key aspect of Roman power and imperialism was funneling communication and activity, as much as possible, through communities that the Romans controlled. Similar to modern social media companies, the Romans seem to have recognized the power in being able to dictate where and how conversations and interactions took place. We can see this in their approach to communities like Veii in the early fourth century and Latin communities in the middle of the fourth century. Things had not changed by the late fourth century. Any rival networks or hubs of interaction represented a threat to Roman control.

Rome and Tarentum first came into conflict in 303, when the Romans pushed into the Tarentines' traditional area of influence while engaging the Samnites—highlighting that Rome's warfare in southern Italy during that period was not solely against the Samnites and likely extended to other networks. The Tarentines knew they could not act against the Roman military system alone, and so they called on their allies—specifically their mother community of Sparta. In response, the Spartans sent the general Cleonymus with 5,000 mercenaries. He was able to raise another 22,000 soldiers from around Tarentum (likely including many mercenaries) and had some success against the Romans before being pushed back. In 302 Tarentum was able to secure a favorable treaty with Rome, establishing zones of control and evidently limiting Roman movement and expansion in the area.

The exact details of the outbreak of the next war with Tarentum are debated, although it evidently stemmed from an incident in 282. In this year, 10 Roman ships were active in the Gulf of Taranto and were attacked by the people of Tarentum. Appian suggests that it was a peaceful mission, unconnected with Tarentum, but that the Romans accidentally breached the treaty of 302, which had forbidden them to sail beyond Lacinium.[14] The Tarentines supposedly attacked, sinking several ships. Alternatively, Cassius Dio suggests that the Roman ships had actually been on a peaceful errand to Tarentum.[15] However, upon arrival, they were evidently insulted by drunken Tarentines, in breach of normal rules of hospitality. Either way, tempers were clearly on edge before this set of events, and war was declared after.

The Tarentines immediately looked to their allies for help, but Sparta was already otherwise engaged and was unable to assist. As a result, the Tarentines invited the Molossian king Pyrrhus of Epirus to intervene. Tarentum was located just across the Adriatic from Epirus and seems to have had a strong relationship with the Molossian kings stretching back centuries. Pyrrhus had emerged as an important figure in the wars of Alexander the Great's successors, was connected to many of the major players, and led a powerful army. The Tarentines, somewhat optimistically, promised him a local force of 350,000 infantry and 20,000 cavalry if he decided to come to their aid. If the Tarentines had had these sorts of numbers, one wonders what they needed Pyrrhus for. This was either a blatant exaggeration or, more charitably, an estimation of the number of soldiers potentially available for hire in the region—and either way, it did not eventuate. However, Pyrrhus accepted the invitation in 281 and began to put plans in place to fight the Romans.[16]

Pyrrhus began his invasion by sending an advance force to establish a beachhead in Italy while he mobilized the rest of his forces. When he accepted the invitation of Tarentum, he evidently did not have the ships needed for the crossing of the Adriatic and was forced to rely on his ally and patron, Ptolemy II Philadelphus of Egypt (who had helped Pyrrhus to the throne in 297) to acquire them. He then mobilized his forces— which included 20,000 infantry, 3,000 cavalry, 2,000 archers, 500 slingers, and 20 elephants—and attempted the crossing from Epirus in winter, in order to reach Italy by the start of the campaigning season in spring. This characteristic impetuous impatience—at least as is typical of Pyrrhus in our sources (he was the archetype of "impatient genius" in literature)— was a mistake, and his forces were caught by a storm and scattered across the coast. Eventually, Pyrrhus was able to regroup at Tarentum, where he was named *strategos autokrator* (effectively "commander in chief") of a unified army and was quickly put on the defensive by the Romans.

The first major engagement between Pyrrhus and the Romans was near Heraclea in 280. Heraclea was a site not far from Tarentum, to the west of the community along the Gulf of Taranto. The community had been founded by settlers from Tarentum in the late fifth century and was allied with Tarentum in this period. The Roman consul Valerius Laevinus had already marched his army into the region and set up on the western side of the Siris River, while Pyrrhus, marching from Tarentum, set up on the eastern side. The two armies faced off for some time until the Romans forced the issue and splashed across the river to attack Pyrrhus. This may have been a strategic decision, designed to stop Pyrrhus from receiving more reinforcements. Alternatively, it may have simply been the fact that keeping several thousand men healthy and supplied in the field was a difficult task at the best of times, particularly in hostile territory, and decisive action was often preferable. The battle was fairly evenly contested, although Pyrrhus' elephants seem to have made an impact, and Pyrrhus is typically considered to have been the victor of a closely fought engagement. Roman losses were suggested to have been between 7,000 and 15,000 compared with between 4,000 and 13,000 for Pyrrhus, depending on the source one follows. Pyrrhus immediately attempted to turn this military "victory" into a diplomatic victory and sent his second in command, Cineas, to Rome to negotiate a favorable peace and alliance. The Senate was initially receptive until a speech by the now-aged Appius Claudius Caecus turned the group against it.

This particular speech is actually quite a famous one, as not only did it effectively change the course of the war, but it was also evidently one of the first pieces of narrative Latin prose to be written down.[17] The later historian Appian records that, while the Senate argued over what to do, the aging Appius Claudius Caecus, now blind due to old age (whence he earned the nickname "caecus," which means "blind") slowly rose to his feet and said:

> I used to be depressed at not being able to see; now I am depressed that I still have my hearing! I did not expect either to see or hear you make such plans. After a single defeat, you have suddenly so forgotten yourselves that you are proposing to treat as friends rather than enemies both the man who did this to you and those who led him against you, and you are planning to give to the Lucanians and Brutii the heritage of your forefathers. What is this but making Rome subject to Macedon? And some of you even dare to call it peace rather than slavery!

Appius then went on to say that if Pyrrhus wanted to be a friend, he could approach them as such, by taking his army home to Epirus from Italy and sending an embassy. But if Pyrrhus stayed in Italy, there should be no chance of dealing with him on friendly terms. The Romans would not bow to the Hellenistic kings. This argument evidently won over the Senate, who immediately sent Cineas packing, supposedly sending him on his way using the exact words given by Appius on the Senate floor. If Pyrrhus wanted a treaty, he should go home to Epirus and negotiate from there.

This was, of course, not something that Pyrrhus could accept and so, in 279 he marched his army north from Tarentum, up the eastern coast of Italy. The Romans came south to meet him, and the combined armies of the two consuls for that year, Publius Sulpicius Saverrio and Publius Decius Mus, confronted Pyrrhus near the site of Asculum in northern Apulia. While Heraclea was not a small battle, this engagement was on an entirely different scale. Our sources suggest Pyrrhus' army now contained 70,000 infantry, while the Roman side contained slightly more. The Roman army contained 20,000 Romans citizens, with the rest being allies. The Romans also had 8,000 cavalry. Pyrrhus' forces were slightly stronger in this area, and he also fielded his 19 remaining elephants.

The size and construction of these armies are fascinating. Given that Pyrrhus had arrived in Italy with slightly more than 25,000 men and would have lost some at Heraclea the previous year, his army of roughly 80,000 men would have been largely composed of locally recruited troops. The core of the army, and the center of his battle line, was still made up of his own Epirote troops (Thesprotians and Chaonians).[18] However, the right wing of his infantry was largely Italian, composed of citizen soldiers and mercenaries recruited through Tarentum, along with contingents of Bruttians and Lucanians drawn from southern Italy. These were supplemented by a small group of mercenaries from Ambracia in northern Greece. Pyrrhus' left wing contained various Greek allies and/or mercenaries (Athamanians, Acarnanians, and Aetolians), but was primarily composed of Samnite troops. So, we seem to have a skeleton of Greek and Epirote troops, fleshed out with Italian allies. On the right side of the infantry, Pyrrhus placed Samnite, Thessalian, and Bruttian cavalry, while on the left he put northern Greek, Lucanian, and Tarentine cavalry. He, personally, seems to have moved about this formation a bit, along with his bodyguard, but his formal position would have likely been with the Samnite, Thessalian, and Bruttian cavalry on the ring wing—as this was the usual position of honor in Hellenistic armies.

Out of the ca. 80,000 troops Pyrrhus fielded at Asculum, our sources record that only 16,000 had come with him from across the Adriatic—meaning roughly 55,000 were Italian.[19] These troops, which would have joined his army in the past year, account for ca. 80 percent of his total forces. This did not mean that the troops were inexperienced, however, either in general or in the practicalities of fighting in a Hellenistic army. As noted, this area was renowned for its mercenaries, and many of these men may have fought in Hellenistic armies previously. But it is worth noting the composite and Italian nature of Pyrrhus' army. Although this conflict is often framed as the Romans fighting off a foreign invader, this would be a battle of Italians against Italians.

Indeed, in terms of the composition of forces, things were not so different on the Roman side. The two consuls evidently lined their combined four citizen legions, or roughly 20,000 men, across from Pyrrhus' main infantry battle line. They then took the 50,000–55,000 allied troops that had accompanied them (which included Latins, Campanians, Sabines, Umbrians, Volscians, Marrucini, Peligni, and Ferentani) and interspersed them among the Roman troops.[20] So, here, we seem to have a skeleton of Roman troops (in contrast to Pyrrhus' Greek and Epirote troops), also fleshed out with Italian allies. From the names, we can see the majority of the Roman force was also pulled from tribes from the central Apennines, who would have fought in a roughly similar manner to the Lucanians, Bruttians, and Samnites of Pyrrhus. So, despite being led by very different leaders, these armies would have looked and operated in similar ways. It is also worth noting that, evidently, this mixing of infantry units did not cause any issues for either the Romans or the army of Pyrrhus in terms of tactics or approach. This may seem like a minor detail, but it stands at odds with most of the traditional models of ancient warfare, which have generally assumed a sort of homogeneity and mechanistic order to things. Breaking up either the Roman battle line or Greek and Epirote phalanx with groups of allies from the central Apennines should, theoretically, interrupt the cohesion and elaborate choreography of the respective battle systems. This did not happen. Indeed, the ability of both Pyrrhus and the Romans to integrate so many Italian forces quickly and easily suggests that those traditional models are likely wrong, and that ancient armies may have fought in a more flexible manner than often supposed (for a more detailed discussion of this type of matter, see the Appendix at the back of this book).

The cavalry figures are more difficult to parse. According to Polybius, each Roman legion should have had 300 Roman cavalry associated with it, resulting in a total Roman force of 1,200, while allies usually supplied three times that number (3,600) for a total of 4,800. With 8,000 cavalry, it is unclear whether this would have been composed of ca. 1,200 Roman cavalry and ca. 6,800 allies, or some other combination or relative weighting. It is clear, however, that the Romans were bringing more cavalry than usual to this engagement. Pyrrhus' cavalry is described as being both more numerous and stronger than the Romans', which would be typical for a Hellenistic army where cavalry formed the most important "strike element"—typically waiting for a gap to appear in the opposing infantry before charging in to exploit it and breaking the enemy formation. And, of course, we cannot forget about his elephants.[21]

The battle at Asculum is remembered as a truly epic affair, full of fabulous details and anecdotes—almost all of which are certainly embellished, and many of which are perhaps entirely fabricated. The battle was once again evenly fought, with the Romans supposedly finding success against Pyrrhus' elephants by using wagons equipped with "fire-bearing grapnels"—scholars have often debated what these might be and whether they actually existed. The Romans also supposedly benefited from divine favor brought about by the heroic self-sacrifice of the consul Decius Mus, mirroring that of both his father and grandfather. However, Pyrrhus' forces also did well, driving back the Roman left wing and, in the end, the sources are mixed on who won or lost. Famously, Plutarch places the famous "Pyrrhic victory" quote ("If we are victorious in one more battle against the Romans, we shall be utterly ruined")[22] in the aftermath. Whatever the result, after the battle Pyrrhus left peninsular Italy to pursue a separate campaign in Sicily at the invitation of Syracuse. The reasons for seemingly abandoning his Italian campaign to pursue one in Sicily are unknown, but it is usually attributed in our sources to Pyrrhus' somewhat fickle nature. He evidently bored easily. This Sicilian campaign put him into conflict with Carthage, which was fighting with Syracuse for control of the island and actually resulted in a short-lived military alliance between Rome and Carthage in 279 against him. Pyrrhus only fought one major engagement in Sicily, a failed siege at Lilybaeum in 276, before leaving the island to return to mainland Italy.

Although Pyrrhus' absence from Italy clearly had a negative impact on the Tarentines and their allies, it did not spell the end of the war which continued for several more years. Indeed, given that the activity all took place in the same area that Rome had been operating in previously and involved many of the same groups, while the Pyrrhic or Tarentine War is traditionally seen as a separate conflict, it could easily be considered a continuation of the so-called "Samnite Wars." Rather than pursuing territorial conquest and domination, the Romans were likely raiding and expanding their influence through alliances—as is suggested by the scattered references we have to actions in this period. While the Romans may have been exerting some wider strategic pressure on Tarentum and its elite families, the Tarentines were not at risk of real "defeat." The Romans were pillaging but not attempting to conquer and control. Or at least, not yet.

This raiding activity was still ongoing in 275 when Pyrrhus returned to Italy, having worn out his welcome in Sicily. He rejoined his allies in Samnium, where he supposedly attempted to surprise a Roman army under the command of the consul Manius Curius Dentatus by using a forced night march. However, his planned assault was slowed by the terrain and his forces were revealed by the dawn, resulting in his tired army fighting a full and refreshed Roman force. Our sources are mixed on the composition of the armies. Plutarch reports Pyrrhus brought 20,000 infantry and 3,000 cavalry from Sicily, which he supplemented with local troops before marching into Samnium, although he does not give the total.[23] The much later writer Orosius suggests Pyrrhus had 80,000 infantry and 6,000 cavalry at the battle, although this is surely an exaggeration, especially since he seems to have been engaging the army of a single consul.[24] Whatever the numbers, the outcome was a defeat for Pyrrhus. Orosius suggests Pyrrhus lost almost half of his army,[25] while Livy and Plutarch comment on the defeat rather perfunctorily and simply suggest that it caused Pyrrhus to leave Italy.[26] Plutarch goes on to note that "He returned to Epirus with eight thousand foot and five hundred horse, and since he had no money he sought for a war by which he could maintain his army."[27]

As suggested at the beginning of this section, this war highlights, more than anything else, the strengths of the Roman system. The Romans were able to mobilize large numbers of troops, on an annual basis, despite significant losses. With an expansive system of allies and citizens, the Roman pool of soldiers was considerable and could evidently suffer significant losses in multiple years without a notable drop in effectiveness. However, it must be noted that Pyrrhus' army was also able to achieve this. Despite suffering significant losses in battles, the Molossian king was able to continue to campaign, and indeed field large, competitive armies. The difference was the system of obligation that allowed each army to achieve this. Pyrrhus relied on the Mediterranean's mercenary networks, supported by coined money. This was incredibly effective as long as his money lasted. However, in the end, his inability to secure sufficient funds in Italy to maintain his army forced him to return to Epirus to seek out different/easier sources of funds. The Romans, by relying on a much cheaper system of obligation, backed by a combination of force and strong social bonds, were able to avoid this pressure. While their armies still sought out wealth and spoils, it was not required for their recruitment and maintenance. They had found a way to leverage the same types of military groups and connections that Pyrrhus had, and indeed among the same types of Italian populations, but without coined money or centralized resources. They relied, instead, upon traditional social bonds of alliance and obligation, backed by the threat of force.

As a brief aside, this was not actually the end of Pyrrhus or his career. He lived to fight another day. Indeed, he likely had to fight, as he needed to replenish his treasury. Once back in Epirus, Pyrrhus turned his attention east and invaded the kingdom of Macedon, sacking and plundering rather than attempting to secure any lasting control. He then ventured south, invited by allies in the Peloponnese, and soon found himself attacking the ancient city of Argos. It was here that Pyrrhus met his end. After successfully breaching the walls of the city, he and his troops found themselves engaged in urban warfare against soldiers and civilians alike. As part of this, Pyrrhus was evidently hit on the head and knocked from his horse by a roof-tile thrown from the top of a nearby building by a grieving mother. Stunned and helpless, he was then finished off by a young Macedonian mercenary named Zopyrus, who happened to be fighting for Argos.

Rome and the Mediterranean

THE THREAT OF CARTHAGE

While the war against Pyrrhus highlighted the strengths of the Romans' federated, imperial system, the situation leading up to the First Punic War illustrates the tradeoff that the Romans had accepted as part of this. While the ability of the Roman military to operate without centralized resources or coined wealth was clearly a benefit in the earlier conflict, it put them on the back foot with Carthage, as it meant they were initially unable to engage equally at sea. Ancient navies, far more than any other aspect of ancient warfare, seem to have required centralized resources and money—from the construction or purchase of warships, to purchasing supplies, to paying sailors, ancient navies were notoriously expensive.[28] If the Romans wanted to participate in the naval sphere in an equal way to their Hellenistic rivals, they were going to have to change their ways.

The conflict with Carthage in the early third century, like Rome's war against Tarentum, seems to have been largely over "influence" and shaped by greed and traditional raiding practices.[29] The Carthaginians and Romans had been negotiating zones of control since the start of the Republic. While they had sometimes worked together, as in the middle years of the war against Pyrrhus, in general their relationship was focused on defining where the other side could and could not operate. This suggests that for all the rhetoric of difference and "otherness" found in our sources, many of which were shaped by the traumatic events of the Second Punic War, Rome and Carthage were, in fact, very similar and, indeed, direct competitors. Both operated as extended networks of powerful families within the region, with the city functioning as a hub of interaction and activity. This is why they seemed almost predestined to come into conflict, as both networks grew within the central Mediterranean.

The nominal cause of the First Punic War was the community of Messana in Sicily, on the north-eastern tip of the island and across the narrow straits from Rhegium in Italy. During the reign of Agathocles, tyrant of Syracuse (361–289), a group of Italian mercenaries known as the "Mamertines," or "Children of Mars," had been hired from Campania to serve in the Syracusan army. After Agathocles' death in 289, the Mamertines settled in the Carthaginian-controlled community of Messana in 288. In

280, issues with the Mamertines were among the reasons the Syracusans cited when seeking help from Pyrrhus, inviting him to the island. These issues continued after Pyrrhus left, with the tyrant Hiero II of Syracuse fighting against the Mamertines regularly in subsequent years. In 267 Hiero finally besieged the settlement of Messana, forcing the Mamertines to call for aid.

The first potential ally the Mamertines approached was Carthage, which had nominally controlled Messana since at least 307, although seemingly with little actual influence. The Carthaginians acted swiftly, sending soldiers and forcing Hiero to withdraw. However, it seems as if the Mamertines also had links to Rome, perhaps through their Campanian connections, and at least some seem to have sought assistance from them as well—although whether this was against Syracuse, or to balance Carthaginian power, is not clear. Indeed, it is not at all clear that the Mamertines should be considered a single group with a coherent foreign policy, and it is entirely possible that different factions within the Mamertines sought help from different powers. This may have been a mixed and diverse collection of mercenaries. The Roman Senate was uncertain how to proceed, and supposedly—and exceptionally—put the matter to a vote of the Roman assembly. While wars were traditionally confirmed by a vote from the people, the issue was usually always decided first by the Senate. The assembly voted to support the Mamertines, and the consul Appius Claudius Caudex (the younger brother of Appius Claudius Caecus) was given command of an army to cross into Sicily and support the Mamertines in 264.

While I have been consciously trying to give the basic narrative of events in this chapter, avoiding the thorny debates that academics have had (and still have) around the ancient evidence, it is perhaps wise to have a short digression here on the subject. Polybius is our main source for much of the First Punic War, supported in places by Diodorus Siculus and excerpts from the surviving summaries of Livy's history. As a historian, Polybius is generally lauded for his accuracy, and it is clear that he was working from a rich historical tradition related to this period, which was only a century or so removed from his own lifetime. As such, most historians generally trust his basic narrative for the war. However, his understanding of the First Punic War was fundamentally shaped by his knowledge of the Second and Third, as well as his overarching historiographical goals, and so we should not push this accuracy too far—especially when it comes to understanding Roman motivations or indeed his wider framing of the conflict. Polybius consciously emphasized both the idealized natures of the Romans and Carthaginians, as well as their supposedly oppositional nature.

Perhaps nowhere is this explicit and somewhat constructed opposition more visible than in Polybius' discussion of their two military systems. The Carthaginians, he notes, "commanded the sea," while the Romans were dominant on land.[30] Polybius then sought to explain how the Romans became "lords over land *and* sea in our part of the world."[31] So, a key part of Polybius' narrative arc for the Romans is to show how they beat the Carthaginians at their own game. As part of this, Polybius consciously—and somewhat oddly—paints the Romans as total novices when it came to the sea in 264. This supposed Roman naïveté at sea, despite its persistence in modern scholarship, stands in stark contrast to virtually every other piece of evidence we have. As suggested in earlier chapters, both our literary and archaeological evidence suggest that Rome had extensive maritime connections going back to the sixth century. We also have the naval activity assumed by the various treaties with Carthage, and regular references to raiding and trading by central Italian peoples in literary sources going back to the fifth century. By the fourth century, the expansion of Rome's citizenship and alliance networks into Campania would have resulted in the integration of a significant number of people with a strong seafaring tradition and history. By the late fourth century, communities like Cumae, which was a major maritime power, held citizen status, while powerful trading communities like Neapolis were allies. In 311 the Romans supposedly created a new set of naval magistrates, the *duumviri navales*, and at least two small fleets. Indeed, the outbreak of the Pyrrhic War was supposedly brought about by the actions of a Roman fleet.

Polybius' description of the Romans being novices at sea is, at the very least, exaggerated and is part of his wider argument around the growth of Roman power in this period. He wanted to explain why the Romans had not pushed beyond the boundaries of Italy before this time and presented the sea as the great barrier to their success. Once that was overcome, Rome's conquest of the wider Mediterranean was inevitable. That being noted, Polybius' focus on the relative weakness of Rome's naval forces is not entirely without substance. Despite this long tradition of maritime activity, at the start of the First Punic War, Rome's naval forces were completely outmatched by those of Carthage—a point that is connected with the nature of Rome's military system.

The details of the First Punic War are beyond the limited space available in this book (for those interested, book 1 of Polybius' history covers the entirety and is an excellent read), but the basic sequence of events can be summarized like this.[32] Between 264 and 256, the war was focused on the island of Sicily. Despite both sides mobilizing large armies—in 263 the Romans supposedly sent both consuls with a total force of 40,000, while the Carthaginians countered with a force of 50,000 infantry, 6,000 cavalry, and 60 elephants—major land battles were limited. Settlements were besieged and raided, indemnities paid (famously Syracuse paid Rome 100 talents of silver after its capture), but the two sides rarely engaged each other en masse. Although somewhat confusing from a modern perspective, this type of warfare was still the norm for both Roman and Carthaginian forces, led by powerful clan leaders who were still largely out to maximize personal gain and glory. Massed battles could be fought but were risky, and it seems like both sides were consciously trying to avoid them here if at all possible. In general, leaders on both sides were out to win individual battles, not the war. The goal was to acquire as much booty as they could in their year of command and then come home safely. The main exception to this, in the early years of the war, was the siege of Agrigentum in 262, which resulted in a costly Roman victory.

In 260 the Romans built a fleet of 120 triremes to combat Carthaginian naval superiority. Although supposedly novices, the Romans seem to have won every naval engagement where their forces were at least equal in number to their Carthaginian opponents, including at the battle of Mylae in 259 and Tyndaris in 257. In 256 the Romans mounted an invasion of North Africa, mobilizing a force of 330 ships that would assist with the landing of 26,000 infantry, led by the consuls Marcus Atilius Regulus and Lucius Manlius Vulso Longus. The Carthaginians countered with a naval force of 350 ships under the command of the generals Hanno and Hamilcar. The navies fought off of Cape Ecnomus in Sicily, in one of the larger naval engagements in antiquity, which the Romans ultimately won. While Manlius returned to Sicily with half of the army and the fleet, Marcus Atilius Regulus continued to North Africa with a force of 15,000 infantry and 500 cavalry. There, he led a series of successful raids before ultimately being defeated in 255 by a force led by the Spartan mercenary commander Xanthippus, who was working for the Carthaginians. After his capture, Regulus was supposedly sent back to Rome to help negotiate peace. When this was unsuccessful, he honorably returned to the Carthaginians, where he was famously tortured to death (see fig. 15 for an early modern depiction).[33]

Between 255 and 248, action returned to Sicily and the seas surrounding it and was again dominated by raids. The Romans were generally more successful on both land and sea, which has led to confusion among scholars over why the war seemed to drag on, although this is once again in line with standard Roman practice as seen in Campania and southern Italy over the preceding century. The Romans were not interested in conquest, in the modern sense, but in extracting wealth along with alliances or promises of obligation. The only significant Carthaginian victory in this period was at Drepanum in 249, which saw 93 Roman vessels captured along with their crews—likely over 15,000 men.

The war ultimately concluded in 241, after the Roman naval victory by a fleet commanded by Gaius Lutatius Catulus over Hamilcar Barca's Carthaginian fleet off the Aegates Islands to the north-west of Sicily. The location of this naval battle has sensationally been found and is the subject of ongoing excavations—although the finds were not exactly what was expected.[34] Despite this being a resounding Roman victory, the rams and equipment found on the sea floor were not entirely or distinctively Carthaginian—and indeed many bear Roman inscriptions. Scholars are still divided on what this might mean, but the most likely answer is that both "Roman" and "Carthaginian" forces were using the same types of equipment, possibly even produced by the same manufacturers. Again,

FIG 15
Regulus Condemned to the Most Horrible Torture. Pierre Chenu after Gabriel de Saint-Aubin. Etching and engraving. Metropolitan Museum of Art. 2007.49.355.

these two powers were not rigidly defined states, but federated networks, that seem to have overlapped in the area of southern Italy. Local workshops and weapon manufacturers were likely selling to families from both sides, as they had always done. Following the Roman victory at the

Aegates Islands, Romans and Carthaginians signed the Treaty of Lutatius, which gave the Romans control over Sicily and nearby islands as well as the payment of 3,200 talents of silver (82,000 kgs)—a truly massive sum. The treaty was renegotiated only four years later, adding a further 1,200 talents to the indemnity and ceding control of Sardinia as well.

There are many interesting features and takeaways from the First Punic War, but here I would like to emphasize just a few, which are of direct relevance to the core themes of this book.[35] First of all, although this was a new war for the Romans, and the first fought off of Italian soil, the Romans still tried to follow their traditional, tried and true practices. In the First Punic War, the Romans were predominantly focused on raiding, in this instance over more than two decades. This raiding was also, evidently, somewhat reciprocal. The Carthaginians are also recorded as raiding, both in Sicily and peninsular Italy, and it is clear that neither side was exclusively focused on the other. Both the Romans and Carthaginians continued to fight and operate against other peoples and communities as well. The conflict between Rome and Carthage was obviously important, but also only part of a wider set of engagements pursued by the families in the two federations. In this context, the seemingly long duration of the war is entirely normal. This was not due to an inability to prosecute it more aggressively, or an inability to "win" it, but rather a lack of desire (or, more accurately, a different definition of "winning"), as territorial conquest and peace did not align with Roman elite aims.

Second, and perhaps more importantly, the Romans were incredibly successful at sea, despite not having a significant navy prior to the war (or indeed after). As suggested above, this situation can be largely explained by the nature of the Roman military system. The Romans would have had access to a large body of experienced shipbuilders and sailors in Italy. Italians had been sailing the Mediterranean for millennia, and the coastal communities of the peninsula—many of which would have been aligned with Rome by the start of the war—would have been full of experienced mariners and vessels. Some may have been "Greek," or from Greek colonies, but many were Italian. The Polybian story of Roman shipwrights being unaware of how to construct a quinquereme (a warship with five banks of oars, instead of a trireme, which had three, or a quadreme with four) and only learning after finding a Carthaginian vessel that had run aground is almost surely a myth. This sort of knowledge would not have been a closely guarded state secret, as indeed these evidently did not exist in this context, but would have been part of the wider shipbuilding industry, of which the Italians were certainly a part.[36] Major ports, like that at Neapolis which had been within the Roman system from the middle of the fourth century, would have certainly been party to this sort of technical knowledge. The issue for the Romans was never a lack of knowledge or ability, but, again, a lack of desire.

While the people of the ancient Mediterranean basin had been using the sea for millennia, large navies, composed of dedicated warships, were a relatively recent phenomenon, and their rise seems to be directly connected with the rise of more centralized states and coinage. From the start of the fifth century, in the eastern Mediterranean, ancient navies were inexorably connected with significant state investment, largely through the new medium of coined money. Perhaps the best example is the great navy of Classical Athens, bought and paid for with silver extracted from both the mines of Attica by slaves and from its allies, although the examples are myriad. From Sparta, to Syracuse and Carthage, to the Persian empire and the later Hellenistic kingdoms, navies and coinage went hand in hand. The reason behind this connection is simple: warships, like triremes and quinqueremes, required significant investment to construct, use, and maintain. Coinage facilitated the quantification, centralization, storage, and distribution of the resources needed. While individuals and families could perhaps maintain a single ship or small fleet, when operating on the sort of scale needed for a substantial navy, the flexibility and efficiency offered by coinage was almost a necessity. Ancient navies were built and run using payment in silver coinage.

The Romans, however, had avoided this centralization of resources and use of coinage. As suggested above, they preferred to mobilize manpower on an ad hoc basis for short-term goals. While individuals, families, and communities likely had small personal fleets, and the Romans had evidently explored the idea of small, community-based fleets previously, the underlying political and economic principles that underpinned larger Hellenistic navies simply did not align with the Roman approach. Like

FIG 16

RRC 20. "Ogulnius *didrachm*." Minted in the first half of the third century BCE. Struck silver didrachm. Obverse: head of Hercules, facing right. Reverse: she-wolf, facing right, with suckling twins. UoA inv. RR1. Image: G. Morris.

many wealthy families throughout history, the majority of the clans at the center of Rome's empire did not want to pool their resources any more than they had to. While they were happy to take advantage of the shared resources and opportunities that came from being within the Roman system, they were primarily interested in extracting wealth for their own benefit. Pooling wealth for the collective good required some convincing. They had done this before, with the introduction of *tributum*, but it is clear that this was an exception to the rule. Polybius was, therefore, likely correct in suggesting that the Romans, as a military alliance, had not regularly engaged in naval warfare before, at least as a group, and that this was not their forte. The nature of Rome's military system, and the contentious and competitive relationships within Rome's Senate, was simply not conducive to it.

In the 260s, however, the Roman Senate seems to have changed its mind and finally began to invest in this area. Pliny suggests that the Romans first minted silver coinage in 269.[37] This was associated with the consulship of Quintus Ogulnius and the issue in question is often called the "Ogulnius didrachm" (fig. 16)—with Hercules on one side and on the other, a depiction of the statue group of Romulus, Remus, and the she-wolf, that the consul and his brother had commissioned when they were tribunes in 300. This exact date for the issue has never been particularly certain, although the coinage does seem to slightly predate the First Punic War, hinting that the Romans were once again exploring the possibility of coinage in this period. With the start of the war, Roman coinage exploded, with a massive upsurge in the number and types of issues minted by both the Romans and their allies. While it is likely that this went toward a number of different expenses, including logistics in Sicily, a significant proportion (likely the majority) of the coinage seems to have gone toward the emergent Roman navy. This would have included paying for ships, as well as likely paying for experienced rowers and crew to man them. The Roman fleet at Cape Ecnomus alone would have needed ca. 60,000 sailors, most of whom were likely recruited from among allies and mercenaries in southern Italy and Sicily. This represented a massive outlay and a significant shift in approach for the Roman elite.

What caused this change of heart within the Senate is uncertain. It was certainly connected with a wider movement toward centralization and a growing sense of *Romanitas* and corporate identity within the wider Roman federation. We can see this with the growing use of the "Roman" label ca. 300, the increased importance of political office in Rome for elites, the rise of Romanocentric myths (including that of Romulus, as seen in the statue group and coin), and even the Senate allowing the assembly to vote on going to war. All of this indicates a growing sense of community, and a distinctively "Roman" people and state beginning to emerge, which surely helped to ease this move. Gone were the days when elite families only passed through Rome, and relationships were ephemeral and transient. By the early third century, the Romans had ensured that the conversations and relationships that ran through Rome were the most important ones within the region. Through either removing or integrating rivals, there was increasingly nowhere else for dissatisfied elites to go. Even in the dark days of the Second Punic War, only a few elites (famously Lucius Caecilius Metellus) sought to leave the Roman network. This granted a certain amount of stability, which was not an intrinsic part of the system.

However, the increasing centralization in Rome during this period was also likely related to practical concerns and personal gain. Coinciding with the rise of the Roman navy and coinage, we also have the increased use of indemnities being applied to defeated communities after warfare, largely in the form of silver. In the fifth century, virtually all wealth acquired in warfare came in the form of portable wealth carried away by the army and funneled through the hands of the general. During the course of the fourth century, while portable wealth remained the most common and popular spoil of war, this was often supplemented by community-held land. In the third century, portable wealth continued to dominate, although a new type of spoils emerged as well—the indemnity payment, to be paid by the defeated community to the Romans as a whole. It is likely that these payments were used to mint most of the coinage the Romans required for their navy, and perhaps even to pay back any initial investment by the tribes or Senate which the navy's introduction necessitated. The Senate may have, therefore, seen the use of coinage and the centralization of resources as a necessary investment in order to achieve wider gains—and perhaps gains that did not necessitate putting their own life and limb on the line. After the war, the Roman economy boomed, and the Roman Senate enjoyed the benefits more than most.

ROME'S FIRST EMPIRE

Rome, at the end of the First Punic War in 241, had reached a pinnacle. In a similar manner to the conquest of Veii in 396, the Romans had just vanquished a powerful regional rival and asserted their superiority on a wider stage. They controlled the dominant social, political, and military system within the region, although this time, "region" meant the entire central Mediterranean rather than just northern Latium/southern Etruria. The Romans had citizen and alliance networks running the length and breadth of the Italian peninsula, bringing a vast number of families, communities, and potential soldiers under their influence. Indeed, the Romans added a final two tribes to their tribal system in 241, bringing their total up to 35, and then rationalized the entire system to enhance its efficiency. The military forces recruited through this system had proven adaptive and effective, generally supporting the traditional raiding tendencies of her elites with ever-larger forces, while also allowing for centralized expenditures and new approaches when needed.

The elite families that had set up the Roman Republic in the late sixth century had benefited immensely from this system, but the opportunities afforded even to new arrivals—at least since the end of the "Struggle of the Orders" in the fourth century—meant that it was an attractive deal for many newcomers as well. While some elite families and networks continued to struggle against the power and control that the Romans exerted over the region, many others were evidently happy to align themselves and join the Roman system. Being part of the emergent Roman empire allowed Italian families and elites to engage on the wider Mediterranean stage on relatively equal terms with the great Hellenistic powers, offering a chance at real power for those able to claw their way to the top of Roman politics. For those further down the social and economic hierarchy, the benefits were also quite real and tangible. Roman citizens became part of the most powerful system in the region, with wealthy and influential patrons, supported by increasingly robust laws, and were able to access more and more social and economic opportunities. They were also part of an extensive "protection racket," which shielded them from raiding and predation—certainly from those within the Roman system, and generally from those outside it who would be scared to provoke Roman ire. All that was asked in exchange was military obligation, or to support military action through contributing resources, which would have been common and traditional in the region anyway. Clans and communities in Italy had long had alliances, and many were linked through traditional patron-client relationships as well. The Roman system simply standardized these relationships and funneled them all through the city and polity of Rome. So long as the Romans remained in an area where the cultures both utilized and recognized similar systems, this approach seemed to work well.

By the middle of the third century, the Roman system exerted a significant amount of control over warfare, land, and elite interaction within Italy, with tendrils of this influence covering the wider Mediterranean basin. However, even at this late date, this was still quite a loose association, with the aims and goals of those at the top of the system largely focused on their personal interests. Despite its increasingly expansive and

Rome and the Mediterranean

territorial focus, Roman imperialism still relied on principles of social integration and leveraging existing political systems and hierarchies in order to function. While Roman dominance was often initially asserted through force of arms, in the third century at least, the Romans did not continue to enforce their will on defeated clans and communities through military occupation or the imposition of an imperial bureaucracy. Indeed, even if they had wanted to, their systems were not set up to allow for that. This was a devolved empire, with a remarkable amount of self-governance.

That being said, there is evidence of something new emerging: a growing sense of pride and community cohesion, a new *Romanitas* unbound from the community of Rome itself. Authors, like the south Italian Quintus Ennius (lived ca. 239–ca. 169), spoke multiple languages but began to write in Latin as it was the language of the Roman system, and indeed wrote epics of the emergent "Roman people" themselves—although who they were and what they represented was still a bit fuzzy. Despite this, however, or indeed perhaps because of its flexible and adaptive nature, an increasing number of Italians began to latch on to the idea of "Roman-ness" as a deep, philosophical, and metaphysical thread that bound together the various peoples within this superficially pragmatic and violent federation. This was, in many ways, the high watermark for the earliest iteration of the Roman "empire." The triumph of the first, imperialist *res publica*.

CLOUDS ON THE HORIZON

It is very tempting to simply stop the story here, with a moment of Roman glory. To end the story on a high note. However, as anyone who is familiar with the broad outline of Roman history knows, this triumph was short-lived. Roughly 20 years after Rome's victory over Carthage in the First Punic War, Rome would once again go to war against the Carthaginians in the cataclysmic Second Punic War (218 to 201). This conflict would fundamentally change the nature of the *res publica* and reshape the later Roman memory of everything that came before. It is the reason why we have struggled, for so many years, to tell the story presented in this book. As a result, we must at least touch on it here.

The specific details of the Second Punic War are beyond the scope of this book and indeed are covered in some detail in Dexter Hoyos' 2015 *Mastering the West* in this same book series, but the impact and scale of the war are vital to understanding the Roman approach to empire and imperialism. The war encompassed the entirety of the western Mediterranean (and some of the east as well). Although many decisive actions took place in Spain, and the final battle occurred in North Africa at Zama in 202, the most important activity for the Romans occurred in Italy as a result of Hannibal Barca's invasion of the peninsula. In 218 Hannibal famously crossed the Alps into Italy and spent the next 15 years marching up and down the peninsula, laying waste to Roman armies and communities, and straining Rome's imperial system to its breaking point.

The Roman *res publica* that emerged from the Second Punic War was a fundamentally different entity from that which entered it. Some of this is due to the nature of the war itself. While the Romans were used to fighting prolonged conflicts, this had typically involved raiding enemy territory over an extended period—as in their wars in central and southern Italy, and seemingly in Sicily as well. The length of early wars was a product of the collected Roman elite wanting to extract as much as possible from the area, rather than their inability to finish it. The Second Punic War was very different. Rather than raiding enemy territory, it was Roman communities in Italy that were being attacked and threatened for 15 straight years—while the Roman state, with its vaunted alliance, was evidently unable to stop it. While the Romans attempted to turn the war into a series of smaller engagements, especially under the command of Fabius Maximus, the early stages were defined by a series of major battles (and Roman losses), including at Trebia, Lake Trasimene, and Cannae. The regular Roman defeats, and their inability to defend citizen and allied settlements, put the entire footing of their military system in jeopardy. While members could excuse losses in aggressive campaigns, the basis of alliances in Italy was their defensive aspect. An ally who could not defend was not an ally at all.

Of even greater importance, however, were the losses Hannibal inflicted on the population of Italy in this war. The three battles of Trebia, Lake Trasimene, and Cannae, in the first two years of the war, resulted in a reported total of over 100,000 Roman and allied dead. The true scale of these losses is hard to grasp, as we are unsure of the total population of Italy at this time. Roman census data suggests that the 35 tribes contained a total of roughly 300,000 citizen men in this period. If we assume that roughly 75 percent were of fighting age, and that Roman citizens represented roughly half of those lost, we can arrive at a figure of roughly 20 percent of Roman citizens lost in just these three battles. Although modern and ancient demographics are difficult to compare, the scale of these early losses is perhaps comparable to French army losses throughout the entirety of World War I. The size of the wider Italian population is even more of an unknown, although it is likely that men from Italy would have been dying on both sides of this conflict as Hannibal also recruited from the region during his 15 years there. And, of course, we should not forget the many civilian deaths that undoubtedly occurred during the period too—victims of both direct aggression and indirect consequences of war (famine, plague, etc.). The war would have been absolutely devasting in terms of the simple human cost. Finally, in first millennium Italian society, not all men were considered equal. These losses would have hit the Roman and Italian elite the hardest, as these men represented the warrior class. These were not conscript armies made up of poor citizens, but collections of powerful, elite clan leaders and their followers. The 20 percent of Roman citizen losses were not spread equally across society, but focused almost exclusively at the top.

These losses would have impacted the Roman military system in a number of ways, but perhaps the most important is that these elite men dying on the battlefield were the sinews through which Rome's military system ran. The personal relationships that the vast systems of obligation and alliance ran through were dictated by individual Italian and Roman clan leaders. The power-sharing arrangement at the core of the Roman *res publica* was shattered by the Second Punic War, and many of the powerful families involved were simply killed off. The Roman Senate was forced to declare a special *lectio* or "recruitment" in 216 to replenish its ranks, as nearly every Senator under the age of 45 was dead—177 of Rome's elite.[38] These men represented the heart of the Roman system. The Senate that emerged after 216 was therefore a very different creation, full of new men, dependent on the traditional power and authority of the Roman Senate rather than their own personal clout and often relying heavily on the voices of the few remaining traditional elites.

Through the military defeats of 218–216, and the Roman elite losses at them, Hannibal effectively carved out the heart and soul of the traditional Roman *res publica*. The wider system was only saved by the traditional power of the bonds of obligation the Roman system relied on, citizenship and alliances, helped along by the growing sense of institutional cohesion and community that had emerged over the previous century with the stable hand and voice of the few remaining traditional elites. These allowed the Romans to stagger on, and ultimately win the war, but at tremendous cost.

The Roman *res publica* of 200 was a changed polity and system. While it remained a power-sharing arrangement among the elites, both the elites in charge and the nature of their power were different. The Senate was no longer full of independently powerful clan leaders, who exerted significant power in their own right, but rather another class of men who relied on Rome's institutions and their new position within them to exert power. They were "new men" (*novi homines*), "system men," hungry for power, and firmly invested in the corporate Roman system which had given them this golden opportunity. This also put them at odds with the wider collection of Italian elites, the old allies (those who had survived at least), which still contained quite a few powerful clan leaders and elites—although these men were increasingly locked out of the Roman system. While it had not mattered greatly whether they were integrated as citizens or allies in the fourth or early third century, and indeed being an ally may have actually been preferred by some of the more powerful, in the early second century it was a significant issue. This tension would ultimately lead to the Social War of the first century, although the ongoing civil wars and various elite purges and proscriptions of the subsequent decades make its resolution both difficult to understand and perhaps a moot point. But in 200, this tension resulted in a unified and aspirational Roman Senate, seeking to make the most of its new position, and very happy to centralize power and resources for their collected benefit. While still competitive, this group seemed to be working in a new type of competition, which both allowed and facilitated Rome's tremendous Mediterranean expansion in the following 30 years.

This period, from ca. 200 to 170, is the second phase of Roman imperialism, and the one which is far better known and researched due in large part to its great proponent, the historian Polybius. This phase was, however, a very different thing from the first. In this second phase, the Romans were united and cohesive, coming out of the crucible of the Second Punic War newly reforged as a vibrant and violently expansionist society. They had been unified by the threat of Hannibal and swept across the Mediterranean in a way never seen before or since. Interestingly, the energy and cohesion seem to have been relatively short-lived, and by the late second century things had returned to something of a status quo. But for a few decades, the Mediterranean bore witness to one of the most violent and aggressive eras of empire-building the region had ever seen—and it had seen quite a few!

It is worth really emphasizing, though, that this second era of Roman imperialism was truly exceptional. It was not how the Romans usually did things, and it had an energy and cohesion that was nothing like the imperialism which we see in the periods before and after. Both the early and later periods were instead dominated by powerful, individual families, who used the Roman system to increase their own wealth and power. It was based on violent negotiation and forceful compromise, with clans working both with and against each other to gain an advantage in a highly competitive context. When seeking to understand the true nature of *Romanitas* and Roman imperialism, we should look beyond the exceptional moments and seek out more regular, repeated, and often quite unexceptional practices and behaviors—like those visible in early Rome.

EPILOGUE

As discussed in the preface at the beginning of the book, early Roman history and the creation of Rome's Italian empire have long been understood as little more than the "opening acts" for the better-documented late Republic and early imperial periods. With uncertain sources, all written many centuries after the fact and full of fantastic anecdotes of dubious historical merit, most scholars have, at best, sought to trace later institutions and themes back into this period. At worst, they have misinterpreted its events to fit their narratives. Most commonly they simply ignored the period. As I hope should be clear by now, we can do better. When we properly interrogate the evidence and view early Rome in context, a more interesting and insightful narrative emerges.

Early Rome, and early Roman imperialism, is not the story of a single people, striving for greatness. Rather, it is the story of a single, albeit evolving, agreement. A federation. A relationship. A bargain. This relationship, arguably, began back at the start of the regal period, when the first king agreed to work with the community of Rome, establishing a mutually beneficial alliance. The community would support the king and fight in his wars, provided he protected them and served as a benevolent patron. The bargain changed at the end of the sixth century, when the position of the king was taken over by a group of elite clan leaders. Rather than struggling to be the sole rulers themselves, they agreed to share power on an annual basis. While these clans and clan leaders did not permanently tie themselves to Rome, and many may have left when they were not in power, the appeal of the arrangement seems to have been

Epilogue

great—as was the appeal of Rome itself. Strategically located on a number of different routes through the region, it was a useful place to meet. Rome evidently attracted new elites on a regular basis, although things remained relatively small and ad hoc for most of the century.

The start of the fourth century marked a third period of transition for Rome and the birth of the first iteration of a proper "Roman empire." The century began with Rome's victory over her local rival Veii, followed soon after by the sack of Rome at the hands of Brennus' Gauls. These two developments pushed Rome's leaders in a new, more aggressive, and expansionist direction, reaffirming the need for cooperation and the importance of Rome as a shared, symbolic focal point for their activities. But the focus of this empire was limited, and almost exclusively based on military obligation. Over the course of the next 150 years, the Romans worked tirelessly to expand their military network, adding both citizens and allies through peaceful treaties and annual warfare. However, the Roman elites continued to utilize this expanding military to pursue personal gain, as they had always done, highlighting the underlying nature of the system. The empire was always a means to an end, and not an end in and of itself.

This growth seems to have had unintended consequences, though, and there was a gradual increase in community focus and involvement over time. The growth, and the changing context, required greater community investment. In response, Rome's armies brought in community land, and later other types of wealth, to repay the corporate investment and leading to a growing sense of community identity. By the middle of the third century, many of these developments seem to have reached a critical mass. Rome's community identity was growing of its own volition, now pushed through art and literature, and Rome's military context increasingly necessitated a far more cohesive and centralized approach—particularly when it came to the sea.

And yet, when Rome was not pushed, the underlying nature of the system was evident. After the First Punic War, the Romans seem to have completely divested themselves of their navy. Without a pressing need, the Roman elites did not naturally seek to pool their resources. Every compromise and investment was negotiated, and always with the personal benefit of powerful elites and their families in mind. We have an

Epilogue

exceptional moment after the Second Punic War, when a new group of elites banded together and pushed Rome's imperialism across the wider Mediterranean. However, even that seems to have run out of steam, and by the late second century, we have a return to the status quo—competing elite families, seeking to increase their personal wealth and power, and doing their best not to share any more resources than absolutely required.[1] The imperial Roman state was only as strong as the ties that bound the elite family heads together at the top.

To try and summarize things briefly here, at the end, the core of the Roman Republic was a power-sharing arrangement among a collection of powerful elite families. It was a grand bargain that they struck, working together to increase their individual wealth and power. Through their extended networks, both individual and corporate, they were able to include most of the population of Italy within its structures by the third century—although it is unclear how much say the wider population had in this arrangement. Some local elites and communities may have joined willingly, others may have simply followed their patrons, while still others were evidently forced to join at the point of sword. It was not, however, like a modern empire, or even like the later forms of Roman imperialism. This was a loose federation between more established and stable entities; the closest modern analogy would be an alliance like NATO. Indeed, this largely military character also fits with this model. It was only as strong as its individual components and the bonds that brought them together. When push came to shove, these core elements showed themselves, often through the rise of independent "warlords." These elements were always there in the Roman military system—in fact, they *were* the Roman military—just labeled differently and typically operating under a wider, shared authority. Roman imperialism was the gradual extension of this bargain and authority across Italy and, later, the Mediterranean basin. This was sometimes peaceful, quite often violent, and always about personal power and ambition.

Our sources present a very interesting view of this imperialism. The authors of our extant literary evidence were not necessarily confused or mistaken about its nature, although they likely had little reliable information about its earliest periods. Rather, they chose to focus on a very

Epilogue

particular moment, and a very particular view of it, which was shaped by their personal goals and context. While they may have recognized the loose and weak nature of the Roman state, they chose not to focus on that aspect and instead argued—almost certainly a bit aspirationally— for a strong and cohesive Roman people and a sense of *Romanitas* that bound the people of Italy together. Many of them, like Livy and Dionysius, did this because they saw the pain and suffering that conflict between elite families within the Roman system could bring. Having lived through the era of the Civil Wars in the late Republic, they viewed anything else as preferable. Others, like Polybius, may have simply preferred to work with more cohesive states and ideals for rhetorical or philosophical reasons. But all of the histories that survived to us today seem to have actively and consciously argued for a more cohesive Roman state and people than actually existed.

All of this is quite relevant to us today in a number of ways. First, it highlights how deceptive or superficial unifying social and political labels can be. Despite claims of uniformity and cohesion, even modern nation-states can also be seen to be based on entirely different sets of social, political, and economic structures, which are often only loosely unified by a few bonds at the top levels. Civil wars and social discord still tear modern societies apart, often revealing these underlying structures in frustratingly violent ways. Second, and perhaps paradoxically, despite their seemingly ephemeral and superficial nature, it hints at how powerful these unifying labels and "grand bargains" are. These ideas helped to drive Roman imperialism, and the period when Roman unity was at its strongest, in the early second century, is also the period of Rome's greatest and most energetic expansion. As modern sociological work has shown, nationalism is an incredibly powerful tool, particularly (and all too often) when directed toward military conquest, and even the sort of proto-nation we can see in the Roman Republic can yield tremendous, and tremendously devastating, results.[2]

APPENDIX

THE NATURE OF THE EARLY ROMAN ARMY

THE NATURE OF EARLY Roman warfare, and Roman imperialism, is—perhaps obviously—directly related to the nature of the early Roman army. The strengths and limitations of the army helped to define what was possible. A small, seasonal, tribal army would have had very different capabilities to a large, permanent, state-supported army. A disparate group of warbands would behave very differently from a cohesive phalanx. Roman generals would have been aware of this. They were limited by the tools at their disposal. So, it is worth thinking about the character of the early Roman army carefully, and how this would have shaped Roman warfare and imperialism in different periods. Specifically, in this appendix, we will explore the details of how the early Roman army seems to have been organized, how it was recruited, how it may have functioned, and how all of this may have changed over time.

Given that ancient authors discussed these points in some detail in their works, it might be natural to wonder why this might require a full appendix and, indeed, why this material wasn't included in the main body of this book. The short answer is that "it is complicated." While the ancient authors did leave us quite a few detailed descriptions of ancient armies, these are neither entirely consistent nor are they giving us the full story—and, in fact, the ancient authors may not have known it themselves. We must always remember that the armies and events we are discussing here occurred many years—sometimes centuries—before the Romans started writing narrative histories. So the detailed descriptions of armies that we have are based, at best, on flexible oral traditions. Further, the ancient authors, for all their emphasis on detail, were not actually concerned with factual accuracy in the modern sense. This was narrative elaboration, not scientific detail. Finally, they were clearly writing for an audience that had a working understanding of ancient armies, meaning they could leave out details without worrying about losing their readers. As a result, figuring out "what really happened?" will once again take some effort. It will require delving into the literary evidence properly, outlining what it actually says, what scholars have interpreted it to mean, and how we might be able to make sense of it within the wider context of archaic Italian society. It also means getting a little more technical and "academic" in our approach. When we can't take an author at their word, we must really interrogate what they are giving us—sometimes word by word—and decide what may be authentic bits of information and what might not. This results in quite a bit of cautious interpretation, as well as some speculation.

So, as a quick summary of where we will be going in this appendix (for those who decide they don't want to wade through the detail), no one has ever doubted the complexity or heterogeneity of the Roman Republican army. All our evidence suggests that it was made up of small units of various types, that it contained a remarkable range of different troop and equipment types, and that it featured a high level of tactical flexibility. There were a lot of specialized, moving parts in the military system of the Roman Republic. This is broadly agreed. Scholars have simply disagreed on how this came about and what it means about the underlying systems.

Traditionally, scholars assumed, following the explicit testimony of our ancient sources, that the Roman Republican army was a stable and deeply practical institution whose form sometimes changed as a result of military necessity. It was an overt symbol of Roman society and Roman power. Just like the city it is thought to represent, the army grew and developed over the centuries, increasing in size, complexity, and sophistication over time. Its core feature was its adaptability, although this did not change its true nature. The Roman army was a shapeshifter. For instance,

Appendix

it has long been argued that the Romans initially had a tribal army under Romulus. This transitioned to a single dense phalanx of citizen soldiers in the late regal and early Republican periods, when the Romans faced off against the Etruscans who fought in this way. It remained a citizen militia, but one that fought in a new way. When the army had to fight in the hilly terrain of Samnium in the fourth century, it supposedly transformed this dense formation into a more flexible one made up of many smaller units. Later, when the Romans would face off against the Gauls in the first century, known by then for their massed infantry charges, the Romans were thought to deploy slightly larger formations to increase tactical stability. The Romans were deeply pragmatic. They would use one system as long as it was effective. When it wasn't, they would adopt a new one, often from their enemies. It just so happens that our sources only start describing the army in any detail during one of its more complex and heterogeneous phases, in the middle Republic.

Superficially, this makes quite a bit of sense. It feels rational and logical, and aligns with the principles of modern military doctrines. However, it is probably incorrect. In reality, the complexity and heterogeneity of the Roman Republican army were likely there at the very beginning, and what we actually have is a relatively linear progression toward ever more homogeneity and cohesion over time. There were no massive reorganizations or radical tactical shifts to respond to specific threats or contexts. There was just slow, incremental change, whereby small units were gradually brought together and merged into larger ones as part of the wider construction of Rome's imperial apparatus. The movement was always in one direction, toward more cohesion, and was driven by social and political forces rather than military ones. A loose collection of clans slowly came together to form a more coherent and state-based army over the course of 500 years. Not only does this model make sense, given our understanding of Roman society and politics, but it is also supported by both the archaeology and comparative data.

This does not mean, however, that the descriptions of the Republican army offered by our sources are wholly incorrect. In fact, they actually seem to have a lot of truth in them. The authors of our sources simply misinterpreted, or perhaps consciously shifted, the starting point. They

Appendix

assumed a strong, stable, and unified army (and community) at the outset, which then became very complex in the middle Republic, before once again becoming a bit simpler and more unified in the late Republic. Their snapshot of the army of the middle Republic, and certainly the army of the late Republic, may be largely accurate—idealized, perhaps, but fundamentally sound. They just put these snapshots into the wrong developmental arc. This appendix will walk us through what that means in real terms.

ROME'S REGAL ARMY

Let us begin, then, with the traditional narrative for the early Roman army—as laid out in its systemized and idealized form by the authors of our sources, and as broadly accepted by scholarship until recently. What the authors of our surviving sources seem to have done—and indeed, were often quite obvious about—is take some real, remembered traditions and reframe them within a narrative that emphasized Roman unity and cohesion. So, as historians, we can be quite critical of the overarching framework and narrative, while still trying to make the most of the remembered detail and institutions.

The story of the Roman army always begins with Romulus. While Aeneas was nominally the founder of the Roman lineage, and evidently had a small "army" of his own, this was never associated with the community or state of Rome. Indeed, while both Romulus and Remus also had bands of followers, who assisted them in their early adventures and evidently helped them found the city of Rome, these were also never considered part of the "Roman army" as traditionally conceived. The "Roman army" was always associated with the physical site and state of the urban community, as founded by Romulus, and only emerged after he had accepted the title of *rex*.

As discussed in Chapter 2, during his initial organization of Roman society, Romulus supposedly created the three tribes and 30 *curiae*, which formed the basis of the first Roman army.[1] Each of the *curiae* supplied 100 infantry and 10 cavalrymen, to create a total force of 3,000 infantry and 300 cavalry. The sources offer very little detail apart from this broad structure, which is likely little more than educated guesswork based on some known,

Appendix

archaic divisions and some important numbers in Roman society (e.g. 3, 10, and 30). The 30 *curiae* were well known and indeed existed down to the late Republic. Historians have assumed that these were somehow connected to the three traditional tribes of Romulus, which were supposedly later superseded by the Servian tribes, although the division of 10 *curiae* per tribe may be antiquarian speculation—as, indeed, may be the tribes of Romulus themselves.[2] As for the 100 infantry per *curia*, this was likely derived from the later tradition of dividing the army using "centuries." While it is clear that Rome's later, Republican centuries were political divisions and did not usually contain 100 men, the number 100 clearly had some meaning in this context and made as much sense as any other figure. The 10 *equites* or cavalrymen per *curia* was also likely a rationalization based on the fact that Roman cavalry were typically organized into *turmae* of 30 men in later periods. So, in short, much of this was likely made up—or, perhaps we can say it is the result of "educated guesswork," trying to make sense of some vaguely remembered divisions. We shouldn't put too much stock in it.

The Roman army, as established by Romulus, supposedly remained stable through the reigns of the subsequent kings, with the only changes being the gradual expansion of the cavalry.[3] Livy reports that the third king, Tullus Hostilius, doubled the number of *equites* from 300 to 600 (although the number of "centuries" evidently stayed the same, at three, with each now containing 200 men).[4] The fifth king, Tarquinius Priscus, doubled the number again to 1,200, this time by doubling the number of centuries.[5] So, in the early sixth century, the Romans supposedly fielded an army of 3,000 infantry and 1,200 cavalry. But the core organizing principles were static and supposedly based upon the 30 *curiae*.

The authors of our sources clearly indicate that they thought this army was, despite its tribal labels and regal context, essentially a civic militia. Men were mobilized and organized, as they would be under the Republic, by civic divisions: in this period, the *curiae*. This is important on a number of levels. First, it allowed later authors to differentiate this entity from not only the personal warbands of Romulus and Remus (and indeed Aeneas before), but also the "personal" or independent armies of the late Republic and civil wars. This army was "Roman," as opposed to "Romulan" (i.e. of Romulus), Numan, Hostilian, or that of some other powerful family. It

Appendix

was a community-based force. While many modern scholars accepted the civic foundation as the natural default for any armed force, for the authors of our ancient sources this was almost certainly a conscious and politically motivated position—particularly given the importance of private groups in warfare and violence down into the late Republic. Indeed, virtually all of our archaeological and anthropological data for this period of Italian history suggests that clan-based warfare was the norm.[6] Community-based militias were certainly possible, and it is likely that members of urban communities would have banded together for mutual defense and that communities represented important points for communication and networking, but the default organizing principle for armed forces was almost certainly the clan or extended family. Additionally, organizing the military by *curiae* provided a point of continuity with later Republican forces, which were mobilized and organized using political structures, most notably the tribes and centuries. As will be discussed later, it is unclear whether this is a real point of continuity or an invented one, but either way, it was an important one, as it helped to create a single conceptual entity with a consistent character throughout Rome's long history.

The next big development for the Roman army was associated with Servius Tullius, Rome's sixth king and the early city's great political reformer. Servius Tullius supposedly reorganized Roman society from top to bottom, recategorizing all Roman citizens by both wealth (into classes and centuries) and physical location (into a new type of tribe, now defined by the community) through a newly created census. Scholars have long argued that this represented the logical evolution of the Roman community as it moved things from family-based associations toward a new set of somewhat arbitrary, state-based divisions.[7] It also, conveniently (perhaps too conveniently), aligns with the famous reforms of the politician Cleisthenes in Athens, which are actually reasonably well attested, demonstrating that this sort of measure might actually be possible at this time. Under the "Servian Constitution," a citizen's civic identity was defined entirely by the state. It was the ultimate victory of community over family, or at least that is how the traditional story goes. The army that emerged from this reorganization was thought to have formed the basis for the army of the Republic, with only minor tweaks and adjustments.

Appendix

The core of Rome's "Servian" army was the "first class," which may have initially been the only class (*classis*), along with the *equites* or cavalry. Livy and Dionysius both say that each of the classes in the Servian system was associated with a particular military panoply or set of equipment, and the first class was equipped in what we might call the archetypal "hoplite" manner: helmet, round shield, body armor, greaves, sword, and thrusting spear.[8] This literary description has been backed up by ample archaeological evidence from across Italy supporting the existence of this bronze equipment and its use across Italy (e.g. see fig. 17). Some scholars have, therefore, associated the reforms with the advent of a hoplite phalanx in Rome, yet again mirroring developments in the Greek world at this time.[9] And indeed, the Romans themselves claimed to have fought in this manner in the early period.[10]

Increasingly, however, doubts have been raised around the existence of an early Roman phalanx. Most notably, while bronze armor was clearly in use in early Italy, it may not be as closely connected to "hoplite" warfare and the community-based, phalanx formation as once thought.[11] While many ancient warriors (especially Greek) certainly seem to have worn lots of bronze armor, even in Greece it was actually more common in the earlier Archaic period (800–480) than the Classical period (480–323), and seems to have been linked to a more individual approach to combat. Indeed, as the Greeks began to utilize denser formations of infantry, they slowly got rid of many pieces of armor, until by the middle of the fourth century some hoplites from Athens were only being equipped with the circular shield and helmet, and men in the Macedonian phalanx of Philip II and Alexander the Great wore even less. As the formation began to provide more protection, soldiers needed less armor.[12] So when we find lots of bronze armor, rather than indicating a dense, community-based formation, it might actually be pointing toward more dueling—which is, incidentally, what the rest of our evidence suggests for early Italy. Indeed, there is a strong possibility that many of the elite "hoplite" burials and sets of bronze equipment found in graves from early Italy may actually be for cavalrymen, as much of the artistic evidence from Italy at that time hints that heavily armored cavalrymen were common. Even the iconic *aspis* or *hoplon* (large circular shield) used by Greek-style hoplites has

Appendix

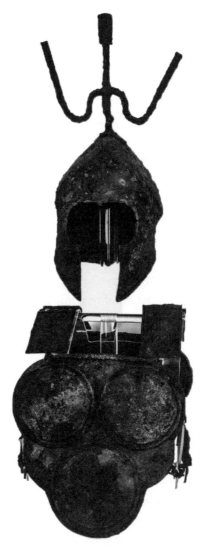

FIG 17
Bronze cuirass and helmet from Paestum, tomb 174, Gaudo necropolis. 390–380 BCE.
Photo: J. Armstrong.

increasingly been reinterpreted in this light, as cavalry seemed to use shields of a similar type.

Breaking the direct link between bronze armor and a hoplite phalanx has been quite liberating, as it has been difficult to align Rome's loose, raiding ethos with the more cohesive and methodical approach to warfare

Appendix

suggested by the phalanx. It is difficult to conduct a fast-paced raid with a slow-moving infantry formation. That being said, no one is suggesting that infantry did not *sometimes* fight in relatively densely packed formations in early Italy. In certain contexts this formation makes a lot of sense. Indeed, we find "shield walls" and similar tactics deployed in a wide range of periods and places, especially against men on horseback. Our current understanding is simply that these formations were not the defining feature of Italian warfare during this period, and that they never reached the size, scale, and complexity that we have reported for Classical and Hellenistic Greece. Quite the reverse, in fact. Our evidence suggests that most Italian warriors probably formed themselves into groups of 80 to 100 men, but these units generally they did not come together to form large, dense formations. Italian armies seem to have favored a more dispersed and flexible mode of operating, where each unit could (and did) act independently—and had both the space and freedom to do this. There was likely always some variability, though. For instance, the behavior of the Roman *triarii* (the third line of Roman Republican infantry in the traditional military structure) suggests that they may have sometimes formed a single, solid defensive line of several hundred men—although the troops in front of them, the *hastati* and *principes*, continued to operate in a much looser fashion.

Returning to the Servian classes then, the second class in the system was equipped comparably to the first, but with an oblong shield instead of a circular one, hinting at a later date for its addition—possibly associated with the fourth century when the oblong *scutum* came into fashion in Italy. The third and fourth classes were equipped in a similar manner to the second but with fewer pieces of armor. The fifth class, which also had the least wealth of the military classes, was made up of slingers and other light infantry. Beneath the fifth class was the *capite censi*, or "head count," made up of everyone whose wealth was valued as less than roughly 11,000 *asses* (*as* = lb of bronze).[13] Each of the classes was also divided by age, into *iuniores* (aged 17–46) and *seniores* (aged 47–60), with the former making up the field army and the latter the garrison for the city. Interestingly, the army did not have a fixed size in this early period. While some scholars have assumed that the centuries initially contained 100 men each—resulting in a total army of

Appendix

19,300 for the full centuriate system or 10,000 if only considering the first class and *equites*—Dionysius explicitly noted that the size of the army was variable and that the centuries were simply used for recruitment.[14] He suggested that "whenever [Servius] had occasion to raise ten thousand men, or, if it should so happen, twenty thousand, he would divide that number among the hundred and ninety-three centuries and then order each century to furnish the number of men that fell to its share." Dionysius also argued that the order of classes also represented their order on the battlefield, with the first class at the front and the other classes ranged behind them by rank, with only the fifth class of light infantry being "outside the line of battle."

Class	No. of Centuries	Required Wealth (*asses*)	Assigned Military Equipment
Equites	18	100,000(?)[1]	Cavalry
1st	80 + 2[2] (40 *juniores* and 40 *seniores*)	100,000	Helmet, round shield, greaves, breastplate, all of bronze, sword, and spear
2nd	20 (10 *juniores* and 10 *seniores*)	75,000	Helmet, oblong shield, greaves, sword, and spear
3rd	20 (10 *juniores* and 10 *seniores*)	50,000	Helmet, oblong shield, sword, and spear
4th	20 (10 *juniores* and 10 *seniores*)	25,000	Spear and javelin [oblong shield, sword][4]
5th	30 +2[3] (15 *juniores* and 15 *seniores*?)	11,000 [12,500][4]	Slings and stones [javelin][4]
Capite Censi	1	<11,000 [12,500][4]	N/A

[1] Equites were required to be of "highest birth" (Dionysius of Halicarnassus, *Roman Antiquities* 4.18), or the "principal men of the State" (Livy 1.43). However, the text does seem to hint at a required level of wealth as well.

[2] The first class included two centuries of engineers. However, it is unknown if these represented one century of *iuniores* and one century of *seniores*.

[3] The fifth class included two centuries of trumpeters and supernumeraries. However, it is once again unknown if these represented both *iuniores* and *seniores*.

[4] Details in square brackets denote variations present in Dionysius of Halicarnassus' account of the Servian Constitution, but not Livy's.

FIG 18

An outline of the Servian Constitution as given in Livy and Dionysius of Halicarnassus.
Adapted from Armstrong (2008), 62.

Appendix

Much of this detail and description of the Roman army during the late regal period is offered as part of specific digressions on the political reforms of Servius Tullius in our sources—short political treatises, within the wider narrative, where the authors of our sources are clearly trying to explain an overall system to their audience. Outside of these isolated passages, the descriptions we have of Roman military activity are often so vague and general that they could apply to almost any army. Those descriptions that do exist, and provide slightly more detail, often raise more questions than answers.

For instance, one of the more detailed battle descriptions we have from the early period is that of the battle of Lake Regillus in 496, in the first years of the Republic. Dionysius provided a relatively detailed account of events, where he suggested a Roman force of 23,700 infantry and 1,000 cavalry faced off against an army of Latins and allies totaling 40,000 infantry and 3,000 cavalry.[15] According to Dionysius, the battle began with trumpets, followed by a massed charge by both sides. The cavalry and light infantry led the way, followed by the "phalanxes" of both sides. However, it seems clear that Dionysius did not mean the traditional, dense, hoplite phalanx, as after the initial engagement of forces we find the Roman commander, Aulus Postumius Albinus, with a body of cavalry, sitting in the center of the Roman "phalanx," actively fighting and pushing back the Latin forces in a style of combat which evidently included javelins—as the opposing commander was wounded by one. Indeed, the entire battle description is dominated by dueling. The infantry commander for the Romans was Titus Aebutius, while the Latin infantry was led by Mamilius Octavius, and the two men evidently found and engaged one another, on horseback, on the battlefield. The duel was inconclusive, with both men wounded and being forced to withdraw. The battle ended when Sextus Tarquinius, the son of the deposed king Tarquinius Superbus, charged into the center of the battle, was "surrounded by the Romans, both horse and foot, and assaulted on all sides with missiles, like a wild beast, he perished, but not before he had killed many of those who came to close quarters with him."[16] The feel of this conflict is more Homeric and heroic than anything else, but still utilizes the basic vocabulary of the Servian system—especially the concept of a "phalanx" of some sort.

Appendix

LIVY AND THE ARMY OF THE EARLY TO MIDDLE REPUBLIC

From the late regal period through the early Republic, the authors of our sources present a remarkably stable vision of the Roman army. While the Romans supposedly experimented with different types of command—moving from kings to the praetors/consuls of the early Republic, to consular tribunes, to the "new" consulship of 367—the army these men commanded does not seem to change dramatically. We may have a gradual expansion of the *classis* to include the other centuriate classes, and perhaps subtle tweaks to the military equipment each used—for instance, Camillus' supposed changes to Roman spears and shields, commented on by Plutarch[17]—but the core organization and structure remained stable. Admittedly, descriptions of the army in action during this period remain quite vague, especially once we lose Dionysius' more detailed account after the middle of the fifth century. It is also clear that Livy, or his sources, were not particularly interested in providing minute and complicated details about the nature of the army in action. While warfare remains a common theme, Livy's narrative consistently focuses on the social and political aspects.

Despite this stability, or at least lack of comment, some things were evidently changing as, by our next detailed snapshot of the army in book 8 of Livy's account, the army looks rather different. In this section, Livy provides another digression on Rome's military structure and is the basis for our understanding of what is now commonly called the "manipular legion" of the middle Republic.[18] The location of this digression in book 8 places it in the context of his narrative for the year 340 and both the so-called "Latin Revolt" or "Great Latin War" along with the First and Second Samnite Wars—indeed, this digression occurs in the context of the battle of the Veseris River, which was discussed in chapter one. This was a time of intensive warfare and expansion for Rome and has long been recognized as one of the pivotal moments of transition in Roman Republican history. The victory over the Latins, and their subsequent inclusion into the Roman state, would have exponentially increased Rome's military power almost overnight. The wars against the Samnites, which occurred in roughly the same time period, marked the first real test of Rome's

Appendix

expanding army and state. The army that emerged from these conflicts was the army that would go on to conquer the Mediterranean world.

While, in general, Livy described battles in broad and often dramatic terms, when he began to discuss the engagement between the Romans and the Latins near the Veseris, he suddenly branched off into a more structural discussion. It stands out in the narrative in many ways. As noted above, Livy often seems unconcerned with relating the "historical" details of ancient combat and almost always prioritizes his own narrative agenda in battle descriptions. It is also noteworthy that this structural description is not connected to any specific reforms or other changes, as was the case with the Servian army. Instead, this description seems to be serving three functions. First, as will be discussed slightly later, the nature of the detail and its clear deviation from his normal narrative style hints that Livy is pulling directly from an existing source. While he is almost certainly adapting and reframing things to fit within his narrative, these structural digressions on the army are not typical of Livy's approach. He is likely getting it from somewhere. Second, it seems as if Livy has become aware that the nature of battle in this period requires some additional explanation. While Livy always prioritized his own agenda, he still tried to stay broadly true to his source material when he could. During the late fourth century, the battle descriptions seem to take on a rather different character—far more dynamic and diverse, with different units and unit types being described beyond the simple "cavalry and infantry" dichotomy. In order to make sense of this for his audience, Livy seems to have felt the need to provide a bit of structural detail to catch his readers up on the changes that had evidently occurred in Rome's military structure. Third, this particular military description is framed as a general discussion of the nature of central Italian armies in this period—indeed, Livy explicitly notes that the Latin army was organized in a similar way to the Roman army. As a result, in addition to showing the changing nature of war, he is able to show how the Romans and Latins were equally matched in this conflict.

Livy begins his structural digression with a discussion of military equipment and immediately notes that this has changed since the time of Servius Tullius. While previously the first class had used circular shields and supposedly fought in a phalanx, now all of the Romans—and all of the Latins as well—used the oblong *scutum* and fought in smaller groups. The *scutum* was a common shield type in Italy during this period, and across the Mediterranean, generally connected with javelin warfare as it protected more of the body and was easier to use when throwing a spear. Indeed, in this period we are able to supplement Livy's narrative with that of Diodorus—a rough contemporary of Livy who wrote a universal history in Greek, the "Historical Library" (*Bibliotheca historica*), which included some aspects of Roman history. Diodorus suggests that the oblong *scutum* was something that the Romans had picked up from their opponents—presumably the Gauls, Samnites, or the Latins—which is part of a wider theme in the literature of the Roman army learning from their enemies.[19] Diodorus goes on to suggest that this was not the only thing that the Romans adopted, as they also imitated their enemies' use of small subunits. He uses the Greek word *speira* for these units, which is usually translated into English as "maniple," although it is also sometimes translated as "cohort" depending on the context.[20] More on this in a moment.

After his brief discussion of equipment, Livy describes the organization of the Roman army in some detail (see fig. 19 for a visual model). He claimed the first line of the Roman army was known as the *hastati*, presumably named after the heavy thrusting spear, the *hasta*, despite the fact that at least some were evidently equipped with javelins. These men were arranged in 15 "maniples" (*manipuli*) which stood at some distance from each other. The word "maniple" is an odd one. It is clearly connected to the word for "hand" (*manus*) and is generally thought to mean "handful," although even our sources seem confused on how or why, and various etymologies are offered. Livy suggests that the men of the *hastati* were the younger, and perhaps slightly poorer, troops—men who were keen and eager for glory and spoils, and so wished to be stationed toward the front. Twenty light infantrymen, or *leves*, were also attached to each of these maniples, while the rest of the unit is described as an irregular group, or *turbam*, of "shield bearers" (*scutati*). The rigid rank-and-file order usually assumed for Roman armies is certainly not seen here. No number is given for the overall size of the unit.

Appendix

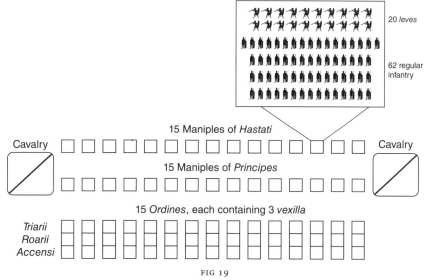

FIG 19
Indicative model of the fourth century manipular legion, as described by Livy.

Behind the *hastati* were the *principes*, who were also organized into 15 maniples, and who were equipped with the "best equipment"—likely indicating their increased social and economic status. The name then makes some sense, as the word *principe* means "foremost" or "preeminent." It is worth remembering that Roman soldiers all supplied their own equipment for battle for the entire period under discussion in this book, so the level of equipment would have varied based on wealth more than experience or age.[21] Altogether, the 30 maniples of the *hastati* and *principes* were known as the *antepilani*, supposedly because they were stationed in front of, or *anti*, the "standards," *pilani*.

When describing the units behind the *principes*, Livy shifts from calling them "maniples" to columns or *ordines*. The change in vocabulary is noteworthy, as it suggests that the army behind the *principes* was organized in a slightly different manner, although it is not clear how or why.[22] Livy suggests the troops in this part of the army were divided into 15 "columns," each of which contained three subunits known as "standards" (*vexilla*) or, perhaps more accurately, "units based around a standard." Each of these units had 60 soldiers, two centurions, and one "standard bearer" (*vexillarius*). The first unit of each rank was made up of *triarii*, the second was made up of *rorarii*, and the third the *accensi*. We are not quite sure where these names are derived from, although *triarii* likely refers to them being the third line of infantry overall.

The *triarii* are described as being veteran soldiers, the *rorarii* as "younger and less distinguished men," while the *accensi* were the "least reliable." So, each column seems to have contained 189 fighting men, which included 60 *triarii*, 60 *rorarii*, 60 *accensi*, and six centurions (two per unit), along with three "standard bearers." Livy suggests the entire legion would

FIG 20

Scene from the so-called "Altar of Domitius Ahenobarbus," now in the Musée du Louvre in Paris. The frieze is dated to the late second century BCE, but the Roman soldiers it shows are broadly indicative of Livy's description. Photo: J. Serrati.

Appendix

usually contain 5,000 infantry and 300 cavalry (incidentally, when discussing these overall numbers, this is the only time the horsemen are mentioned in this passage). Doing some quick math based on the unit numbers Livy provided suggests that the columns, including the *triarii*, *rorarii*, and *accensi*, should number roughly 2,835 men in total (15 columns × 189 men), the light infantry attached to the *hastati* would be 300 men (15 maniples × 20 men), leaving 1,865 men for the 30 maniples of the *hastati* and *principes*. While Livy does not provide specific numbers for these, assuming they were roughly similar in size, each would contain around 62 men.

Following this detailed (and, frankly, somewhat confusing) description of the organization, littered with technical vocabulary, Livy then goes on to describe the usual mode of battle. He suggests that the maniples of the *hastati*, supplemented by their light infantry, engaged the enemy first. If they were not able to win the battle on their own, they would retreat through gaps in the *principes*, who would take over the battle in turn. If the *principes* were also unsuccessful, they would fall back to the line formed by the *triarii*. In contrast to the maniples of *hastati* and *principes*, which seem to have been quite fluid and open, Livy records that the *triarii* would form a more stable battle line with their spears planted in the ground to form a palisade of sorts. If the *principes* and *hastati* had been pushed back to the line of the *triarii*, then the entire force of troops would charge en masse and hopefully break the enemy with this final push.[23] This is quite an interesting description, as it suggests that the Romans usually expected battles to be fought and won by less than half of the army. By Livy's figures, the *hastati* and *principes* together made up less than 40 percent of the infantry but were expected to do the majority of the fighting.

It seems clear that Livy is working from a rich source tradition for this section of his narrative. His account for the year 340 is particularly detailed and includes two famous military anecdotes on either side of this lengthy structural digression: Manlius Torquatus' execution of his son for breaking ranks takes place before, and the heroic sacrifice (*devotio*) of Publius Decius Mus takes place immediately after. The opening lines of Livy 8.8, and his discussion of military equipment, also find resonance with other accounts relating to this rough period, most notably that of

Appendix

Diodorus Siculus and the text of the so-called *Ineditum Vaticanum* which both relate to the start of the First Punic War. It is possible, then, that they were all working from the same source tradition when writing these sections. When combined with references to units and divisions that bear a striking resemblance to Hellenistic military systems, we can hypothesize that Livy was working from an early third-century Hellenistic source—perhaps the history of Hieronymous of Cardia or that of Timaeus of Tauromenium. While this might give us some reason to doubt the details and nuances, it is clear that these sources were both interested and knowledgeable about the way Italian peoples fought, and so we can perhaps put some stock in the broad outline.

THE MANIPULAR ARMY IN POLYBIUS

Although Livy's account is largely internally consistent, and seemingly based on at least some sort of early source material, many scholars have adjusted or amended it by combining it with the description of the manipular army given by Polybius. The army to which Polybius was referring dates to a full two centuries after that of Livy, ca. 140, and so one can assume some changes would have occurred—most notably during the course of the Second Punic War. However, because Polybius' legion still features maniples (or at least maniple-like divisions), because he provides more detail than Livy, and because he is generally viewed as a more reliable source (largely because he was a military man himself and would have spent a significant amount of time within the Roman army), his account is often put forward as the "better" version.[24] Livy, on the other hand, was famously not a military man and, in book 8, was writing about an army 300 years before his time based on uncertain evidence. Most scholars try to find a sort of "middle ground" between Livy and Polybius' descriptions as a sort of "idealized" or standard version of the Roman army across the late fourth to early second centuries—often leaning heavily on Polybius for many of the details. As a result, and despite the fact that it relates to a later army, it is worth discussing Polybius' description in some depth here.

Appendix

Importantly, in his structural description of the Roman army given in book 6 of his *Histories* (see fig. 21 for a visual model), Polybius identifies the same troop types that Livy described—the *hastati, principes,* and *triarii*—and even uses Greek transliterations of these Latin labels, so there can be no doubt about what he is describing. This is perhaps the most significant and striking linking feature between their accounts, and why they are often read together to create a composite picture of the Roman army in the middle Republic. The *rorarii* and *accensi* were evidently gone by Polybius' time, although they seemed to be little more than "support staff" for the *triarii* in Livy's description anyway. Polybius provides slightly different numbers for the army. In his description, a legion is about 4,200 men (only exceptionally up to 5,000), made up of 1,200 *hastati,* 1,200 *principes,* 600 *triarii,* and 1,200 light infantry (he calls them *grosphophori,* literally "those who carry javelins"). How these are organized, however, is not entirely clear given the varied and complex military terminology Polybius uses, much of which is evidently derived from the armies of the Hellenistic east.

Polybius begins with a broad discussion of the army, laying out its basic attributes. First, we have the overarching command structure. This includes the two *hypatoi,* which means "highest commanders" (we can assume he means "consuls" here), followed by the election/appointment of 24 *chiliarchoi* which is commonly translated "military tribunes" by

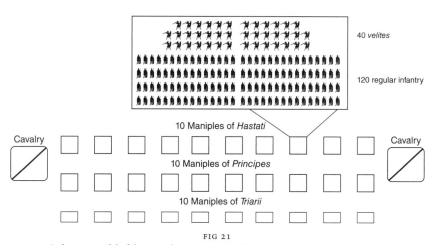

FIG 21
Indicative model of the second-century manipular legion, as described by Polybius.

Appendix

modern scholars, based on our wider understanding of Rome's military apparatus and the (perhaps questionable) assumption that the Romans always used Latin terms for their military officers and positions.[25] I will generally use the Latin terms here, as it is easier than using the Greek, but it is worth remembering that these are merely translations of what Polybius actually says. Indeed, it is interesting that Polybius does not try to provide Greek transliterations of the Latin words for these officers, as he does at other points in this same description and for the troop types. Rather, Polybius uses ranks and positions that would have been common in a Hellenistic military system. *Chiliarchos*, for example, was an established rank within Hellenistic armies and would generally be in command of a unit of roughly 1,000 men. In the Roman system, these men performed a similar role in that they ran the *dilectus*, or levying of troops (which will be discussed in detail slightly later), and provided the overall command of the army.

After the *dilectus* or levy had occurred, Polybius goes on to describe the internal structure of the legion.[26] From each of the three main classes of infantry within each legion (with the exception of the light infantry) the soldiers elected 10 taxiarchs, another well-established rank within Hellenistic armies, followed by a further set of 10, resulting in a total of 20 taxiarchs per troop type or 60 taxiarchs per legion. Polybius explicitly notes of these officers that "they named all of these taxiarchs" and does not try to give a Roman or Latin label in this section.[27] As a result, we will generally keep with Polybius' terminology here. Later, he does hint they might be equivalent to the Latin centurion, but it isn't entirely certain. There was a clear hierarchy among these men, both within those elected from each class (the first 10 elected from each class are superior to the second 10), and overall, with the very first taxiarch selected from the legion being given a seat on the military council.[28] The 60 taxiarchs then selected an equal number of men from the ranks to serve as *ouragoi* or rear commanders (commonly translated into Latin as *optiones* by modern scholars, based on much later models of the legion).

With this structure in place, Polybius says that the three main classes of soldiers (*hastati*, *principes*, and *triarii*) were then divided into 10 groups each by the taxiarchs, for a total of 30 units over the three classes.

Appendix

Each of these subunits was then assigned two "leaders" (*hēgemones*), presumably drawn from the taxiarchs, supported by two of the rear commanders, for a total of four officers in each unit. Later, Polybius adds a further two "standard-bearers" (*sēmaiphoroi*) to each unit, who supported the leaders.[29]

Given Polybius' initial figures for the numbers of each troop type (1,200, 1,200, and 600, respectively), most scholars have assumed that the *hastati* and *principes* each had 10 units of 120 men, while the *triarii* had 60 men in each unit. Each unit would also have six officers: two leaders or taxiarchs, two rear commanders, and two standard-bearers. The light infantry was supposedly divided equally among these units. With 30 units in total, the 1,200 light infantry would work out to 40 per unit, giving total unit sizes of 160 for the *hastati* and *principes* (120 + 40) and 100 (60 + 40) for the *triarii*. Polybius does not give these figures explicitly, although he does elsewhere confirm that each unit of the *hastati* and *principes* contained more than 100 men, not including the light infantry.[30]

A subtle point that is worth emphasizing here is how Polybius breaks up the various types of officers in the army into two distinct levels in his description.

At the top level, we have a group of elected magistrates: two consuls, each commanding an army composed of two legions, followed by 24 tribunes or *chiliarchoi* which are split across the four legions—six for each. The consuls and tribunes were all elected/appointed before the mobilization of the army by the assemblies of the community and therefore had a close relationship with the political "state."[31] They were in charge of initiating and running the levy and seemed to be tasked with the overall command of the army on behalf of the state. During the levy, Polybius' attention shifts to the collected soldiers, who are described in detail and according to their class. From these men, a further officer class emerges. There are 60 taxiarchs elected by, and from, the assembled soldiers for each legion, and a further 60 rear commanders selected by the taxiarchs. The taxiarchs and rear commanders are the ones tasked with dividing up the classes into their subunits and the men who directly command and lead them in battle.[32] However, only one of these men per legion, the first taxiarch selected, is allowed to join the military council,

Appendix

made up of the consuls and tribunes—a somewhat singular exception that arguably highlights the otherwise general division between the two officer groups.

Many modern scholars have likened this division among the Roman officers to that which exists between commissioned and noncommissioned officers in many modern armies. In this analogy, the taxiarchs, often discussed as "centurions," are the gritty and respected noncommissioned officers, career soldiers who came up through the ranks, while the consuls and military tribunes are the more political "top brass," who flit in and out of the military as suits their wider ambitions. By the time Polybius was writing, in the middle of the second century, there may have been some truth to this. However, it was not always this way. One must remember that all of Rome's soldiers in the early and middle Republic were fairly well-off, and the ranks of the legions likely included a fair number of men with social and political status and ambitions—even without considering the cavalry/*equites*. Although most men serving in the ranks would likely not have been able to break into the highest echelons of Roman society and politics, this does not mean they did not have quite a bit of local power and influence, outside of the army. The men who were elected to positions of authority by the assembled army were almost certainly men of some substance, and probably local leaders. Indeed, in 342 Livy preserves a fascinating anecdote about a military mutiny, evidently instigated by some centurions, and a subsequent law being passed which stated that "no one might afterwards be a military tribune when he had served as a centurion."[33] It has been argued that it was only at this point that the division between the two officer groups was formalized, severing the pathway that previously existed for centurions to climb the ranks into the upper levels of Roman military magistracies.[34]

The division between the taxiarchs and rear commanders on the one side and the consuls and tribunes on the other, certainly seems to have involved a difference in status—but, perhaps, not as great a difference as is often supposed. Instead, these two groups of officers may represent two different parts of the Roman military system. The consuls and the tribunes are clearly those in charge of the overall system and were connected with the political community of Rome. They were elected magistrates,

Appendix

who gained power and authority through the central political assemblies. The taxiarchs and rear commanders derived their authority from the mobilized soldiers. They were likely preexisting local leaders who had brought their family and followers to the levy due to their military obligation as citizens and who were subsequently confirmed into a position of leadership once that levying process had been completed. They represented existing military hierarchies within Rome's citizen body. This is important, as it suggests that the Roman army, even as late as Polybius' era, was not a monolith but a composite entity. While it was commanded from the top by a group of officers elected by the assemblies of Rome, the army itself was made up of local groups, and perhaps even local units, led by local elites. Polybius explicitly notes this was the case with Rome's allied troops, the *socii*, but it seems to have been the case with Rome's citizen levies as well—despite the seeming dispersal caused by the *dilectus* process, as will be discussed.

Indeed, being composed of preexisting, local units may help to explain the dispersed structure of the manipular legion overall.[35] Scholars have traditionally latched on to the passage in Diodorus Siculus that claims the Romans shifted from a hoplite phalanx to the manipular structure during the Samnite Wars (perhaps due to the mountainous terrain of the region), as a means to explain this formation. However, this has been consistently challenged in recent years—not least because the very existence of an early Roman phalanx has been largely discarded.[36] The idea that the manipular legion was simply a "broken up phalanx" falls apart if there was no phalanx to begin with. Instead, it is likely that the Roman army was always composed of small groups of men, representing the constituent families, clans, and communities of the wider Roman citizen body, which were organized and fought based on their preexisting groupings. Given the short-term and seasonal nature of most Roman warfare down to the third century, where soldiers were typically only mobilized for a few weeks at a time, it would have made little sense to break up existing units and divisions, which would have certainly had a negative impact on both morale and effectiveness. Rather than the irregular oscillation between dense formations and looser ones, which our ancient authors erroneously suggest,[37] the overarching trend in Rome's military organization

Appendix

is generally toward greater cohesion and larger units as the Republic progresses. It is perhaps noteworthy that Polybius' second-century maniples are larger than Livy's fourth-century maniples, and Caesar's first-century cohorts are larger than Polybius' units. This likely reflects the increased time that armies spent mobilized and together in the field across these centuries. From the regal period to the late Republic, we can see ever increasing size, organization, and cohesion among these units—although, even by the end, the Roman army is still composed of a series of discrete units that could, and often did, operate independently.

While Livy is quite open about the varied nature of the units in his description, with maniples, columns, and various other subunits all individually listed, Polybius generally disguises any variability by using ambiguous turns of phrase—often referring simply to "divisions" within the army—and, of course, deploying standardized Hellenistic military terms. In most modern translations, this has been cleaned up and rationalized even further, with the Greek word "taxiarch" almost always translated into English as "centurion" and the 30 subunits of the Polybian legion assumed to be "maniples." But this is by no means certain and may not be what Polybius intended.

Much of the assumed equivalency between taxiarchs and centurions relies on a short statement toward the end of Polybius' structural description where he suddenly complicated his previous discussion by noting that "these units are called *tagma* and *speria* and *sēmaia*, and their *hēgemonas* are called centurions and taxiarchs."[38] *Tagma* seems to refer to a band of soldiers generally. While *syntagma* could be argued to be a specific unit in a Hellenistic army (roughly 256 men) by this period, *tagma* is more nebulous, and the closest Latin word might be *ordo*, meaning "order" or "rank." *Sēmaia* refers to a "banner" and is not a particularly common unit label in Hellenistic army descriptions. The closest Latin word is usually thought to be *vexillum*, which also refers to a "standard" or flag and certainly later takes on the meaning of a military grouping of some sort, but here it is not certain.

Speira is the word that is most often translated as "maniple" and is also used by Diodorus for this unit type, although it is not a specific or exact translation, nor is it strictly Roman Republican. The original Greek term refers to something that has been twisted or wound together tightly,

Appendix

like a rope or leather binding, but it eventually came to mean a close association, for instance a religious group or even a trade guild. It clearly could mean a military unit as well, but not necessarily or always a "maniple." Indeed, it is a term used by other sources to refer to tactical units of both the Ptolemaic army and later Roman imperial army. So it may be that Polybius is simply offering a number of different Greek words that might plausibly apply to the single type of unit (the "maniple") that the Romans fielded, or it may be that he is saying that the Romans fielded a number of different units types, which corresponded to these labels. The difference is perhaps a subtle one, but important, as it means that Polybius may be hinting at a more heterogeneous army than often supposed. Polybius also uses the same varied terminology to describe the units of the Roman allies, or *socii*.[39]

We then have his reference to centurions and taxiarchs. This is the only place in his work where Polybius uses the Greek transliteration of "centurion" (*kenturion*). As with the labels for the units, it is uncertain whether Polybius meant that these leaders, or *hēgemones*, might be called either centurions or taxiarchs, or whether both titles could be somehow applied. Elsewhere, when describing activities that we would usually associate with centurions in the better-attested army of Caesar, Polybius uses the word "taxiarch." This includes when discussing their position of honor in the first tent of each row of the camp, and overseeing the entrenchment, and so broadly supports the traditional usage, where we should simply read "taxiarch" as "centurion." However, the fact that Polybius specifically notes, twice in the same passage, that the Romans called at least one of their officers a "taxiarch" is intriguing and hints that the term carries some meaning here. It is entirely possible that many groups of Italian soldiers, which had been incorporated as Roman citizens, referred to their military leader as a taxiarch.

Before continuing on, we should also touch on the cavalry, which Polybius says were divided up into 10 *turmae* of 30 men with three officers (called *decuriones*) each. The section on cavalry is both linguistically straightforward and doesn't have a direct parallel in Livy (or any other source) to compare with and complicate matters—so we have generally taken it at face value. It is noteworthy that Polybius is not particularly

Appendix

flattering of the Roman cavalry, suggesting that they were initially lightly equipped and quite ineffective. Given their elite character and, indeed, dominance in the Servian system, where they supposedly made up perhaps a third of the army, this is interesting and perhaps shows an outsider's view of this force in the second century. Polybius indicates they only recently became more effective militarily, after adopting Greek arms and armor, although it is clear that the majority of cavalry in Roman armies would have been supplied by allies and not the Roman state itself. They are presented as something of an afterthought in the description, outside of the core army as described.

Trying to summarize this complex passage and situation, we can say that Polybius certainly thought that the Roman army contained troop types known as the *hastati*, *principes*, and *triarii*. Polybius suggests that these troop types were each divided into 10 units, which could be variously described as *tagma*, *speria*, or *sēmaia* to a Greek audience. None of these terms are particularly technical or descriptive, but they give the sense of relatively small groups of troops that might contain about 100–200 men each and where a "standard" or flag seems to have been quite important. Each of these units, whatever they were called, was seemingly commanded by two leaders who were evidently supported by at least two others. We are not entirely certain what these men were called. Polybius labels them as *hēgemones* taxiarchs, and *ouragoi*, and indicates they may have also been called "centurions." In the end, it seems as Polybius felt that quite a few different labels could be applied to both the individual units of the Roman army and their leaders. While it is possible that he was simply struggling to settle upon one single word that best encapsulated each, a more likely option is that the units and leaders were diverse enough that they defied a single label. We know that, from the fourth century onward, the Roman army mobilized citizens from across Italy and from regions and communities with widely varying military traditions and norms. In many ways, it would be quite shocking if a single label, position, or unit type could be applied across this spectrum.

While the original Greek account is not anywhere near as clean and straightforward as many modern translations suggest, it does broadly

Appendix

match Livy's description of an army that is composed of many smaller units, perhaps of varying size, and certainly different troop types. Livy's legion had 30 maniples, each with roughly 62 men, and 15 columns of roughly 189 men each, all with different equipment and seemingly different roles. We actually do not know how Livy's maniples were organized, but the columns each had three subunits, which contained 60 men each in addition to two "centurions" and a standard bearer. Polybius' legion contains 30 units, which seem to have ranged from roughly 160 to 100 men each, including their contingents of light infantry. Each unit was led by two to four men, who were evidently chosen from and elected by the units they led. Polybius' units are equipped in a more homogenous fashion, with the notable exception of the *triarii* having a thrusting spear instead of the javelin carried by the *hastati* and *principes*. One must always take this with a pinch of salt, however, as Dionysius suggests that the *principes* of the third century were equipped with a two-handed thrusting spear.[40]

THE POLYBIAN *DILECTUS*

Of at least equal interest to his description of the army's organization is Polybius' description of how it was levied, as this highlights many of the more subtle features of its character. Polybius begins with a discussion of the officers, emphasizing the top-down nature of the Roman military structure—at least in his model.[41] First, the two consuls are elected by the *comitia centuriata*. Second, 24 military tribunes are appointed/elected. Then, a day for the levy is declared. On that day, male citizens who were eligible for military service were supposed to report to the Capitoline hill in Rome. Polybius notes that there was consideration of age (18–46 years of age) and experience—with infantrymen expected to serve for 16 years, and cavalry for 10—although the traditionally assumed property qualification, dictated by the Servian classes, is not discussed.

When the men had assembled, the 24 military tribunes would be divided into four groups for the four legions that were typically levied in this period—six tribunes for each. The levy then progressed by tribe. Four men of roughly comparable age and status, and so presumably of the

Appendix

same classification within the *velites/hastati/principes/triarii* system, were selected from each tribe. The first group of four would be brought forward and the military tribunes from each legion would select which of these four men they wanted, with the first legion having first choice. Then another four men would be brought forward and, in this round, the military tribunes of the second legion would get the first selection. In the third round, the military tribunes of the third legion would select first, and so on. This would continue until all the legions were at full strength. The military tribunes would then administer an oath, the *sacramentum militum*. This was a deeply personal oath, which bound the soldiers directly to the general, and was likely tied closely to the grant of *imperium* that gave consuls and praetors the right to command the army. Despite the personal nature of this obligation, Polybius records that the military tribunes usually selected only one man, who they felt was "most suitable," to take the full oath and then simply asked others to confirm that they would do the same.[42] Following on from this, the military tribunes would set a day and a place for each legion to muster in full military gear, and the men were then sent home. The allies were also informed of the date when they were expected to join the army. While these were evidently raised and organized locally, following local customs, Polybius describes them using the same terminology as he does for the Romans, including the same types of units.[43]

How the citizen *dilectus* would have worked in real terms has always been debated, as the system as reported has long been recognized as being deeply impractical and indeed somewhat implausible. First of all, recruiting the 16,800 men required for the four legions using groups of four men would be shockingly inefficient and time-consuming, as it would require 4,200 individual rounds of selection. This would have taken days to complete. That being said, we do know that levies could take many days—for instance, in his account for the year 169, Livy noted that the levy was completed within 11 days, and seemed to consider this speedy.[44] However, what Livy appears to mean is that the levy took 11 days "all-inclusive," so from the date the levy was declared until the actual selection and not just for the selection process itself. Looking elsewhere in Livy, that seems to be how the time for a levy was measured, as many levies took far

Appendix

longer—perhaps averaging about 40 days—due to the travel time required to get to Rome. It may have even included the time between selection and final muster. Adding further time, to run 4,200 individual rounds of selection, has always seemed unlikely.

Additionally, summoning all Roman citizens of military age to Rome each year—possibly a quarter of a million men, according to Livy's census figures for the mid-second century—in order to recruit only 16,800–20,000 would have been both logistically difficult and wasteful. It also would have been impossible to fit all of these men on the Capitoline hill at one time, although this may have been managed by organizing things by tribe—which is actually what Polybius suggests. Taking Livy's total of roughly 250,000 male citizens in this period, if that was divided roughly equally across Rome's 35 tribes (after 241) it would come out to roughly 7,200 citizens per tribe. Not all of these men would have been eligible for service, either due to their age or service history, let alone property qualification, meaning an actual recruitment pool of perhaps 5,000 per tribe at most. This brings the overall number of citizens who might be in Rome down to roughly 175,000 and, if the tribes were summoned individually, 5,000 would have been a manageable figure to have on the Capitoline at one time—although it still would have been a tight squeeze.

This does not address, though, the issue of almost 200,000 people descending on the city of Rome for several weeks each year, on relatively short notice, and the havoc that would have caused for local food and water supplies. It also does not account for the fact that most of those 175,000 men would have not actually needed to be there. In a normal year, with four full-strength legions, and if every tribe contributed equally, each tribe would only contribute about 488 men out of its notional recruitment pool of ca. 5,000—meaning more than 90 percent of the men eligible for service might not be selected. There is also no mention in Polybius' description of men being turned down and sent away. The selection process he outlines has each group of four being fully distributed. Obviously, the military tribunes would have wanted a good selection of men to choose from, in case there were any who were clearly unfit and in order to fill out the various parts of their legions. However, given the logistical challenges involved in bringing so many men together, one

Appendix

must wonder whether every single eligible man actually attended the levy each year. Indeed, the variable time required for levies in different years does suggest that not everyone attended each. Could the Roman tribunes have really summoned every eligible citizen to Rome and run the full levy process in less than two weeks?

We should also consider that Rome's legions and military classes were not recruited equally from Rome's citizen population. If each of the 35 tribes knew it would be ultimately responsible for roughly 488 men per year—which would need to include ca. 140 *velites*, ca. 140 *hastati*, ca. 140 *principes*, and ca. 68 *triarii*—it would make sense for them to only bring these numbers, or something close to them. This would have required some planning, as the men eligible for each class would not have been equally represented within the tribe. There would have likely been fewer men able to serve as *principes* and *triarii* within each tribe, while the *velites* would have likely been easier to source—although it is worth noting that the simple ability to afford equipment does not equate to being able to use it. But even if each tribe brought most or all of its possible recruits, it is likely there was some accounting done beforehand to make sure that they had sufficient numbers in each category.[45] It is, therefore, likely that the levy was more of a ritual practice than a practical mechanism for selection and organization. Tribes and their members would have been broadly aware of their obligations in advance and evidently supplied not only the troops but many of the leaders themselves. The *dilectus* may have been a ritual confirmation of who would be joining the army that year, reaffirming the nature of command, and a convenient means to pass on how and where they would be mustering.

The Polybian *dilectus* reinforces Polybius' vision of the Roman army as a bureaucratic, state-based institution. For Polybius, the army was nothing without the state that mobilized it. It was, first and foremost, a collection of citizens who were brought together and organized solely by the state. In this context, it is worth remembering that, unlike Livy's structural digressions on the army, Polybius' description occurs during a wider discussion of the Roman constitution. This is explicitly part of his understanding of the Roman political system. However, despite this overt narrative, we can still see some interesting themes beneath the surface. The most significant

Appendix

feature is how the entire process seems to be managed by the tribes. The levy was run by military tribunes, at least some of whom were elected by the tribal assembly (others were evidently appointed by the consuls), and the recruitment itself occurred by tribe. Out of all of Rome's varied institutions, the tribes represented the most diverse and decentralized, initially referring to individual clans and communities that had joined the Roman system in the sixth and fifth centuries and gradually coming to represent the wider population of Roman citizens across Italy by the fourth and third centuries. The tribes were how the Romans integrated new populations, and so it is noteworthy that they are also the primary, and indeed only, institution involved in recruiting and organizing the army in Polybius' account. They were the mechanism by which the Romans leveraged the manpower they were acquiring through warfare and seem to be the closest approximations to preexisting political and military groupings that we have. Even in Polybius' second-century model, then, we have a somewhat federated approach.

THE ROMANS AT WAR

For all that Livy and Polybius emphasize large, state-based structures and ideas in their descriptions, it is still clear that the underlying framework was always based on the tribe and, ultimately, the individual clan or family. When looking at the tribes created by Servius Tullius, which survived down to the late Republic, the clan-based names are obvious. All 15 of the rural tribes associated with Servius Tullius carry the names of known clans, as well as 16 of the 17 created before the start of the fourth century (only Clustumina, evidently derived from Crustumerium and created in 495, does not). Thus, down to at least the reorganization of Rome's tribes in the 240s, even if we assume that Polybius' description of the levy is at least indicative of actual norms, the legion would have been mobilized based largely on clan affiliation. The power of *imperium*, which military leaders like kings, dictators, praetors, and consuls wielded, was clearly derived from the power of the *paterfamilias*. It largely mirrored the powers, responsibilities, and obligations that a family head had over the members of his *gens* and, even in later periods, was understood to operate within that same realm. Famously, in 213 Quintus Fabius Maximus Cunctator approached his son, Quintus Fabius Maximus, who happened to be consul at that time, and there was a tension over whether the authority of the *paterfamilias* trumped the *imperium* of the consul or not.[46] In the end, the *imperium* of the consul was deemed to be superior, but they were evidently thought to have functioned within a similar realm. Even the subdivisions of the Roman legion, from its maniples or columns and subunits, seem to look like clan-based units. They evidently operated independently, with locally selected commanders. In fact, the clear similarities between these citizen units and the locally raised and led allied units are marked. So, despite the emphasis on state-based structures, the underlying systems were largely clan-based, at least down to the middle of the third century.

In addition, virtually all of our evidence outside of the explicit testimony of our ancient literary sources suggests that warfare in Italy was dominated by clans and not states down to at least the third century—and indeed possibly longer. We can see this in the use and burial of military equipment in archaic contexts, which seemed to form a vitally important part of clan-based displays and rituals. It is well established that individual soldiers supplied their own military equipment down to the late Republic, but the implications of this have not often been explored in detail.[47] Military equipment was a family investment. It was part of the family's wealth and property, was acquired through family connections (likely commissioned from a craftsperson, at least down to the fourth century), and evidently formed an important part of a family's status. It was placed in the burials of deceased family members, dedicated at shrines, and captured arms and armor were displayed outside of private houses. This equipment was not strictly, or even primarily, associated with the state. It was deeply personal and symbolized the status of both the individual and their family. Although certain classes in the Servian Constitution were associated with panoplies, this was evidently more descriptive than prescriptive. While there may have been some social pressure to conform to certain norms, soldiers would have shown up equipped with whatever their family owned. It is also likely that these

Appendix

families used this equipment outside of the Roman military system. The military equipment did not stay in a locked cabinet, waiting for the man of the house to be called up through the *dilectus*. Low-level violence and raiding were common throughout Italy, and it is likely that this equipment saw regular use in personal and clan-based conflicts, in addition to state-based warfare. Even our literary sources, which emphasize the state-based nature of things, record quite a few instances of clan-based military actions. The so-called "private war" between the Fabii and the community of Veii in the 470s is perhaps the most famous, whereby a single clan evidently led a relatively successful campaign against a major community for several years until suffering a major defeat at the Cremera River in 477. But beyond this, we have quite a bit of evidence for private warfare in early Rome—from the mythical raiding of Romulus and Remus, to the inscription on the Lapis Satricanus seemingly discussing the private warband of a Poplios Valesios (possibly the late sixth-century Roman politician Publicola), to the attack on Rome by Appius Herdonius and his followers in 460. While there seems to be slightly less of this sort of activity the later we get, inscriptions like that of Caso Cantouios, dated to ca. 300 and describing the victories of a Marsic clan chief and his allies against various local communities, suggest that private warbands were still active in the region as late as the start of the third century.[48]

Further, and perhaps most strikingly, when one looks beyond the detailed structural digressions of our sources, the way the early Roman army seems to behave is much more aligned with clan-based warfare than it is with a state-based ethos. Scholars have often puzzled over the nature of Roman warfare during the regal period and early Republic, because despite the fact that Rome was evidently a large, powerful community that engaged in almost annual conflicts, Roman warfare seems to have been incredibly ineffective—at least if one assumes that the Romans sought to conquer and control. For much of the sixth and fifth centuries, and indeed the fourth and third, the Romans fought wars against a wide range of communities and people, almost every year, many seemingly much weaker and smaller than they were, but emerged with very few long-term gains to show for it. This issue was seemingly recognized by the authors of our ancient sources, who chalked it up to both internal

Appendix

disagreements between the patricians and the plebeians, and the nascent nature of the Roman state, which was still developing the laws and systems needed to take advantage of its power. There may be some truth in this. However, a key feature that modern scholarship has begun to recognize is that Roman warfare may have actually been quite successful during this period, but was simply focused on the short-term goals of individual leaders. Clan-based, federated armies in the regal and early Republican periods all seem to have been primarily focused on raiding for portable wealth, despite their nominal association with Rome. Control of land seems to have only become a focus of warfare toward the end of the fifth century, and a real focal point of Italian warfare in the fourth century, although even there it is not clear how truly communal this was.[49] Indeed, even after this period, and down into the third century, raiding for portable wealth remained an important goal of Roman warfare and may have even defined major conflicts like the Samnite Wars and the First Punic War. These wars may have lasted so long, not because the Romans couldn't finish them, but because they didn't want to. There were still spoils to be had.

CONCLUSIONS

Pulling these various threads of argument and evidence together is a difficult task, and there is not a single, universally agreed-upon model of the early Roman army, nor is there consensus among modern scholars on this subject. However, the broad outline of the current debate may give us enough of a foundation to move on. Roman warfare, especially during the Republic, makes the most sense if one understands the state-based systems to be working within a wider context dictated and defined largely by clan-based warfare. The Republic is generally acknowledged to have been a power-sharing arrangement among the clan-based elite of Rome, and the early Roman army was effectively a pooling together of clan-based military resources. The basis of the power and organization always resided firmly in Rome's varied clans and patronage networks. These were preexisting social, political, and military entities that, increasingly regularly,

Appendix

came together to form a federated force, mobilized under the banner of "Rome" and led by one or more of their own clan leaders selected by the group. They also often, and indeed increasingly, augmented this force by incorporating other groups and communities through bonds of military obligation and alliance. This federated force was not the only, or indeed primary, mechanism through which these clans engaged in warfare. Many likely engaged in their own private wars or raiding, and they may have also fought for or as part of other forces—for instance, the armies of the so-called Latin or Etruscan Leagues—or even as mercenaries for other states. But they were also involved in the army of Rome, which is what the authors of our sources were interested in and attempted to chronicle.

This sort of federated model also helps us make sense of the somewhat idiosyncratic nature of the Roman army as described by our sources. Although all of our ancient writers work to present a unified Roman force, they cannot help but talk about its diverse and heterogeneous character. Even in its early iterations, it was full of different troop types with different functions. And when we get the "manipular" armies of Livy and Polybius, the situation is even more complex. The manipular Roman army was supposedly composed of up to 60 different units of varying sizes and compositions, separated from each other, and spread across the battlefield. Each could, and evidently did, operate independently, led by its own commanders, many of whom (including the most important unit commanders) were evidently selected from the units themselves. While some scholars have seen this as the height of Roman bureaucracy and organization—the creation of a complex machine—an alternate, and far simpler explanation is that this merely represents a collection of the various entities that contributed to Rome's military. The Romans did not take a large, undifferentiated body of troops and divide them into maniples and columns and subunits, creating this complex system out of nothing. Instead, the Romans took a collection of existing military groups, which were already broken up into maniples and columns and subunits based on where they had come from and their native organization, and simply put them together on the battlefield together. The Roman state supplied a thin level of military hierarchy over the top, the consuls and

Appendix

perhaps military tribunes (although these also seem to have been tribal in nature), but the vast majority of the organization was determined by the existing divisions of the various clans and communities that supplied the forces. This would help to explain the incredibly confusing number of labels, divisions, and types of officers we find in our descriptions.[50]

Rome's ability to field this federated army was both the key to its success and its greatest weakness. It was a tremendous strength, as it was almost infinitely expandable. Rome did not need to worry about integrating individual soldiers into an existing system and training them to operate in a specific "Roman" manner, but could instead simply bring in new units—as either citizens or allies—and allow them to deploy and operate independently on the battlefield. We can see the clear benefits of this in both the war against Pyrrhus and the Second Punic War, where Rome was able to regularly return to the battlefield with a new army after defeats which would have caused other militaries to crumble. The Roman military system was an empty shell that could be regularly refilled with local units, drawn from Italy's vibrant military context. However, the system was also a weakness, precisely because it relied on a strong, clan-based military context to supply it. Rather than drawing on individuals, it drew upon groups, which came with their own politics and associations which could sometimes work against the interests of the Roman state. While working and fighting together gradually brought these groups closer, the only "Roman" structures and systems were typically those at the top level, while the vast majority of the army was defined and organized based on strong local associations. These Roman systems could be manipulated or broken more easily than those of a *polis* like Athens or a modern nation-state, which were imbued with deeper meaning and symbolism. It is clear that the Romans began to address this, and both gave the Roman state greater symbolic power over time and also worked to break down some of the clan-based affiliations, but the core of the military seems to have remained relatively federated.

TIMELINE OF EARLY ROMAN HISTORY

All dates are BCE.

ca. 1150	Traditional date for Aeneas' arrival in Italy
753	Traditional date for Romulus' foundation of the city of Rome
715	Traditional date for the death of Romulus and the beginning of the reign of Rome's second king, Numa Pompilius
672	Traditional date for the beginning of the reign of Tullus Hostilius
640	Traditional date for the beginning of the reign of Ancus Marcius
616	Traditional date for the beginning of the reign of Tarquinius Priscus
578	Traditional date for the beginning of the reign of Servius Tullius
534	Traditional date for the beginning of the reign of Tarquinius Superbus
509	End of the monarchy and beginning of the Republic
452/1	Creation of the Laws of the Twelve Tables
444	Election of the first consular tribunes
443	Election of the first Roman censors
396	The Roman sack of Veii
390/387	The sack of Rome by the Gauls
376–367	Period of political anarchy, ended with the passing of the Licinio-Sextian reforms (creation of the consulship)

Timeline of Early Roman History

343–341	The First Samnite War*
340–338	The Latin War*
326–304	The Second Samnite War*
298–290	The Third Samnite War*
280–275	The war against Pyrrhus of Epirus
264–241	The First Punic War
218–201	The Second Punic War

* These are modern labels for these conflicts.

ROMAN NAMING CONVENTIONS

IN THE EARLIEST PERIODS of Roman history, Roman men may have only had one or two names (e.g. Romulus or Numa Pompilius). However, by the middle Republic, most Roman men had three, and some of the most illustrious even had four. Each name gave very specific information. The first name was the *praenomen*. The Romans only used about 35 first names regularly for men, and they often related to things like birth order, the month in which they were born, or the specific circumstances of their birth—for instance, Agrippa is often thought to refer to a child born feet-first or breach, while Lucius may refer to a child born at dawn. The second Roman name was the *nomen*. This was arguably the most important name and gave the clan or family. The third name was the *cognomen*. This gave the specific branch of the family they were in. Finally, some Roman men had a fourth name, or *agnomen*, which referenced a specific feat or achievement.

Using the example of Publius Cornelius Scipio Africanus, the great Roman hero of the Second Punic War. Publius is his *praenomen*, or first name. The *nomen* Cornelius indicates that he is part of the Cornelii clan or family. Scipio is his *cognomen*, showing he is part of the Scipio branch of the Cornelli. Africanus is his *agnomen*, which he was given due to his victory over the city of Carthage in North Africa. So, the further one goes in the name, the more specific it is. There would have been millions of men named Publius in Italy, possibly tens of thousands in the Cornelii clan (if we include freedmen), thousands among the Scipiones, but only one Africanus. Taking the full name together, though, and even without the *agnomen*, we can pinpoint people and their families quite specifically.

Roman Naming Conventions

In modern history books, most Romans are referred to by either just their *cognomen* or their *nomen* and *cognomen*. For instance, Gaius Julius Caesar is often referred to as either "Caesar" or "Julius Caesar." Marcus Vipsanius Agrippa, the great friend and commander of Augustus, is typically just referred to as "Agrippa." For those with an *agnomen*, like Publius Cornelius Scipio Africanus, we often use either the *agnomen* on its own (so just "Africanus"), or a combination of the *cognomen* and *agnomen* ("Scipio Africanus").

For women, Romans often just used a feminine form of the family name. So women in the Julii family would just be called "Julia." If there were two sisters, they would have had either *major* ("the older") and *minor* ("the younger") added—so "Julia major" or "Julia minor." If there were more than two sisters, they would have been numbered first, second, third, etc. Rome was a deeply patriarchal society.

GLOSSARY

antipilani	The rear part of the Roman Republican army, as described by Livy (book 8). The word means "behind the standards" and it included the 15 columns made up of units of *triarii*, *rorarii*, and *accensi*.
Apulia	Region in south-eastern Italy, effectively the "heel" of Italy. Traditionally home to the Apulians.
Asia Minor	Region in the eastern Mediterranean that roughly aligns with the modern Republic of Türkiye.
aspis	Large circular shield made out of wood and usually covered in a thin layer of bronze. Commonly associated with the Classical Greek hoplite warrior.
Bruttium	Region in south-western Italy, effectively the "toe" of Italy. Traditionally home to the Bruttians.
capite censi	A Latin phrase that literally means "those counted by head." This refers to the lowest class of Roman citizens who did not have enough wealth to qualify for either taxation or service in the legions.

Glossary

centurion	A military officer in the Roman army. There were 60 in each legion. They were the primary commanders of Roman soldiers in battle, often leading by example, as well as handling logistics and discipline in camp. The name probably derives from the centuriate assembly and system, and not the size of the units they commanded—which never seem to have contained 100 men.
cohort	From the Latin *cohors*, it can be translated as "military unit" in a generic sense. By the late Republic and Empire it seems to take on a more specific definition as a formal part of the legion.
consul	Roman military commander. During the Republic, from at least 367 BCE, there were two consuls elected each year. They were given a grant of *imperium* by the *curiae* and were the primary commanders of Rome's legions.
consular tribune (military tribune with consular power)	A special type of tribune that served as the primary type of military commander in Rome from the 440s to 370s BCE. Somehow connected with Rome's tribal system, although little is known about them.
cuirass	Body armor.
curia (pl. *curiae*)	Archaic divisions of the Roman community. There were 30 of them, supposedly created by Romulus, which could pass very specific laws (including granting *imperium*) and were connected with shrines dotted throughout the city. By the late Republic, the *curiae* were little more than an archaic vestige with limited ritual duties, but they seemed to represent the main administrative units of the early urban community.

Glossary

decurion	A Roman cavalry commander in charge of 10 men.
didrachm	A silver coin worth two *drachmae*. Usually weighing about 8.6 grams, these were minted across the Mediterranean from the fifth century onward. When Rome started using coinage ca. 300, they minted and used didrachms. They kept this currency until the period of the Second Punic War, when they shifted to a new coinage and weight standard known as the *denarius*.
dilectus	The Roman levy, or system for raising a legion of Roman citizen soldiers.
Dionysius of Halicarnassus	A late first-century BCE Roman historian from the city of Halicarnassus in Asia Minor. Was a teacher of rhetoric in Rome and wrote in Greek.
equites	The label given to the Roman cavalry, from *equos* or "horse," as well as a socioeconomic and political class within Roman society. Occupied the level just below the senatorial elite.
Etruria	The region north of Rome, bordered to the west by the sea, and the north and east by the Apennine mountain range. Traditionally home to the Etruscans.
Eutropius	A fourth-century CE Roman historian who summarized all of Roman history, down to his own lifetime. Wrote in Latin.
Faliscan	Refers to the culture associated with a region in central Italy, east of Etruria, and sandwiched between the Etruscans, Sabines, Umbrians, and Latins.

Glossary

formula togatorum	A list of Roman allies and their obligations that was published in Rome by the early second century BCE.
gens	The Latin word for clan or extended family.
greaves	Leg armor, worn over the shins.
hasta	Thrusting spear.
hastati	A class of soldier within the Roman army of the Republic. Despite the name, which is connected with the *hasta*, these men used *pila* and swords. Along with the *principes*, they formed the core of the Republican legion.
Hernici	A people, traditionally based in *Latium adjectum*, to the east of Rome. One of Rome's first conquests and also one of Rome's first allies.
Hesperia	Originally from the Greek, it refers to evening, the setting of the sun, and generally means "western lands." As Italy was to the west of Greece, this could include the Italian peninsula. By the Roman period it was more commonly applied to Spain.
imperium	A grant of power given by the Roman *curiae*. In real terms, it gave certain magistrates the right to command armies, although its actual nature is debated. It is likely it gave generals the effective power of a father, or *paterfamilias*, over the men under his command.
iuniores	Literally means "young men." These were male Roman citizens, aged 17–46, who qualified for military service based on wealth and were therefore able to serve in the legions.
Jupiter	Chief god of the Roman pantheon.
Latium	Region in central Italy, bordered to the north by the Tiber River, the east by the Apennine mountain range, and to the south by

Glossary

	Campania. Location of the city of Rome and home to the Latin people.
Latium adjectum	Means "added Latium" and refers to a strip of land to the east of Latium proper. The people who resided there were often thought of as Latin, but more rugged and pastoral.
lectio senatus	The process for deciding the membership of the Senate.
Livy	A late first-century BCE/early first-century CE Roman historian. Wrote in Latin and had a strong moralizing agenda.
Lucania	Region of southern Italy, roughly in the modern region of Basilicata. Traditionally home to the Lucanians.
maniple	Derived from the Latin word *manipulus*, it literally translates as "handful." Used to refer to a Roman military unit of roughly 120 men.
Marsi	An Italian people from central Italy who were renowned for their military ability. They fought against the Romans in the Samnite Wars and were defeated and integrated ca. 300.
ordo (pl. *ordines*)	A Latin word that means "column" and generally refers to more rigid blocks of troops.
Oscan	A language spoken in central and southern Italy, usually associated with the peoples from the mountainous interior of the peninsula.
paterfamilias	Male head of household. Held tremendous power in Roman society, including being the official owner of all family property and having the power of life or death over individuals in his family.
peltast	A light infantryman, common in Greek and Hellenistic armies of the fourth and third centuries BCE.

Glossary

phalangite	A soldier fighting within a phalanx formation, from the Greek φαλαγγίτης.
phalanx	A dense infantry formation made up of rows and ranks of heavy infantry. Commonly associated with the Classical Greek hoplite warrior and *polis*.
pike	A two-handed thrusting spear.
pilum	Heavy javelin used by both the Romans, along with other central Italian peoples, from the fourth century BCE onward. Seems to have been brought into Italy by Gauls from the north.
polis	A Greek city-state.
Polybius	A mid-second-century BCE Roman historian. Originally from Greece, he lived in Rome as a hostage (in the house of the Scipiones) and wrote in Greek.
Plutarch	A late first-/early second-century CE historian and biographer. Traveled widely and wrote in Greek.
praetor	Roman military commander. The Latin word simply means "leader." This was the name given to the earliest military commanders of the Republic. When the consulship was created in 367 BCE, praetors were placed below them in the social and military hierarchy. They were given a grant of *imperium* by the *curiae* and so could command armies.
principes	A class of soldier within the Roman army of the Republic. They were equipped the same as the *hastati*, but with slightly more and better-quality equipment. Along with the *hastati*, they formed the core of the Republican legion.
quadreme	An oared warship, popular from the fourth century onward, which had both a bronze ram at the front and sails to support longer voyages.

Glossary

	The name means "four oars," and so it is usually thought to have had four banks of oars in contrast to the trireme's three. However, it may simply indicate a slightly larger and faster vessel than the trireme.
quinquereme	Like the quadreme, this was an oared warship, popular from the fourth century onward, which had both a bronze ram at the front and sails to support longer voyages. The name means "five oars," and so it is sometimes thought to have five banks of oars in contrast to the quadreme's notional four and trireme's three. However, this has always seemed somewhat implausible, and it likely indicates a slightly larger and faster vessel than the quadreme and trireme.
Sabinum	A hilly region in north central Italy, east of Etruria. Traditionally home to the Sabines.
sacramentum	The sacred oath that was taken by Roman soldiers as part of the *dilectus* or Roman military levy.
Samnium	A hilly region in south central Italy. Traditionally home to the Samnites.
sarissa	The name of the long spear used by many Hellenistic armies. It can refer to either the two-handed pike used by infantry in the *sarissa*-phalanx or to the lance used by the cavalry.
scutum	This is a Latin word for "shield." It generally seems to refer to the oval or rectangular "body shields" the Romans favored in later periods, in contrast to the circular *aspis*. However, it is not a technical label for a specific shield type and is used to refer to a wide range of shield forms by Roman authors.

Glossary

Senate	The Senate was the collected elite of Rome. In the regal and early Republican periods, it seems to have been reasonably informal and fluid, but by the third century BCE, membership had been formalized. The Senate was the most important entity in Rome, not because of legal powers (they had few officially), but because it contained the most powerful men in the state.
seniores	Literally means "older men." This term would refer to any older men, but in a military context referred to male Roman citizens, aged 47–60, who qualified for military service based on wealth and who sometimes served as military garrisons for communities.
stipendium	Payment to Roman soldiers, supported by *tributum*. It began ca. 400 BCE.
"Struggle of the Orders"	Social and political conflict in Rome between the patrician and the plebeian groups during the fifth and fourth centuries.
Tacitus	A late first-/early second-century CE historian and biographer. Was part of the Roman elite and wrote in Latin.
triarii	A class of soldier within the Roman army of the Republic. They were equipped with long thrusting spears and formed the third and last line of infantry. Traditionally composed of the most experienced Roman soldiers.
tributum	A "war tax" paid by families to the Roman "state" through the tribal structure. It began ca. 400 BCE and ended in the mid-second century.
tribus	Can be translated as "tribe," but is far more specific in a Roman context. Refers to a Roman sociopolitical division.
tribune	A magistrate connected with Rome's tribal system. The "tribunes of the plebs" are the

Glossary

	most famous, but there were several other types of tribunes (military, fiscal, etc.).
trireme	An oared warship, popular from the sixth century onward, which had both a bronze ram at the front and sails to support longer voyages. The name means "three oars," and so it is usually thought to have three banks of oars. Used extensively by Greek and Phoenician navies from the fifth century onward.
turma	A Roman cavalry unit composed of 30 men.
Umbria	A hilly region in north central Italy, east of Etruria. Traditionally home to the Umbrians.
velites	Roman light infantry, usually equipped with javelins and limited armor.
Velleius Paterculus	A late first-century BCE/early first-century CE Roman historian. Was part of the Roman elite and wrote in Latin.
vexilla	The Latin word for "banner," which is commonly used to refer to a discrete unit that can operate independently. In the Republican legion, each *ordo* or column of the *antipilani* contained three *vexilla* or subunits.

FURTHER READING

FOR THE PREFACE

Bradley, G. (2020) *Early Roman Italy to 290 BC: The Origins of Rome and the Rise of the Republic.* Edinburgh: Edinburgh University Press.

Cornell, T. (1995) *The Beginnings of Rome: Italy and Rome from the Bronze Age to the Punic Wars (c. 1000–264 BC).* London: Routledge.

Helm, M. (2021) *Kampf um Mittelitalien: Roms ungerader Weg zur Großmacht.* Hermes Einzelschrift 122. Stuttgart: Franz Steiner Verlag.

Lomas, K. (2018) *The Rise of Rome: From the Iron Age to the Punic Wars.* Cambridge, MA: Harvard University Press.

Raaflaub, K. (1986) *Social Struggles in Archaic Rome: New Perspectives on the Conflict of the Orders.* London: Wiley-Blackwell. Second edition published in 2005.

Terrenato, N. (2021) *The Early Roman Expansion into Italy: Elite Negotiation and Family Agendas.* Cambridge: Cambridge University Press.

FOR CHAPTER 1: THE ORIGINS OF EMPIRE

Armstrong, J. (2016) *War and Society in Early Rome: From Warlords to Generals.* Cambridge: Cambridge University Press.

Bernard, S. (2023) *Historical Culture in Iron Age Italy: Archaeology, History and the Use of the Past, 900–300 BCE.* Oxford: Oxford University Press.

Eckstein, A. (2009) *Mediterranean Anarchy, Interstate War, and the Rise of Rome.* Berkeley: University of California Press.

Flower, H. (2010) *Roman Republics.* Princeton, NJ: Princeton University Press.

Hodos, T. (2020) *The Archaeology of the Mediterranean Iron Age.* Cambridge: Cambridge University Press.

FOR CHAPTER 2: SONS OF VENUS AND MARS

Fox, M. (1996) *Roman Historical Myths: The Regal Period in Augustan Literature.* Oxford: Clarendon Press.

Galinsky, K. (2015) *Aeneas, Sicily, and Rome.* Princeton, NJ: Princeton University Press.

Holloway, R. R. (1994) *The Archaeology of Early Rome and Latium.* London: Routledge.

Hopkins, J. (2016) *The Genesis of Roman Architecture.* New Haven, CT: Yale University Press.

Further Reading

Keegan, P. (2021) *Livy's Women*. London: Routledge.

Malkin, I. (2011) *A Small Greek World: Networks in the Ancient Mediterranean*. Oxford: Oxford University Press.

Wiseman, T. P. (1995) *Remus: A Roman Myth*. Cambridge: Cambridge University Press.

Wiseman, T. P. (2004) *The Myths of Rome*. Exeter: University of Exeter Press.

FOR CHAPTER 3: VEII, THE GAULS, AND ROME REBORN

Bernard, S. (2018) *Building Mid-Republican Rome: Labor, Architecture, and the Urban Economy*. Oxford: Oxford University Press.

Bernard, S., L. Mignone, and D. Padilla Peralta (eds) (2023) *Making the Middle Republic: New Approaches to Rome and Italy, c.400–200 BCE*. Cambridge: Cambridge University Press.

Kagan, D. and G. Viggiano (2013) *Men of Bronze: Hoplite Warfare in Ancient Greece*. Princeton, NJ: Princeton University Press.

Williams, J. (2001) *Beyond the Rubicon: Romans and Gauls in Republican Italy*. Oxford: Clarendon Press.

FOR CHAPTER 4: THE ROMANS, THE LATINS, AND THE SAMNITES

Armstrong, J. and M. Fronda (eds) (2019) *Romans at War: Soldiers, Citizens and Society in the Roman Republic*. London: Routledge.

Dench, E. (1995) *From Barbarians to New Men: Greek, Roman, and Modern Perceptions of Peoples from the Central Apennines*. Oxford: Oxford University Press.

Scopacasa, R. (2015) *Ancient Samnium: Settlement, Culture, and Identity between History and Archaeology*. Oxford: Oxford University Press.

FOR CHAPTER 5: ROME AND THE MEDITERRANEAN

Hoyos, D. (2015) *Mastering the West: Rome and Carthage at War*. Oxford: Oxford University Press.

Kent, P. (2020) *A History of the Pyrrhic War*. London: Routledge.

Lazenby, J. (1996) *The First Punic War*. London: Routledge.

Thonemann, P. (2016) *The Hellenistic Age*. Oxford: Oxford University Press.

FOR EPILOGUE

Isayev, I. (2017) *Migration, Mobility and Place in Ancient Italy*. Cambridge: Cambridge University Press.

Mouritsen, H. (1998) *Italian Unification: A Study in Ancient and Modern Historiography*. London: Institute for Classical Studies.

Smith, C. and L. Yarrow (eds) (2013) *Imperialism, Cultural Politics, and Polybius*. Oxford: Oxford University Press.

FOR THE APPENDIX

Armstrong, J. (2016) *War and Society in Early Rome: From Warlords to Generals*. Cambridge: Cambridge University Press.

Bishop, M. and J. Coulston (2009) *Roman Military Equipment: From the Punic Wars to the Fall of Rome*. Oxford: Oxbow Books.

Goldsworthy, A. (2003) *The Complete Roman Army*. London: Thames & Hudson.

Keppie, L. (1998) *The Making of the Roman Army: From Republic to Empire*. Norman, OK: University of Oklahoma Press.

Further Reading

Lintott, A. (1999) *Violence in Republican Rome*. Oxford: Oxford University Press.

McCall, J. (2001) *The Cavalry of the Roman Republic*. London: Routledge.

Pearson, E. (2021) *Exploring the Mid-Republican Origins of Roman Military Administration: With Stylus and Spear*. London: Routledge.

Roselaar, S. (2010) *Public Land in the Roman Republic: A Social and Economic History of* Ager Publicus *in Italy, 396–89 BC*. Oxford: Oxford University Press.

Smith, C. J. (2006) *The Roman Clan: The* Gens *from Ancient Ideology to Modern Anthropology*. Cambridge: Cambridge University Press.

NOTES

Any works not listed in full below can be found in Further Reading.

NOTES FOR CHAPTER 1

1. Livy 8.7–10.

2. This model is often referred to as "bricolage" and has been championed most notably by Nicola Terrenato. See particularly N. Terrenato (1998), "The Romanization of Italy: Global Acculturation or Cultural Bricolage?," *Theoretical Roman Archaeology Journal* 97: 20–7; and more recently N. Terrenato (2023), "The Paradox of Innovation in Conservative Societies: Cultural Self-Consistency and Bricolage in Iron Age Central Italy," in J. Armstrong and A. Rhodes-Schroder (eds), *Adoption, Adaption, and Innovation in Pre-Roman Italy: Paradigms for Cultural Change*, 33–46 (Turnhout, BE: Brepols).

NOTES FOR CHAPTER 2

1. Vergil, *The Aeneid* 6.752–853.

2. For a more in-depth discussion of these ideas, see Fox (1996).

3. See particularly P. Wiseman (1995), *Remus* (Exeter: University of Exeter Press); and (2004), *The Myths of Rome* (Exeter: University of Exeter Press).

4. The literature on Aeneas is truly vast, with much of it focused on Virgil's famous epic poem *The Aeneid*. For a discussion of the myth in a slightly broader and more historical context, see Galinsky (2015).

5. The seemingly tenuous connection between these two heroes, linked by the so-called "kings of Alba Longa," has caused historians, both ancient and modern, quite a bit of trouble. See A. Grandazzi (2008), *Alba Longa, histoire d'une légende. Recherches sur l'archéologie, la religion, les traditions de l'ancien Latium* (Rome: École française), for a full outline of the evidence and some compelling interpretations.

6. For more in-depth summaries, see the relevant sections in K. Lomas (2018) and G. Bradley (2020).

7. The exact nature of the power-sharing arrangement, and particularly the ways in which the elite families shared power with the wider population of the community, is still contested. H. Mouritsen (2017), *Politics in the Roman Republic. Key Themes in Ancient History* (Cambridge: Cambridge University Press) provides some excellent discussion of the wider debate, although focused on the late Republic. For the early Republic, see Bradley (2020).

8. Plutarch, *Life of Camillus* 1.1, trans. Perrin.

Notes

9. It is possible that Aeneas was initially tied more closely to the site of Rome, as suggested by some early Greek writers like Hellanicus of Lesbos and Damastes of Sigeum, who both wrote in the fifth century. However, by the time of writers like Fabius Pictor, in the late third century, this was not the case. It has been suggested that Aeneas and his lineage's shift toward the (possibly mythical) community of Alba Longa may have been a conscious move to "Latinize" this hero. Alternatively, this may simply represent two different traditions, with Aeneas' close association with Rome being more common outside of Italy, while his Latin (and Alban) connections were more popular within central Italy itself. See Grandazzi (2008) for discussion of this wider debate.

10. Plutarch, *Life of Numa* 20.2.

11. RRC stands for "Roman Republican Coinage," which is the two-volume catalogue of Roman coinage from the Republic compiled by Micheal Crawford and published in 1974. Crawford's catalogue numbers represent the dominant way of referring to specific coin issues from the Roman Republic in modern scholarship.

12. Homer, *Iliad* 20.291–340.

13. These figures and their stories are commonly grouped together under the label "*Nostoi*," which means "the Returns" and refers to the return of the various Greek heroes home after the war, although it also often includes the wider journeys of "heroes" during this period. See Hornblower and Biffis's (2018) edited collection, *The Returning Hero: Nostoi and Traditions of Mediterranean Settlement* (Oxford: Oxford University Press), for recent discussion.

14. See Galinsky (2015) for a more detailed discussion.

15. Thucydides 6.2.3. As will be noted later, Cicero (*In Verrem* 4.33) evidently thought Segesta was founded by Aeneas, although we do not know how early this particular story was circulating and whether it was the basis of their fifth-century claim with Athens.

16. Dionysius of Halicarnassus, *Roman Antiquities* 1.72.2.

17. The terracotta statuette is from Veii (500–450), and now in the Museo Nazionale Etrusco di Villa Giulia, Rome (Inv. 40272) LIMC 44268. The intaglio is now in the Bibliothèque Nationale, Paris (de Luynes collection, Inv. 276). See Galinsky (2015) for discussion.

18. These are collected in the *Lexicon Iconographicum Mythologiae Classicae* (*LIMC*).

19. For a summary of the site, see Ross Holloway's description in his (1994) *The Archaeology of Early Rome and Latium* (London: Routledge).

20. The bibliography on this subject is vast, but see Galinsky (2015) for a relatively recent summary.

21. Cicero, *In Verrem* 4.33.

22. Wiseman's work, and especially his (1995) *Remus: A Roman Myth*, has been foundational in this discussion.

23. Ethnicity is obviously a complex topic. For a broad discussion, see J. Mcinerney (2012), *A Companion to Ethnicity in the Ancient Mediterranean* (London: Wiley-Blackwell). For the close connection between family and ethnicity in the ancient (and especially Roman) world, see E. Gruen (2020), *Ethnicity in the Ancient World—Did It Matter?* (Berlin and Boston: De Gruyter).

24. A.-M. Bietti Sestieri's (1994) work at the site of Osteria Dell'Osa (*The Iron Age Community of Osteria dell'Osa: A Study of Socio-political Development in Central Tyrrhenian Italy* [Cambridge: Cambridge University Press]), near Rome, has been particularly important in helping us understand central Italy's early clans.

25. Livy 1.4.1.

26. Dionysius of Halicarnassus, *Roman Antiquities* 1.77, trans. Cary.

27. Livy 1.7.

Notes

28. Ancient religion is obviously complex, and a detailed discussion is beyond the confines of this book, but for some excellent discussion of more detailed concepts see the works of Jörg Rüpke—particularly, for an excellent and accessible recent work, his (2020) *Pantheon: A New History of Roman Religion* (Princeton, NJ: Princeton University Press).

29. For an excellent and accessible summary of recent research and directions on this topic, see Greg Woolf's (2020), *The Life and Death of Ancient Cities: A Natural History* (Oxford: Oxford University Press).

30. See Manning's (2020), *The Open Sea: The Economic Life of the Ancient Mediterranean World from the Iron Age to the Rise of Rome* (Princeton, NJ: Princeton University Press) for a discussion of these principles.

31. Livy 1.9–13.

32. Livy 1.9–13; Dionysius of Halicarnassus, *Roman Antiquities* 2.7–10; Plutarch, *Life of Romulus* 14. Our earliest evidence for the tribes of Romulus actually comes from Cicero (*De republica* 2.14), and the evidence for them is far from secure. Like so many bits of early Roman history, there is a high likelihood that this early structure is largely based on later reconstruction. See J. Richardson (2022), "Varro and the Romulean Tribes," *Classical Philology* 117: 724–35, for discussion.

33. A. Momigliano (1963), "An Interim Report on the Origins of Rome," *Journal of Roman Studies* 53: 109.

34. Livy 1.13; Dionysius of Halicarnassus, *Roman Antiquities* 2.13; Varro, *Lingua Latina* 3.89.1; Plutarch, *Life of Romulus* 13.

35. Varro, *Lingua Latina* 5.91.

36. Livy 1.16.

37. Livy 1.18; Plutarch, *Life of Numa* 1.1.

38. Livy 40.29; Plutarch, *Life of Numa* 22.

39. Livy 1.19.1, trans. Foster.

40. Plutarch, *Life of Numa* 21.

41. Livy 1.22.

42. Livy 1.29–30.

43. See particularly Malkin (2011) and L. Donnellan et al. (2016), *Conceptualising Early Colonisation* (Turnhout, BE: Brepols).

44. See Hopkins (2016).

45. It must be noted that the *equites* were not strictly a military unit. While they did seem to have military duties, the group also represented the community's social, political, and economic elite, occupying an important position beneath the Senate.

46. L. R. Taylor (1960), *The Voting Districts of the Roman Republic: The Thirty-Five Urban and Rural Tribes* (Rome: American Academy in Rome).

47. The *equites* may be the exception. Scholars usually assume they had wealth at least equal to the first class (100,000 *asses*), but they were fundamentally a social class.

48. Livy 1.54; Dionysius of Halicarnassus, *Roman Antiquities* 4.56.

49. Livy 1.58.10. There are two points that probably bear noting here. First, Livy was a man, writing for a male audience, and his characterization of Lucretia in this moment of trauma was clearly written in that context. The attitudes and ideas expressed by the character of Lucretia should be seen as the idealized views of Roman men, and not Lucretia herself. Second, Lucretia was an important example for Livy and one of several important female characters who drive the narrative forward through both their adherence to Roman virtue and personal sacrifice.

50. Tacitus, *Annales* 1.1.

Notes

51. *Imperium* and *auspicium* are incredibly complex and hotly debated topics, even for the better-documented late Republican period. For some useful discussion, however, see Drogula (2015), *Commanders and Command in the Roman Republic and Early Empire* (Chapel Hill: University of North Carolina); and Vervaet (2016), *The High Command in the Roman Republic. The Principle of the* summum imperium auspiciumque *from 509 to 19* BCE (Stuttgart: Franz Steiner Verlag). For the early period in particular, see Armstrong (2016).

52. Cicero (*Epistulae ad Brutum* 1.5.4) indicates that the "patricians" (whatever this group might have been in this early period) managed to establish a monopoly on both *imperium* and *auspicium* in the early Republic. While both powers were gradually opened up to the plebeians by the fourth century, as part of the so-called "Struggle of the Orders," this early monopoly still carried some force, even in Cicero's day, as he claimed that at least *auspcium* reverted to the patricians as a group (*auspicia ad patres redeunt*) if it was ever left vacant.

53. Yet again, we are only scratching the surface of a wide and complex issue. For an overview of the Roman Republic's political systems, Lintott's masterful (1999) work, *The Constitution of the Roman Republic* (Oxford: Oxford University Press), remains an excellent source. See also K.-J. Hölkeskamp (2010) *Reconstructing the Roman Republic: An Ancient Political Culture and Modern Research* (Princeton, NJ: Princeton University Press) for a more thematic approach.

54. For recent discussion of this fascinating figure, see Ronald Ridley's (2023) *Marcus Furius Camillus,* fatalis dux*: A Documentary Study* (Gottingen: Vandenhoeck & Ruprecht).

55. Livy 5.49; Plutarch, *Life of Camillus* 28–9.

56. Diodorus Siculus 14.116.

57. Polybius, *Histories* 2.18.

58. This position was put forward, most famously and extremely, by Georges Dumézil in his (1980) *Camillus: A Study of Indo-European Religion as Roman History* (Berkeley: University of California Press). However, various other versions are also current—see Bruun (2000), "'What Every Man in the Street Used to Know': M. Furius Camillus, Italic Legends, and Roman Historiography," in C. Bruun (ed.), *The Roman Middle Republic: Politics, Religion, and Historiography, c. 400–133 B.C.,* 41–68 (Rome: Institutum Romanum Finlandiae) for discussion and other mythic connections.

59. Scholars have long fretted over this, with some suggesting he is actually standing in for the entire *gens Furia* and the mid-twentieth-century historian Georges Dumézil provocatively suggesting he was actually properly mythic (the personification of the sun god). See G. Dumézil (1980) *Camillus: A Study of Indo-European Religion as Roman History* (Berkeley: University of California Press).

60. Polybius, *The Histories* 6.11.

61. Plutarch, *Life of Camillus* 40.

NOTES FOR CHAPTER 3

1. The origins of "individualism," as a philosophical and political concept, can be traced back to Classical Greece and the works of Greek sophists. However, while the individual and "individuality" were sometimes discussed, it was often through the lens of understanding one's place within society. As a result, the current understanding of individualism, emphasizing the centrality and worth of the individual, is generally accepted as a modern concept—see Morrison (1995), *Marx, Durkheim, Weber. Formations of Modern Social Thought* (London: Sage) for discussion. The ancient world, in contrast to modern society, has long been seen as based on the collective—see, famously, Fustel De Coulanges (1864), *La cité antique: étude sur le culte, le droit, les institutions de la Grèce et de Rome* (Paris: Durand). While this collective basis has been questioned and explored over the years, the role and importance of individuals in ancient society and politics—and particularly Roman society and politics—is still

Notes

rightly understood to be very different from today. See also Trapp (2007), *Philosophy in the Roman Empire. Ethics, Politics and Society* (Aldershot: Ashgate).

2. See Smith (2006) for a detailed discussion of the Roman clan. Perhaps surprisingly, there are some interesting plausible parallels here with medieval Scottish clans as well—see A. Cathcart (2011), *Kinship and Clientage: Highland Clanship, 1451–1609* (Leiden: Brill) for discussion.

3. This term was coined by Nicola Terrenato to refer to this phenomenon—see Terrenato (2019).

4. The "Crisis of the Fifth Century" is a scholarly idea that came to prominence in the 1980s in an attempt to explain Rome's lack of growth during the century. It usually involved increased attacks from tribes from the mountainous interior, coupled with a changing relationship with the Greeks of the eastern Mediterranean. For a recent reappraisal, see Smith (2017), "The Fifth-Century Crisis," *Antichthon* 51: 227–50.

5. See both Sheira Cohen and Christian Heitz's chapters in Armstrong and Cohen (2022), *Production, Trade, and Connectivity in Pre-Roman Italy* (London: Routledge), as well as Marijke Gnade's excellent chapter on the Volscians and Hernicians in G. Bradley and G. Farney (2017), *The Peoples of Ancient Italy* (Berlin: De Gruyter).

6. See F. Fulminante (2014), *The Urbanization of Rome and Latium Vetus: From the Bronze Age to the Archaic Era* (Cambridge: Cambridge University Press) for discussion of the archaeological evidence.

7. See J. Armstrong (2008), "Breaking the Rules: Recruitment in the Early Roman Army (509–450 BC)," in E. Bragg et al. (eds), *Beyond the Battlefields: New Perspectives on Warfare and Society in the Graeco-Roman World*, 47–66 (Cambridge: Cambridge Scholars Press) for a discussion of these instances.

8. For a discussion of these developments, see Armstrong (2016).

9. It should be noted that there would have been a similar period of pastoral movement in the autumn, although this would have coincided with the busy harvest season and so seems to have been more peaceful—hinting that the instigators in this violence were in fact the farmers and communities which sat along this pastoral route and not the pastoralists themselves.

10. Seth Bernard's (2018) *Building Mid-Republican Rome: Labor, Architecture, and the Urban Economy* (Oxford: Oxford University Press) has an excellent chapter covering Rome from the sack of Veii to the Gallic sack, which is well worth a read for those interested in the details of this period.

11. Veii is a fascinating community and an amazing archaeological site. For an overview of the current state of research on it, see Tabolli and Cerasuolo's excellent (2019) volume, *Veii* (Austin: University of Texas Press). For an exploration of the sack of the city, see J. Crooks (2019), "Irregular recruitment and the siege of Veii," in J. Armstrong and M. Trundle (eds), *Brill's Companion to Sieges in the Ancient Mediterranean*, 217–40 (Leiden: Brill).

12. Williams's (2001) *Beyond the Rubicon: Romans and Gauls in Republican Italy* (Oxford: Clarendon Press) offers an excellent account of the lead-up and sack of the city by the Gauls.

13. Much of this discussion builds upon recent reinterpretations of ancient cities and communities. For recent work on this area, see Zamboni et al. (2020), *Crossing the Alps: Early Urbanism between Northern Italy and Central Europe (900–400 BC)* (Leiden: Sidestone Press); and Cowley et al. (2019), *Rural Settlement: Relating Buildings, Landscape, and People in the European Iron Age* (Leiden: Sidestone Press). For recent reinterpretations of Italy in particular, see Robinson (2014), *Papers on Italian Urbanism in the First Millennium B.C. JRA Supplementary Series* 97 (Portsmouth, RI: Journal of Roman Archaeology). See Hopkins (2016) for Rome specifically.

14. See Terrenato (2019) for more expansive discussion.

15. For an overview, see Williams (2001) and Armstrong (2016). For historiography, see Richardson (2012), *The Fabii and the Gauls: Studies in Historical Thought and Historiography in Republican Rome* (Stuttgart: Franz Steiner Verlag). For Livy's account in particular, see Ogilvie (1965), *A Commentary*

Notes

on Livy, Books 1–5 (Oxford: Clarendon Press); and Oakley (1997–2005), *A Commentary on Livy, Books VI–X* (Oxford: Clarendon Press). For the archaeological evidence, or possible lack thereof, see Delfino (2009), "L'incendio gallico: tra mito storiografico e realtà storic," *Mediterraneo Antico* 12: 339–60, and the summary in Bernard (2018).

16. Livy 5.36.

17. Justin 20.5.

18. Traditionally, see Griffith (1935), *The Mercenaries of the Hellenistic World* (Cambridge: Cambridge University Press). More recently, see Tagliamonte (1994), *I Figli di Marte: mobilità, mercenari e mercenariato Italici in Magna Grecia e Sicilia* (Rome: Bretschneider).

19. In 390 Rome had six consular tribunes—three were members of the Fabii, joined by members of the Sulpicii, Servilii, and Cornelii. At the battle of the River Allia against the Gauls, Plutarch (*Life of Camillus* 1.8.4) suggests the Roman force numbered 40,000 (against a comparable number of Gauls), Dionysius (*Roman Antiquities* 13.12) suggests roughly 35,000 Romans (four full legions with allies), and Diodorus (14.114) suggests 24,000.

20. This is a contested etymology for *moneta* on a number of levels. The link to the Latin verb *monere* ('to warn') is strongly implied by Livy's narrative for the Gallic sack, but not explicitly given. Cicero also supports this etymology (Cicero, *De Divitatione* 1.101), but claims the original warning was in reference to an earlier earthquake and not the attack by the Gauls. However, the most significant issue is that Juno Moneta was evidently worshipped outside of Rome and so not directly linked to the city or hill at all. This hints there may be another origin for the label that the Romans conveniently ignored.

21. Plutarch, *Life of Camillus* 22.3.

22. Livy 5.39; Plutarch, *Life of Camillus* 21.

23. Livy 4.59–60.

24. These "campaigning seasons" were sometimes quite short as well. The longest Spartan invasion of the Peloponnesian War was in 430 BCE and lasted 40 days. The shortest, in 425 BCE, was only 15 days.

25. See Armstrong (2023), "Early Roman Spoils: From the Regal Period to 390 BCE," in M. Helm and S. Roselaar (eds), *Spoils in the Roman Republic: Boon and Bane*, 75–100 (Berlin: Franz Steiner Verlag) for a more detailed discussion.

26. This relationship was so personal and direct that the name for it was *manubiae*, derived from the Latin word *manus* or "hand," and seemingly meaning "passing through the hands of the general."

27. Pliny, *Natural History* 33.16.

28. The early fourth century is recognized as an important and pivotal time in the growth of the community, visible particularly in the attention paid by elites and elite families to the urban community of Rome. For an excellent discussion of the current state of research on this period and area, see Bernard, Mignone, and Padilla Peralta's (2023) *Making the Middle Republic: New Approaches to Rome and Italy, c.400–200 BCE* (Cambridge: Cambridge University Press).

29. Livy 6.35–42. See Drogula (2015) for a discussion of both this specific incident and the wider principles of command in this period.

30. The 10 years of political anarchy, reported by our sources, hints at the seeming importance of the measures, but is likely a literary fabrication—a combination of a nice literary device, linking it to important moments like the sacks of Veii and Troy, and a convenient way of bringing the Roman historical timeline in line with Greek time-keeping (they were evidently slightly out of sync).

31. It must be acknowledged that our understanding of the consulship in 367 is complicated by two factors. First, although Livy admits that the highest office in Rome at the start of the Republic was called the praetorship, he assumed that this office was fundamentally the same as the later consulship.

Notes

Thus, for Livy, the Licinio-Sextian reforms simply reintroduced the old office (which had fallen out of favor, increasingly replaced by the consular tribunate). This seems somewhat inconsequential and does not warrant the fuss that the reforms evidently provoked. He, therefore, suggests that the real issue was that the tribunes wanted to require that one of the consuls must be plebeian. This, however, is contradicted by his own later narrative, as this requirement was evidently not brought in until the passing of another law, the *lex Genucia*, several decades later. So, in short, our sources seem a bit confused and contradictory, which means we are also left a bit confused.

32. *Imperium*, even in the middle and late Republic, was granted by the *curiae*, and seems to reflect a very special relationship. Rather than simply representing an elected leader, a general imbued with *imperium* took on the role of both *pater* ("father") and patron.

33. This is not to say, however, that this sort of movement did not have a cost. There would almost certainly have been an economic cost, in terms of lost resources and investment, and very possibly a social and emotional cost, due to a possible severing of local connections and bonds.

NOTES FOR CHAPTER 4

1. On the early coinage, see Kroll and others in William Metcalf's (2012), *The Oxford Handbook of Greek and Roman Coinage* (Oxford: Oxford University Press). For its role and importance in mercenary/military expenditure, see Callataÿ (2021), "Money and Its Ideas: State Control and Military Expenses," in S. Krmnicek (ed.), *A Cultural History of Money in Antiquity*, 43–62 (London: Bloomsbury).

2. As Lily Ross Taylor (1957), "The Centuriate Assembly before and after the Reform," *The American Journal of Philology* 78: 337–54, suggested more than 60 years ago, Rome's centuriate system must have been based on the tribal structure initially. The census would have typically occurred by tribe and would have created the various centuriate classes within each tribe.

3. As an aside, scholars have often wondered about the origin of the title "consul." It is typically understood to be derived from the Latin words *con* (meaning "with") and *sul* (from *salio* meaning "to go" or "move") and so means "those who go together." This is often argued to refer to the collegial nature of the consuls, as there were traditionally always two. However, there are many collegial magistracies in Rome, so it is not clear why this one might have been singled out in this way. One other option may therefore be that the two things going together are not the consuls themselves, but the powers of the tribes and *curiae*.

4. The fourth century has long been known for the creation of the so-called "patricio-plebeian state"—a term made famous by Ferenczy's seminal work from 1976 (*From the Patrician State to the Patricio-Plebeian State* [Budapest: Akadémiai Kiadó]). This development was traditionally thought to be the result of internal political pressure brought by a stable plebeian population but is likely the result of an expanding—and increasingly powerful—group of new, plebeian clans brought in by Roman expansion.

5. This, arguably, was the beginnings of what would be known as the "*pax Romana*" or "Roman peace" in later centuries. Ironically, the "Roman peace" was never particularly peaceful overall. In fact, it often led to increased warfare on the grand scale. The "peace" referred to here was an "internal peace," between the families associated with Rome.

6. Gianluca Tagliamonte's (1994) book, *Figli di Marte: mobilità, mercenari e mercenariato Italici in Magna Grecia e Sicilia* (Rome: Bretschneider), remains the key work on the subject.

7. Almost all of the traditional labels for these wars (e.g. the "First Samnite War," "Second Samnite War," and "Latin War") are modern. Our ancient sources did not label or divide up the conflicts in this way, and it is likely that they are all far more connected than the modern labels imply.

8. For an accessible discussion of the archaeology of Latium, see Holloway (1994).

Notes

9. Andreas Alföldi's 1965 *Early Rome and the Latins* (Ann Arbor: University of Michigan Press) remains one of the better compilations of the surviving literary evidence for this group—although Francesca Fulminante's chapter in Bradley and Farney's (2017) *The Peoples of Ancient Italy* represents an important update, for the archaeology in particular.

10. It is likely that the number 30 is more symbolic than actual and just means "all." We can see this with the number of central Italian structures that are nominally divided into 30—including the Roman *curiae*, the *turmae* of the cavalry, etc.

11. As with so many aspects of early Roman history, our evidence for this period comes from much later sources. As a result, it is likely that significant parts of the Roman and Latin relationship, as preserved in our sources, were shaped by later perceptions—and particularly by the events surrounding the Social War of the first century. During the first century, the Romans seem to have used the old, traditional relationship between "the Romans" and "the Latins" as part of their model for both the wider integration of Italian peoples into the Roman citizen body and for the categorization of other non-Romans in this context. A. N. Sherwin-White's (1939) *The Roman Citizenship* (Oxford: Oxford University Press) remains the standard on this topic, although many of his positions have been nuanced over the years.

12. Dionysius of Halicarnassus, *Roman Antiquities* 1.73. Scholars have long suggested that this myth relates to the history and politics of the fourth century, although the exact context and meaning are much debated. By far the most common interpretation is that it reflects the "Struggle of the Orders," although it is difficult to see the connection beyond the concept of feuding siblings. See Wiseman (1995) for a discussion of this interpretation.

13. It must be noted that Velitrae and Antium are somewhat difficult cases here, as Velitrae was treated quite harshly otherwise and it is not entirely clear what type of citizenship Antium was given from Livy's report—he merely notes *civitas data*.

14. Livy (8.14) suggests this was because they could not be trusted and had allied with Gauls.

15. The so-called *socii ac nominia Latini*, or "allies and those named Latins" (Livy 41.8). For instance, we find the label *socii Latini nominis* ("allies of the Latin name" or "Latin allies") in a *lex agraria* ("agrarian law") of 111.

16. Livy 1.9.1–3, trans. Foster.

17. Dionysius of Halicarnassus, *Roman Antiquities* 8.69.

18. Dionysius of Halicarnassus, *Roman Antiquities* 6.95.

19. Livy 6.10.

20. For a more complete discussion, see Baronowski (1984), "The '*Formula Togatorum*,'" *Historia: Zeitschrift Für Alte Geschichte* 33(2): 248–52.

21. Polybius (*The Histories* 6.21), writing in the second century, also seems to support the idea of an allied obligation to fight on demand for the Romans, and Livy (27.10) indicates that he thought this was in place, and determined by the formula or list, as early as 209.

22. Livy (6.9) suggests we should think about this as a "reacquisition," as he indicated the community had previously been allied to Rome, was "captured by the Etruscans," and then the Romans recaptured it.

23. Frustratingly, we have few explicit mentions in our sources of the various treaties or alliances made by the Romans in this period—and what we do have raises more questions than answers. For instance, we know the Romans granted a treaty to the Etruscan community of Caere in 353, negotiated by the dictator Manlius Torquatus (Livy 7.19–20). This was a rather peculiar treaty, though, which lasted for 100 years and seems to have represented a specific classification—sometimes called the "Caerite franchise" by modern scholars, as it seems to sit awkwardly somewhere between full citizenship and allied status. Our sources are muddled on whether this was a good thing or a bad

Notes

thing, but the unique position of Caere was clearly recognized, as the phrase "to be put on the Caeretan list" became a proverbial saying that referred to the disenfranchising of a Roman citizen by the Augustan period. It evidently became synonymous with the phrase *aerarium facere*, or "to be made an *aerarius*," which was a class of Roman citizens not included in the tribal organization and so lacking political rights.

24. Livy 23.17.

25. For the named cohorts in this period, see Livy 28.45, 41.1–4, 44.40.

26. See Stewart (2017), "Citizenship as a Reward or Punishment? Factoring Language into the Latin Settlement," *Antichthon* 51: 186–201, for discussion.

27. See Terrenato (1998), "*Tam Firmum Municipium*: The Romanization of Volaterrae and Its Cultural Implications," *Journal of Roman Studies* 88: 94–114, for the specific example of Volterrae.

28. Livy 8.14.

29. Livy 7.16.

30. Livy 7.38.

31. Polybius, *The Histories* 3.24.

32. Contrary to popular belief, the Romans actually seem to have had quite a lot of naval interests in this period. We have the *coloniae maritimae* mentioned previously, but also Livy (7.26) reported that in 349, Camillus had marched an army down into the Pontine plain of southern Latium to fight against "Greek pirates." Livy does not provide much detail on the action, but the fact that the "pirates" were seaborne once again hints at this naval interest and also limits the number of options—as, despite featuring a long coastline, the number of safe harbors on the Tyrrhenian coast is limited. There is a strong likelihood that this action occurred around Antium in southern Latium.

33. The Samnites seem to have had a particular, shared tribal structure, whereby *vici* or villages were grouped together into *pagi*, or regions, which were in turn organized into *touto* or tribes. See Scopacasa (2015), *Ancient Samnium: Settlement, Culture, and Identity between History and Archaeology* (Oxford: Oxford University Press), for discussion. However, this does not mean they identified as a single group. Indeed, it has been argued that the very concept of "the Samnites" as a distinct people is perhaps a later, artificial, Roman construct—a way for the Romans to conveniently group and label a rather complex collection of opponents. On this, see Emma Dench's excellent (1995) book, *From Barbarians to New Men: Greek, Roman, and Modern Perceptions of Peoples from the Central Apennines* (Oxford: Oxford University Press).

34. This is certainly not the traditional interpretation (cf. Polybius, *The Histories* 36.4.1–3), which assumes that citizenship was always an honor and privilege. However, given the Roman penchant for making defeated enemies citizens, and the obligation which it evidently placed on them, this may be the most appropriate way to look at it.

35. This detail is offered by Roman historian Velleius Paterculus (1.14).

36. E. T. Salmon's 1967 work, *Samnium and the Samnites* (Cambridge: Cambridge University Press) has long shaped scholarly opinion on this matter, and he argued for a highly strategic Roman approach to the region that saw the Romans slowly push into Samnium using military colonies before ultimately provoking the "Second Samnite War." This highly organized approach to warfare in the region is slowly being reevaluated.

37. On triumphs in this period, see Rich (2014), "The Triumph in the Roman Republic: Frequency, Fluctuation and Policy," in C. Lange and F. Vervaet (eds), *The Roman Republican Triumph: Beyond the Spectacle*, 197–258 (Rome: Edizioni Quasar).

38. Livy 9.2–6.

39. See Richardson (2017), "The Development of the Treaty-Making Rituals of the Romans," *Hermes* 145: 250–74, for discussion.

Notes

40. Livy 9.10–11.

41. Livy 9.45.

42. It must be admitted that these divisions are not entirely modern. For instance, the fourth-century CE scholar Eutropius offers 290 as the end of the Second Samnite War. He notes (2.9.3) that they (Publius Cornelius Rufinus and Manius Curius Dentatus, consuls for 290) brought the war to an end; a war that had lasted for forty-nine years. So we have some attempts to draw divisions in antiquity. However, Eutropius clearly elided the so-called "Second" and "Third" wars, highlighting the somewhat arbitrary nature of this division, and indeed his understanding that these two wars were actually one.

43. Livy 10.11–12.

44. Livy 10.17.11–12.

45. van Sickle (1987), "The Elogia of the Cornelii Scipiones and the Origin of Epigram at Rome," *The American Journal of Philology* 108: 41–55.

46. Livy 10.26–9.

47. Livy (10.30.5–7) does note that his sources were conflicted on this point, although he suggests this was due to their desire to exaggerate the size and significance of the battle. He says: "some writers have so exaggerated as to over-shoot the credible, and have written that in the army of the enemy—including, of course, the Umbrians and Etruscans, for these, too, were present in the battle—there were 600,000 infantry, 46,000 cavalry, and 1,000 chariots; and, to enlarge in like manner the forces of the Romans, they add to the consuls as a commander the proconsul Lucius Volumnius, and his army to their legions."

48. The year 292 is when Livy concluded his tenth book, which is the last book of his history that survives until we get to book 20, which picks up the narrative in the year 240.

49. Eutropius 2.9.3.

50. These summaries are known as the *periochae* and may have been compiled as early as the fourth century CE.

51. Interestingly, none of these communities are located near the traditional region of Samnium. Rather, they are in the rough region of Sentinum, in north central Italy, near the Adriatic coast. This again hints that we should take labels like "Samnite" as being quite flexible and fluid in this period.

52. It is worth remembering that Eutropius was writing over 500 years after these events, that Livy had previously mentioned the renewal of a Samnite treaty without it marking the end of hostilities, and that the absence of evidence for triumphs over the Samnites (and others) is not particularly compelling, as this period represents a major gap in our source material more generally. Not only do we lack Livy's full narrative, or any other literary sources, but there is also a gap in the Capitoline Fasti, which records military magistrates. We also have a gap in the *Fasti Triumphales*, which record triumphs, between 291 and 282. Further, a point conveniently overlooked by many is that in the summary of Livy's book 12, which covers the years down to 280, we find still more warfare against the Samnites, Etruscans, Lucanians, and Gauls. Indeed, the few other mentions we have for this period, from sources like Pliny (*Natural History* 34.32) all indicate ongoing conflicts of various types throughout the same regions. Rather than ending, the regular conflicts and raiding against the Samnites, Etruscans, and Gauls seem to have continued largely unabated throughout the 280s—although, perhaps, redirected and ever more tightly circumscribed by alliances and extensions of citizenship.

NOTES FOR CHAPTER 5

1. The birth of the "Hellenistic Age" has been a subject of intense scholarship for well over a century, and the bibliography is therefore vast. For relatively recent, and accessible, summaries of the current state of thinking, see the brief introductions to the period in Green's (2007) *The Hellenistic*

254

Notes

Age (New York: Modern Library), and Thonemann's (2016) *The Hellenistic Age* (Oxford: Oxford University Press). For a more detailed account, see Shipley's (2014), *The Greek World after Alexander 323–30 BC* (London: Routledge).

2. Griffith's seminal work from 1935, *The Mercenaries of the Hellenistic World* (Cambridge: Cambridge University Press), remains one of the best collections of evidence for this.

3. This is a vibrant field of study at present, but some key works to see are P. Horden and N. Purcell (2000), *The Corrupting Sea: A Study of Mediterranean History* (Oxford: Oxford University Press); C. Broodbank (2013), *The Making of the Middle Sea: A History of the Mediterranean from the Beginning to the Emergence of the Classical World* (Oxford: Oxford University Press); and T. Hodos (2020), *The Archaeology of the Mediterranean Iron Age* (Cambridge: Cambridge University Press).

4. See Trundle (2004) for an excellent overview of the ancient institution, which was based, first and foremost, on social bonds. See, more recently, Jeffrey Rop (2019), *Greek Military Service in the Ancient Near East, 401–330 BCE* (Cambridge: Cambridge University Press).

5. For wider discussion of this across ancient Mediterranean world, see Armstrong, Pomeroy, and Rosenbloom (2024), *Money, Warfare and Power in the Ancient World: Studies in Honour of Matthew Freeman Trundle* (London: Bloomsbury).

6. L. Reitsema et al. (2022), "The Diverse Genetic Origins of a Classical Period Greek Army," *Proceedings of the National Academy of Sciences* 119(41): e2205272119.

7. Polybius, *The Histories* 5.63–79.

8. See James Tan's work on this subject, and particularly his chapter in Bernard, Mignone, and Padilla Peralta's (2023) *Making the Middle Republic: New Approaches to Rome and Italy, c.400–200 BCE* (Cambridge: Cambridge University Press).

9. Varro, *De lingua Latina* 5.181. This is depicted by the Roman playwright Plautus (*Aulularia* 526).

10. Admittedly, this is not incredibly late in the grand scheme of things. While we have cohesive bureaucracies in both the Persian empire and the Greek *poleis*, the kingdom of Macedon only shows clear evidence of this by the early fourth century.

11. Diodorus Siculus 18.4.2–6.

12. The use of a Greek inscription on this coin is likely because the community that minted it was originally a Greek colony and used Greek for its coinage and inscriptions anyway. However, the use of Greek in Italy was common. Greek was the main language used across the Mediterranean in this period. It enjoyed a similar position and role as English today or French in the eighteenth century (the classic *lingua franca*). Even as late as the second century, Greek was therefore probably the most commonly shared language across the Italian peninsula. Latin only came to dominate later.

13. The idea that the Romans introduced prorogation to keep more effective commanders in the field is not borne out by the evidence and likely represents a later rationalization. At the time, it was almost certainly to allow individual commanders the opportunity to complete the personal war that they had initiated.

14. Appian, *The Samnites* 7.

15. Cassius Dio 9.39.

16. This war frustratingly falls into the lost books of Livy—specifically books 12–14, known only from the later summaries—and so has often sat as a somewhat irregular episode in Rome's early history. Although relatively well attested, most notably in Plutarch's *Life of Pyrrhus* as well as the work of Cassius Dio and in fragments from Appian and Dionysius of Halicarnassus, scholars have struggled to fully integrate it into our broader picture of Roman society and history at this time. The events themselves seem reasonably clear, and indeed the surviving narrative is quite detailed, as one might expect given the period and nature of contemporary literature within the Hellenistic world. The early third century was known for its histories, especially in southern Italy and Sicily, with Timaeus of

255

Notes

Tauromenium (a community on the eastern coast of Sicily) being one of the more famous writers associated with it. We are, therefore, fairly certain that much of our evidence was based on what can be considered "first-hand" accounts. However, our extant accounts all focus on the figure of Pyrrhus, with the Romans representing a somewhat nebulous opponent in his struggle for greatness. On the one hand, this is both useful and fascinating, as we so rarely have this point of view in this period. However, this also makes it much more difficult to integrate into the wider narrative of Roman history. Plutarch's *Life of Pyrrhus* provides a wealth of detail and many fascinating anecdotes and is well worth a read for those interested in the details of this war. See also Kent's (2020) *A History of the Pyrrhic War* (London: Routledge), which provides a useful and detailed summary of events.

17. Many later writers refer to this speech, and it seems like quite a few, from Ennius to Cicero, had copies—see Cicero, *Brutus* 61 and *De senectute* 16.

18. Dionysius of Halicarnassus, *Roman Antiquities* 20.1 gives a detailed breakdown of Pyrrhus' army at this engagement.

19. This figure is given explicitly by Dionysius in his description and seems to fit what we know about the situation.

20. Dionysius of Halicarnassus, *Roman Antiquities* 20.1 .

21. There is likely little benefit in pushing our ancient literary descriptions of these events any further, as the figures and details are, as always, likely indicative at best. That being said, it should be noted that, with this war, we are moving into a new period with slightly more plausible evidence. While we should obviously take the figures and details supplied by the authors of our sources with a dose of skepticism, as some "flexibility" with the facts was allowed by the ancient genre of history, with these events at least we have reached the birth of the "historical period" in Italy, when first-hand accounts would have been available. Indeed, as noted above, the speech by Appius Claudius Caecus that helped initiate this battle was famously recorded for posterity and represented one of the first remembered pieces of narrative prose in Latin. So, although the figures are subject to the usual biases and issues of the genre, they seem to be trying to capture the essence of a real, remembered event.

22. Plutarch, *Life of Pyrrhus* 21.9, trans. Perrin.

23. Plutarch, *Life of Pyrrhus* 24.

24. Orosius 4.2.

25. Dionysius of Halicarnassus, *Roman Antiquities* 20.10–11.

26. In contrast, a fragment of Dionysius (*Roman Antiquities* 20.12) offers vivid details of the Roman victory over Pyrrhus' elephants.

27. Plutarch, *Life of Pyrrhus* 26.2, trans. Perrin.

28. See e.g. Gabrielsen's (1994) *Financing the Athenian Fleet: Public Taxation and Social Relations* (Baltimore: Johns Hopkins University Press) for discussion and examples.

29. For an excellent and detailed account of Rome's conflicts with Carthage, see Dexter Hoyos's (2015) *Mastering the West: Rome and Carthage at War* (Oxford: Oxford University Press).

30. Polybius, *The Histories* 1.7.

31. Polybius, *The Histories* 1.3.

32. For a wide-ranging discussion of the period, sources, and the war's impact, see Hoyos's (2011) *A Companion to the Punic Wars* (Oxford: Blackwell).

33. The death of Regulus is often thought to be mythic, or at least heavily embellished, and the reports of his torture vary. Cicero (*De officiis* 3.99–115) suggests he was starved to death. Augustine (*De civitate Dei* 15) claimed he was put in a narrow box with spikes, forcing him to stay awake and ultimately killing him through lack of sleep.

34. See Royal and Tusa (2020), *The Site of the Battle of the Aegates Islands at the End of the First Punic War: Fieldwork, Analyses and Perspectives, 2005–2015* (Rome: L'Erma di Bretschneider) for one of the more recent summaries of the finds.

Notes

35. For those interested in a more detailed analysis, see Hoyos' (2015), *Mastering the West: Rome and Carthage at War* (Oxford: Oxford University Press) as well as Lazenby's (1996), *The First Punic War* (London: Routledge), which remains an important work.

36. For a useful discussion of ancient military technology, see F. Echeverria (2010), "Weapons, Technological Determinism and Ancient Warfare," in M. Trundle and G. Fagan (eds), *New Perspectives on Ancient Warfare*, 21–56 (Leiden: Brill).

37. Pliny, *Natural History* 33.44.

38. C. Barber (2019) "Uncovering a 'Lost Generation' of the Roman Republic: Demography and the Hannibalic War," in J. Armstrong and M. Fronda (eds), *Romans at War: Soldiers, Citizens, and Society in the Roman Republic*, 154–70 (London: Routledge).

NOTES FOR THE EPILOGUE

1. This may also be connected to the supposed manpower crisis of the late Republic and other social and economic issues. As both recent archaeology and the ability of individual commanders to mobilize thousands of "volunteers" has illustrated, Italy was still full of well-equipped soldiers able to fight in this period. When an attractive war was pitched by a popular leader, there was no manpower shortage. The issue seemed to be a shortage of soldiers who desired to serve the "Roman state."

2. See Wimmer (2012), *Waves of War: Nationalism, State Formation, and Ethnic Exclusion in the Modern World* (Cambridge: Cambridge University Press) for discussion.

NOTES FOR THE APPENDIX

1. Plutarch, *Life of Romulus* 13.1; Livy 1.13; Dionysius of Halicarnassus, *Roman Antiquities* 2.13; Varro, *De lngua Latina* 5.89, 5.91.

2. Smith (2006) offers a relatively recent exploration of the *curiae*.

3. Early Roman cavalry remains a poorly studied subject for the most part, although McCall's (2001), *The Cavalry of the Roman Republic* (London: Routledge) is a good exploration of the group before the Imperial period.

4. Livy 1.30.

5. Livy 1.36; Cicero, *De republica* 2.20.

6. Military equipment formed an important part of elite male burials in archaic Italy, hinting at a highly individual, competitive, and family-based environment. Across the ancient Mediterranean, as warfare becomes more communal in nature, there seems to be a direct correlation between decreasing evidence for it in individual burials and increased evidence for it in public or community-based contexts.

7. The scholarship supporting this line of argument is too vast to list here, but summations can be found in virtually any wider work on the Roman army—see, for example, Keppie's (1998) *The Making of the Roman Army: From Republic to Empire* (Norman: University of Oklahoma Press); and Goldsworthy's (2003) *The Complete Roman Army* (London: Thames & Hudson).

8. Livy 1.43; Dionysius of Halicarnassus, *Roman Antiquities* 4.18.

9. For an early expression, see Meiklejohn (1938), "Roman Strategy and Tactics from 509 to 202 B.C.," *Greece & Rome* 7(21): 170–8. For a recent reassessment, see Rosenstein (2011), "Phalanges in Rome?," in M. Trundle and G. Fagan (eds), *New Perspectives on Ancient Warfare*, 289–303 (Leiden: Brill); and Armstrong (2016).

10. Diodorus Siculus 23.2; Livy 8.8; Dionysius of Halicarnassus, *Roman Antiquities* 4.16; the *Ineditum Vaticanum*. See Armstrong (2016), 111–26, for a detailed discussion.

11. H. van Wees (2004), *Greek Warfare: Myths and Realities* (London: Duckworth).

12. The nature, origin, and evolution of the Greek hoplite phalanx remains hotly debated. For one of the better and more even-handed summaries of the current situation, see Kagan and Viggiano's (2013) *Men of Bronze: Hoplite Warfare in Ancient Greece* (Princeton, NJ: Princeton University Press).

Notes

13. The figure is 11,000 *asses* after the coinage reform of ca. 210. It should be noted, though, that while rough lumps of bronze are common in the archaeological record and evidently served as a type of currency in early Italy, we should not imagine every citizen actually having this quantity of material in their home. An *as* was simply a mutually accepted method of quantifying value in this period, and individuals would have their overall property (goods, animals, etc.) assessed using this standard. It must also be remembered that all property within a family was held by the *paterfamilias*. So this assessment was not done by individuals, as we would imagine, but rather by families.

14. Dionysius of Halicarnassus, *Roman Antiquities* 4.19.

15. Dionysius of Halicarnassus, *Roman Antiquities* 6.5–12.

16. Dionysius of Halicarnassus, *Roman Antiquities* 6.13.5.

17. Plutarch, *Life of Camillus* 40.

18. Livy 8.8.

19. Diodorus Siculus 23.2.

20. By the first century CE, *speira* was used by Greek authors (e.g. *Book of Acts* 10.1; Josephus *Bellum Judaicum* 3.4.2, etc.) to refer to the subdivisions of a Roman legion that we would call "cohorts."

21. Some nuance is required here, as the very nature of individual property in the Roman Republic is complicated. Technically, the *paterfamilias* of a family (male, "head of household") held all property, so it might be best to think of this as family-owned equipment. However, as families could be quite large, and include tens, if not hundreds of people, one should not necessarily be thinking of a single, nuclear family handing down equipment from father to son—although this likely did happen. It is entirely possible that many families or clans held equipment corporately and had family-based armories they could draw from. The key point is that equipment was privately held, and not state-owned.

22. Whether we should understand *ordines* as being a technically different unit from maniples in Livy's account is uncertain. While Livy certainly implies this here—see esp. 8.8.5—he is not consistent across his work. In the famous speech which Livy gives to Sp. Ligustinus in 171 (Livy 42.34), Livy claims that Ligustinus was given command of the "tenth *ordo* of *hastati*" (*decumum ordinem hastatum*) by Flamininus, hinting that Livy at least thought that the *hastati* were organized by *ordines*. Slightly later in this speech, Livy reports that Ligustinus is assigned by the consul Cato the Elder to the "first (rank?) of the *hastati* of the first century" (*primum hastatum prioris centuriae*) and later, by M. Acilius, to the "first (rank?) of the *principes*' first century" (*primus princeps prioris centuriae*). This entire speech is likely fabricated by Livy, and it is unclear whether he understood the nuances of the ranks and divisions he was describing, or whether they were appropriate in this period and context. Indeed, it is noteworthy that this is one of the few references we have to the "century" where it is described as something resembling a tactical division in the Roman army (see also the fragment of Livy book 11, discovered at Gebel el Naqlun in Egypt, which also hints at this), and the use of the terms "*prior*" and "*decumum*" hints that Livy is perhaps thinking of the cohortal army of the late Republic and blending the armies form various periods together. However, his terminology is interesting, as it hints at a certain fluidity and lack of specificity.

23. Livy (8.8.9) explicitly references a saying about this: "From this arose the adage, 'to have come to the *triarii*,' when things are going badly."

24. See e.g. Ebeling's critique from 1907. More recently, see Erdkamp (2007), "Polybius and Livy on the Allies in the Roman Army," in E. Lo Cascio and L. De Blois (eds), *The Impact of the Roman Army (200 BC–AD 476): Economic, Social, Political, Religious and Cultural Aspects*, 48 (Leiden: Brill) who notes: "Livy gives us no general account of the Roman army, comparable to book six in Polybius' Histories, since he is not interested in analysing the Roman state and its institutions. However, his narrative of Roman war in books 21–45 seems to give a good view of the [system] as it functioned during the half-century from 218 to 167 BC."

Notes

25. While we have little direct evidence from the fourth century, during the third and second centuries it is clear that many Roman elites could at least read, write, and speak in Greek. Further, as Roman influence spread across Italy during these years, they expanded into areas of, and incorporated as both citizens and allies, many peoples and communities which spoke Greek. While Latin was certainly an important language in many official contexts, including legal, political, and religious, it was unlikely to be only language spoken by most Italians or most Romans.

26. This Greek term, like so much of Polybius' language, is actually quite vague and can apply to any number of groups. It does often apply to armies, especially when encamped, but also to squadrons of ships and even regal courts. Interestingly, Polybius uses the same term for both citizen "legions" and the assembled groups of allies. See Erdkamp (2007).

27. Polybius, *The Histories* 6.24.1–2. A "taxiarch" was generally someone who commanded a *taxis*, as the label simply combines the unit name with *archos*, meaning "commander." The fifth-century Athenian army was divided into 10 *taxeis*, each of which led by either a general (*strategos*) or taxiarch, depending on the army. By the Hellenistic period, the term *taxis* seems to have become a generic term for "unit" (although generally about 128 men) and "taxiarch" was simply "commander."

28. This is usually thought to be the *primus pilus prior*, or the senior centurion of the first maniple of the *triarii*. See Walbank (1957), *A Historical Commentary on Polybius* (Oxford: Clarendon Press), ad loc., for discussion.

29. Polybius, *The Histories* 6.64.6.

30. Polybius, *The Histories* 6.33.9.

31. Whether all the *chiliarchoi*, or military tribunes, were elected is debated. Polybius seems somewhat inconsistent, as he claims at 6.12.6 that the consuls are able to appoint them, while at 6.19.1 and 6.19.7 he says they were elected. Livy (7.5.9) suggests military tribunes were first elected in 362, although it is not clear exactly what that might mean—as he also reports various types of military tribunes being elected previously, famously the military tribunes with consular power. Further, in his account for the year 311, Livy (9.30.3–4) reports that the people were given the power to elect 16 of the military tribunes "which before (with exceedingly few posts left over for popular election) had usually been the *beneficia* of dictators and consuls." See Clark (2016) for discussion. It seems likely, therefore, that this was always mixed—with some of the *chiliarchoi*/military tribunes (by Polybius' time likely the majority) elected and others appointed by the consuls.

32. The situation is not so clear when encamped, however. Polybius reports (6.33.5) that, when encamped, three units of *hastati* and *principes* are assigned by lot to each of the six *chiliarchoi* within a legion to help pitch their tent, guard baggage, etc. The remaining two units of *hastati* and *principes* took care of the central ground within the camp, used by the entire army.

33. Livy 7.41.4–5.

34. Taylor (2021), "Centurions in Early Rome," *Ancient Society* 51: 101–21.

35. For a more detailed discussion of this argument, see Armstrong (2019).

36. Diodorus Siculus 23.2 notes: "For example, in ancient times, when [the Romans] were using oval shields, the Etruscans, who fought with round shields of bronze and in a phalanx formation, impelled them to adopt similar arms and were in consequence defeated. Then again, when other peoples were using shields such as the Romans now use, and were fighting in maniples, they had imitated both and had overcome those who introduced the excellent models." For challenges and discussion, see Rosenstein (2011); Armstrong (2016) and (2019).

37. This, of course, prompts the question of "why did ancient authors ascribe to this idea?" The answer is likely twofold. First, it becomes something of a literary trope for the Romans to "learn from their enemies." This trope is traceable to the early third century and is found in a remarkably similar set of digressions tracking Roman military development from the Archaic period down to the

Notes

Hellenistic—perhaps originally derived from Timaeus or Hieronymus. Although now accepted to be little more than speculation, the principle of adaptiveness evidently appealed, and this narrative became entrenched in Roman historiography. Second, the Roman army did change, and particularly during the period of the Samnite Wars. However, it was not due to adaptation but integration, as it was this period more than any other which reshaped Rome's citizen body due to the expansion of Roman *imperium*—as is discussed in the later chapters of this book.

38. Polybius, *The Histories* 6.24.5.

39. Erdkamp (2007).

40. Dionysius of Halicarnassus, *Roman Antiquities* 20.11.

41. Polybius, *The Histories* 6.19.

42. Polybius, *The Histories* 6.21.1.

43. See Jehne (2006), "Latiner und Bundesgenossen im Krieg. Zu Formen und Ausmaß der Integration in der republikanischen Armee," in M. Jehne and R. Pfeilschrifter (eds), *Herrschaft ohne Integration? Rom und Italien in republikanischer Zeit*, 243–67 (Frankfurt: Verlag Alte Geschichte).

44. Livy 43.15.

45. Even with some provisional planning done at the tribal level, this would have been a messy and complicated process, which is broadly supported by the literary tradition. Livy (43.14) reports that the Romans conducted a *dilectus* quite hastily in 169, and that still required 11 days. Each tribe would have 35 rounds of selection for each of the *velites*, *hastati*, and *principes*, and then 17 rounds for the *triarii*. Even if the tribunes were only working with a select group that the tribes had provided, if Polybius is to be believed the *dilectus* would have still involved an incredible 4,200 rounds of selection.

46. Plutarch, *Life of Fabius Maximus* 24.

47. On the equipment itself, see Bishop and Coulston (2009). For self-supply, this is the accepted interpretation of the panoplies associated with the various classes of the centuriated system—see Forysthe (2007), "The Army and Centuriate Organization in Early Rome," in P. Erdkamp (ed.), *A Companion to the Roman Army*, 24–42 (Oxford: Blackwell), for discussion.

48. *Corpus Inscriptionum Latinarum* I², 5.

49. For more detailed discussion, see Armstrong (2016); and Roselaar (2010), *Public Land in the Roman Republic* (Oxford: Oxford University Press).

50. For instance, one possible explanation for the position of *taxiarch* in Polybius' description of the manipular legion discussed above is that it represents a local clan or tribal leader—operating below the state-level of the tribunes or *chiliarchoi*, but above the maniples and lower-level commanders.

INDEX

For the benefit of digital users, indexed terms that span two pages (e.g., 52–53) may, on occasion, appear on only one of those pages.

Aeneas 6, 14, 16–25, 27–30, 60, 109, 194–5
 Aeneid 14
accensi 205–7, 209, 231
Alba Longa 25, 30–1, 40–1, 109–10
Alexander III of Macedon (the Great) 3, 37, 102, 145–6, 150–1, 156, 161, 197
Allia (river and battle) 82–3, 90, 140
allies 3, 22, 94, 105–6, 109, 113, 115–21, 124, 126, 128–9, 132, 137, 142, 149, 153, 161, 164–8, 171, 176, 178, 184, 188, 201, 215–16, 218, 223, 226, 234, see also *socius*
Apennine Mountains 42, 67–8, 81, 107, 109, 129, 133, 140, 165, 233–4
Ancus Marcius 39, 41
antepilani 205
Aristotle 24, 83
armor 1, 2, 4, 30, 73, 133, 197, 198, 199, 216, 222, 232, 234, 239
aspis 142, 197, 231, 237
Athens 3, 23, 47, 85–6, 149, 176, 196–7, 226
Augustus (emperor) xiii, 6, 14, 17, 19–20, 55, 230
Aventine hill 32, 35, 42
auspicium 53–4, 159

Battle of Veseris River 1–2, 4–5, 115, 202–3
Brennus (Gallic chieftain of the Seones) 56, 76, 81–2, 84, 99, 188

bronze 1, 6, 124, 154, 158, 197–200, 231, 236–7, 239, *see also* coinage
Bronze Age 14–15, 17, 43, 148
(Lucius Junius) Brutus 18, 50–2, 92
(Marcus Furius) Camillus 16, 18–20, 55–8, 77, 83, 92, 202

Campania/Campanians 105–6, 109, 113–16, 127–133, 135–6, 142, 152, 155, 158, 160, 165, 169–71, 173, 235
Cannae (battle) 182
Capitoline hill 29, 31, 34–5, 82, 156, 217, 219
Carthage/Carthaginians/Phoenicians 3, 10, 22, 43, 78, 122, 128, 146, 148, 150, 154, 166, 169–176, 181, 229, 239
 First Punic War 10, 159, 169–72, 175, 178–9, 181, 188, 208, 224
 Second Punic War 10, 121, 178, 181–3, 185, 189, 208, 226, 229, 233
cavalry 38, 41, 44, 46, 126, 151–2, 162, 164, 166–7, 172–3, 194–5, 197–8, 200–1, 203, 205, 207, 209, 212, 215–7, 233, see also *equites*
census/censor/censorship 46, 55, 72, 90, 95, 97, 100, 107, 138, 155, 183, 196, 199, 200, 219, 231
centurion 46, 205, 206, 210, 212, 214–17, 232
Cicero 24

261

Index

citizenship 25, 60, 94–8, 100, 106, 111, 116–18, 120–1, 126–7, 130–3, 136–7, 143, 171, 184

classis/first class 90, 197, 200, 202–3

coinage 6, 86, 103, 124, 148–51, 155, 157–9, 168–9, 176–9, 233, *see also* bronze, *denarius, didrachm*, silver

(Lucius Tarquinius) Collatinus 49

comitia centuriata 53, 217

consul(s) 2, 5, 19, 51–4, 57, 66, 71, 88, 92–4, 98–100, 115, 119, 125, 127–8, 132–3, 135, 137, 138–41, 155, 162, 164–7, 170, 172–3, 177, 202, 209, 211–12, 217–18, 221–2, 225, 232, 236

consular tribune(s) 19, 55, 58, 72, 76–7, 93, 95, 97–100, 202, 232, *see also* military tribunes

Cremera (river and battle) 223

cuirass 198, 232, *see also* armor

curia (pl. *curiae*) 36–38, 53–4, 61, 92, 94, 194–6, 232, 234, 236

Curia Hostilia 41

(Publius) Decius Mus 2, 5, 115, 140, 164, 166, 207

denarius 21, 233

devotio 78, 140, 207

didrachm 177, 233

dilectus 210, 213, 217–18, 220, 223, 233, 237, *see also* levy

Dionysius of Halicarnassus 11, 12, 15, 23, 30, 47, 112, 119, 124, 190, 197, 200–2, 233

Dionysius I of Syracuse 82, 84, 99

equites 44, 46, 90, 195, 197, 200, 212, 233, *see also* cavalry

Etruria 42, 76, 105, 109, 122, 136–8, 140, 157, 179, 233, 237, 239

Etruscan/s 1, 23, 25, 36, 42, 44–5, 105, 110, 120–1, 137–41, 193, 233

Etruscan League 225

Eutropius 141, 233

evocatio 78

Gabii 47–8, 51, 65

gens/gentes 26, 44, 46, 64, 76, 95, 222, 234

Hannibal Barca 11, 106, 141, 182–5

hasta 142, 204, 234

hastati 199, 204–5, 207, 209–11, 216–18, 220, 234, 236, *see also* infantry

Hiero II of Syracuse 170

Hieronymus of Cardia 208

Homer 21–2, 39, 43, 76, 201

Iliad 21–3

Odyssey 22, 43

honor 49, 51, 56, 83, 96, 112, 130, 164, 173, 215

imperialism 8, 10, 11, 15–16, 41, 55, 64, 69, 98, 116, 124, 126, 141, 155, 160, 181–2, 185, 187, 189–91

imperium 37, 53–4, 65–6, 92–4, 99, 126, 135, 139, 159, 218, 221–2, 232, 234, 236

infantry 38, 41, 126, 146, 151–2, 162, 164–7, 172–3, 193–5, 197, 199–201, 203–7, 209–11, 217, 235–9

javelin 2, 58, 142, 200–1, 204, 209, 217, 236, 239

(Gaius) Julius Caesar xiii, 17, 38, 41, 214–15, 230

king(s) 10, 17–21, 25, 30–1, 33, 36–42, 44–5, 47, 49, 51–4, 63, 65–6, 69, 71, 88, 92, 109, 119, 160–1, 163, 168, 187, 195–6, 201–2, 221, see also *rex*

Lake Regillus (battle) 201

Latium/Latins 2–6, 10, 25, 32, 40, 42, 45, 67–9, 74, 85–6, 93, 104–5, 107–13, 115, 118–22, 125, 127–9, 130–1, 135, 142, 157, 160, 165, 179, 201–4, 233–5

"Great Latin War" 2, 104, 107, 116, 131–2, 202–3

Latin League 64, 110, 225

Latin rights 110–11, 117–18, 122

Lavinium 23, 25

leves (light infantry) 204–5, see also *velites*

levy 122, 140, 210–11, 213, 217–18, 220–1, 233, 237, see also *dilectus*

Licinio-Sextian reforms (367 BCE) 57, 71, 73, 92–3, 97, 99–100, 102, 202, 232, 236

Index

Livy 5, 11–12, 15, 23, 30, 38–40, 47, 50,
55–6, 74, 77–8, 81, 86, 99–100, 113,
115, 117, 120, 124, 126–7, 129, 131,
133, 136–41, 152, 167, 170, 190, 195, 197,
200, 202–9, 212, 214–15, 217–21, 225,
231, 235
Lucretia 49–52

Mamertines 169–70
maniple/manipular 115, 152, 202, 204–5, 207–9,
213–15, 217, 222, 225, 235
Manlius Torquatus 2, 5, 115, 207
mercenaries 81–2, 84–6, 90, 99, 101, 103, 105–6,
112, 126, 132, 137, 142–3, 148–53, 161, 164–5,
168–70, 173, 178, 225
military tribunes 46, 93, 98, 125, 209, 212,
217–19, 221, 226, *see also* consular
tribunes

navy 149, 154–6, 169, 171–3, 175–9, 188, 239
Numa Pompilius 20, 39–41, 44, 229

ordo (pl. *ordines*) 152, 205, 214, 235, 239

Palatine hill 32, 34–6
patrician(s) 54, 57, 70–3, 89–90, 102–3, 112, 128,
144, 224, 238
phalanx/phalangites 151–2, 165, 191, 193, 197–9,
201, 204, 213, 236–7
Philip II of Macedon 3, 37, 151, 197
pilum (pl. *pila*) 58, 142
plebeian(s) 54, 57, 70–3, 89, 91, 99, 102–4, 112,
127–8, 144, 224, 238
Plutarch xv, 18–19, 29, 30, 39–40, 55–6, 78,
166–7, 202, 236
Polybius 11, 57–8, 64, 94, 147, 151–3, 166,
170–2, 175, 177, 185, 190, 208–21,
225, 236
pomerium 37, 46, 96, 135
pontifex maximus 40
praetor(s) 53, 57, 66, 73, 93, 98, 99–100, 103, 125,
140, 202, 218, 221, 236
principes 199, 205, 207, 209–11, 216–18, 220, 234,
236, *see also* infantry
Pyrrhus of Epirus 10, 24, 106, 141, 146,
160–71, 225

Remus 17, 30–2, 111–12, 177, 194–5, 223
rex (pl. *reges*) 17, 36–7, 39, 65, 194,
see also king
roarii 205–6
Romanitas 61, 144, 153, 178, 181, 185, 190
Romulus 6, 16–19, 28, 29–33, 36, 38–41, 44–5,
55, 59, 69, 111–12, 118–19, 177–8, 193–5, 223,
229, 232

Sabine women 36, 41, 69
Sabinum/Sabines 36, 40, 42, 45, 68–9, 110, 141,
165, 233, 237
Sack of Rome (390 BCE) 9–10, 19, 24, 56, 76,
80–5, 89, 97, 103, 121, 142–3, 188
Samnium/Samnite(s) 10, 82, 105–6, 113–6, 122,
127–42, 160–1, 164–5, 167, 193, 204, 224,
235, 237
First Samnite War 107, 113, 115, 122,
129–31, 202
Second Samnite War 131–7, 202
Third Samnite War 141–2
scutum 58, 142, 199, 204, 237
scutati 204
semaia 214, 216
Senate 37–8, 41, 44, 54, 86, 119, 129, 130, 132–3,
135, 143, 155, 159, 163, 170, 177–9, 183–4,
235, 238
Servius Tullius 19, 25, 39, 44–7, 94, 196, 200–1,
203, 221
shield(s) 58, 142, 197–9, 200, 202–4,
231, 237
Sicily 3, 22–4, 27, 82, 129, 146, 148–50, 166–7,
169–70, 172–3, 175, 178, 182
silver 21, 172, 175–7, 179, 233, *see also* coinage,
denarius, didrachm
socius (pl. *socii*) 105, 117–22, 124–7, 130, 213, 215,
see also allies
Sparta 85, 110, 149, 160–1, 173, 176
spear(s) 2, 142, 197, 200, 202, 204, 207, 217,
236–8, see also *hasta* and *pilum*
speira 204, 214
spoils 4, 38, 45, 65, 73, 75, 86, 88, 120–1, 132, 135,
151, 168, 179, 204, 224
stipendium 85–7, 100, 151, 153–4, 159, 238
"Struggle of the Orders" 57, 70–3, 89, 104, 112,
144, 180, 238

Index

Tacitus 52–3, 238

Tarquinius Priscus 39, 42–5, 51, 195

Tarquinius Superbus 18, 39, 44, 47–9, 51, 53, 119, 201

taxiarch 210–16

Tiber 31, 34–5, 44, 76, 107, 234

Timaeus of Tauromenium 24, 208

triarii 199, 205–7, 209–11, 216–18, 220, 231, 238, *see also* infantry

tribe(s) xviii, 5, 36, 40, 45–6, 58, 68–9, 90, 93, 95, 97–9, 101, 103, 105–6, 115, 121–2, 129–31, 135–7, 142, 150, 153–5, 160, 165, 179, 183, 194–6, 217–21, 238

tributum 85–7, 97, 100, 116, 122, 127, 151, 153–4, 177, 238

trireme(s) 149, 175, 237, *see also* navy

Tullus Hostilius 39–41, 59, 195

turbam 204

"The Twelve Tables" (laws) 18, 72

Umbria(ns) 42, 122, 136, 139–41, 165, 233, 239

Veii 9, 38, 55–7, 76–80, 83–6, 89–90, 95–6, 98–9, 117, 121, 160, 179, 188, 223

velites 209, 218, 220, 239

vexilla 152, 205, 239

vexillarius 205